Knowing the Rules of the Game

Knowing the Rules of the Game

Conrad Prophet

To order additional copies of this book, contact:
Xlibris Corporation
1-888-795-4274
www.Xlibris.com
Orders@Xlibris.com
23693

Contents

In memory of my beloved sister-in-law, Tina Rochelle Prophet-Thomas, who was like a sister to me. Thank you for your love and support. You will always be missed.

Introduction

Before one can empathize with the frustration and pain of another, they must be aware of the experiences that they have in common. Being Black in America is a common factor that affects the average Black person and, at times, affects those who appear to have achieved professional, financial, and general personal success. Until all of us have "arrived," none of us have truly "arrived." A person's blackness is not something that can be removed with the accumulation of wealth, change of environment, or accumulation of knowledge.

This semi-autobiography is designed to allow young Black people to learn from the difficulties and hardships I had to endure in my efforts to earn an honest living after I graduated from high school and college. It will also give Black women a first-hand account of what the men they love—their sons, husbands, brothers or male friends—may go through in their attempts to handle their responsibilities and maintain a decent standard of living.

I realize that every Black person does not have the ability or even aspire to be a successful entertainer, professional athlete, or preacher. Nor do they want to be a drug dealer or pursue any other lifestyle that would inevitably cause them to become a part of the penal system. There have been numerous books and movies glorifying the lifestyles of the rich and famous, which sometimes include the lifestyles of people who earn their living through illicit means. I am concerned about the young Black men and women who work diligently to make an honest living, yet may still encounter difficulties because they are unaware of the realities of living and surviving in the real world.

* * *

Unfortunately, while growing up, I experienced an enormous void that is common for thousands of Black children across America—the misfortune of being raised in a Black urban community without a father. I am not stating that growing up without a father is a guarantee that a Black person cannot succeed. But the absence of a responsible father does make life much more challenging in a country whose systems are not conducive to the success of the average Black person. I will briefly tell my story in an effort to provide greater insight into the premise that application of the "rules of survival" in a Black urban community does not easily transfer into "the real world," which is controlled by the White power structure.

While growing up in Royal Oak Township, a small Black community outside of Detroit, and in Inkster, Michigan, I had to constantly fight for respect. Either I had to fight to defend myself or be bullied, tormented, and disrespected everyday as a youth. Because of the influence and expectations of my brothers in Royal Oak Township and Inkster, being disrespected was not a viable option. For thousands of Black youths across America, this same mentality was branded into their minds. It was the Black communities' self-imposed theory of "survival of the fittest." Early in life, I developed the motto, "I will get with you mentally, verbally or physically, preferably physically." Fighting for survival was basically a right of passage for myself and other youths who lived by the code of the streets. My environment significantly impacted my perspective on life and the most effective means to sustain it. If you did not give me respect, I would have to take yours. Fortunately, I grew up in the late 1970's and early 1980's. During this time, most disputes among young people were resolved with our hands and not with guns.

This mentality was not only developed in young boys in the communities in which I was raised, but also in girls. Growing up without fearing anyone creates an aura of invincibility and confidence that is unparalleled. In Inkster, Michigan, tough love and the fear of God and my mother forced me to exhibit good behavior daily. In Royal Oak Township, a docile and passive demeanor would cause a young person to be disrespected and bullied. So the behavior that I exhibited in Inkster was unacceptable in the streets of the township, if I wanted to survive. Because of my street mentality I could not be forced to control my temper, respect authority, or fear and revere God. I became rebellious and confrontational because that was the attitude necessary for my survival.

By the time I reached high school, I was able to positively re-direct my anger, frustration, and uncaring attitude toward academics. Although my acts of aggression decreased, the survival instincts that I learned in the streets of Royal Oak Township were not forgotten. They were only locked away, patiently awaiting the opportunity to be unleashed on anyone who I considered to be my enemy.

My way of dealing with reality after graduating from college was based on how I dealt with issues as a youth. I was never told that utilizing the same survival instincts from the Black communities that I was raised in would not be effective in my pursuit of success in corporate America, government, and other employment sectors. It was not until I walked across the graduation stage into adulthood and a new reality, that I realized who my true enemy was—me. I would soon learn, through personal experiences with institutionalized racism, that I would need to examine my thought processes, my motivation, and myself. I would also need to examine the people and influences that ultimately made me who I was and make the choice to conform or develop a more reasonable and effective way to become empowered to achieve success in a system that was not created for me to do so.

* * *

I was never told to assimilate, acclimate, pacify, tolerate, stroke egos, and just go along with the programs that are common in corporate America and government employment. The assumption was that if I graduated from high school or college, I would be given the same professional opportunities as my White counterparts. There was no one to explain to me that in order to be successful and have a good paying job, I had to accept my role based on the norms set for Black people. I did not have a father to tell me that the freedom of speech is not applicable to Black people in America, if we want to keep our jobs. I was not told that in order for me to be financially successful, even after I received my college degree, I still had to make a choice. I could speak out on the issues that concerned the best interest of Black people or remain silent and allow injustice to occur. Throughout my life, I have observed many Black men and women who chose to remain silent and ignore blatant inequality for the sake of maintaining seemingly successful careers. My question is: Where would we be if Malcolm, Martin, Medgar, Harriet, Rosa, and thousands of other Black people had remained silent while our rights were being violated? Again, I ask, where would any of us, even the successful Blacks, be today?

That is the question I sometimes ask myself as I think about all of the career opportunities that I have forfeited. I have continuously stood for the same causes for which others sacrificed their standard of living and at times, their lives, so that those who came after them could enjoy opportunities they never had. And like those before me, I had to always remind myself that my allegiance, first and foremost, is to God. Then it is to the race that God blessed me to be born into.

Throughout my personal trials and tribulations, I had to come to the realization that, "All my skin folks are not my kin folks." I had to learn the hard way that there are Black people who appear to be in positions of power but are cowards who are apathetic and only concerned about their own personal gain. There are thousands of Black people with money but no purpose.

Since Black people are not monolithic, my life experience is not identical to every other Black man's experience. The mentality, attitude and views of Black men concerning the Black experience in this country varies from the far right of the spectrum where Supreme Court Justice Clarence Thomas stands and spans to the far left where the White media has Minister Louis Farrakhan. I do not stand and speak for every Black person in this country. I do think that my upbringing mirrors that of thousands of Black people in this country. I also believe that what I have endured since high school is similar to what countless Black men have endured or will endure in the future. There are many Black men and women my age who have not experienced any of the hardships that I have. For those successful

Black men and women who never experienced blatant racism, Black-on-Black betrayal and general inequality in the workplace, welcome to my world.

The primary purpose of this book is to educate our young Black men and women about the reality of attaining success, and the potential costs or compromises that may be unavoidable to achieve that goal. I want them to know that being assertive, ambitious, fearless and outspoken can be a hindrance to career growth. I want to share my experiences with others, so my fate will not involuntarily be their fate. On many occasions, it was due to decisions that I made with a lack of knowledge. There is a chance that the knowledge I am providing now was available, but I was unaware of its availability in high school and college. I believe that this book can serve as a very effective road map to success. One must decide to read it and learn from it or to ignore it and remain ignorant, and possibly experience some of the same trials and tribulations that I had to endure because of ignorance.

Another matter of great concern for me, which is also the additional purpose of this book, is enlightening the Black children whose parents have worked hard and moved to affluent neighborhoods to shield them from the negative influences that exist in most inner-city neighborhoods. Certainly, they were present in the community I grew up in and thousands of other Black communities across America. Once these young people walk across the graduation stage, the success of their parents will not be able to protect them from the realities of adulthood and independence. Racism and Black-on-Black hatred do not discriminate based on the financial success of one's parents. Just because racism may not have existed in the microcosm that successful Black people are able to raise their children in, does not mean that it does not exist in the United States. I applaud those parents for attempting to shield their children from the ills of the world as long as possible, but one day, reality will hit your child also. It is my hope that your child will be able to handle it successfully.

Another concern is the high number of young Black men and women who are being incarcerated everyday in America. It is unfortunate that we live in one of the richest nations in the world and we cannot provide jobs for everyone who wants to work. Our government and Black America are failing young Black people. Why do our young people feel they have to sell drugs and participate in criminal activities in order to survive? Why do Black parents fail to prepare their children for the future? The lack of knowledge is the primary reason that our young people choose the roads in life that they do. I recently heard that the only time Black men read is when they go to prison. I hope that this is one book that every young Black man and woman will read and I pray they are not within the confines of prison when they read it. There have been too many young men and women who did not have the opportunity to live a productive life because they were incarcerated at an early age. Most of them had dropped out of school and entered the life of violence and crime. This trend of self-destruction must be stopped. In order for this to occur, parents and the Black community must take the responsibility to prepare our children for the future.

I am now able to share the knowledge I have obtained from my experiences, and possibly prevent other young Black men and women from making the same decisions and choices that I made in different employment sectors. I hope to improve or at least positively impact the future of all young Black men and women who read my story. If you are a young Black person, I pray that your decisions will allow you to be successful, in spite of racism, Black-on-Black hatred and any other seemingly insurmountable obstacles that you face as you journey through life. Everyday when you wake up in America as a Black person, racism will be there, but God will also be there to assist you in fighting that battle and any other battle that may come your way.

Before we can blame anyone else for our failures, we must look into the mirror. Even without racism, we continue to contribute to our own failure. Our complacency, self-hatred, low self-esteem, inferiority complex, lack of knowledge, carnal mind, addictions, negative associations, and habits contribute to our downfall, despite the tactics of racist Whites. Our worst enemy is not the White man or any other man. Our true enemy is sin and evil principalities in high places.

As you read this book, you will learn how I faced racism and other obstacles head-on, and lived to write about it and attained success. One way to increase your chances of success is by "knowing the rules of the game," before the game begins.

Chapter 1

NORTHWOOD UNIVERSITY

"When I was a child, I spake as a child, I understood as a child,
I thought as a child: but when I became a man,
I put away Childish things."

I Cor. 13:11

Northwood Business Institute as it was called in 1982 is located in Midland, Michigan. Midland is located 150 miles North of Detroit. Saginaw was the closest city to Midland with a Black population over 20 percent. In 1982, the population of Black people living in Midland was 1.5 percent.[1] Today it is approximately 3.0 percent. When Midland, MI is mentioned, Dow Chemicals and Dow Cornings come to mind. Northwood definitely was not a place where a Black student went to feel at home. It was all about obtaining an excellent education.

You may be asking yourself: why is he telling me this? As you read the details of some of my experiences and how they led to my decision to attend Northwood, it may assist you in making better decisions. Northwood University was a prestigious college of higher learning in 1982 and is still regarded in high esteem today. There are times when a person has to come to reality and accept the fact that if you are not properly prepared for certain academic challenges in life, it is okay to acknowledge your limitations. Even though my time at Northwood was not very long, the experience was priceless.

In 1982, Northwood University was a private university that specialized in the areas of Automotive Management; Economics Management; and Hotel, Restaurant and Resort Management to name a few. In recent years, Northwood has begun to offer 15 dual majors. One characteristic that separates a private college from a public college is that private colleges and universities do not receive any government assistance. That means tuition at private colleges and universities is extremely high in comparison to public colleges and universities.

Financing for college is a major obstacle for most students. USA Today states, "Two-thirds of the nation's wealthiest 25% of students enroll in a 4-year college within two years of graduating from high school, but just one in five from the bottom 25% do so."[2] Because of my limited financial resources at that time, I was able to attend with a Pell Grant and guaranteed student loan I received. Most of the Black and White students attended by the same means. The Black athletes attended on athletic scholarships. There were a number of Black students on academic scholarships also. A considerable number of White students came from wealthy families who could afford the cost of tuition, which seemed astronomical at that time. Inadequacies that are yet characteristic of financial funding for low-income students continue to keep them at a disadvantage for higher education. "In the mid-1970s, for example, the maximum Pell Grant for low-income and working-class families covered 40% of the average cost of attending a 4-year private college; now it covers about 15%."[3]

Unfortunately, when it comes to colleges and universities, student demographics in America are always brought to the forefront. From my observation, I would guess that in 1982 out of the approximately 1,950 full-time students, 85 were Black. Out of the 85 Black students, 30 were athletes. Since I graduated from a predominately White high school outside of Detroit, being outnumbered was not a shock to me.

Life on Campus

Living on campus in a predominantly White environment for the first time in my life was an experience in itself. As a policy for most colleges and universities, all freshmen were required to stay on campus in college housing during their first year. Many colleges and universities still have a similar policy in effect today. This meant that despite your preference, you would probably be assigned a room with a White student if you did not already have your roommate(s) selected. I cannot remember how my roommates were selected, but it worked out. My roommates were two White students from Troy, Michigan. Both of them were down to earth and never exhibited any racist beliefs. There were never any disagreements or any racial conflicts. One of my roommates loved Olivia Newton John and rock music. In 1982, the selection of music was not as enormous as it is in 2004. Plus, the student who owned the stereo, television, or anything else called the shots most of the time. Not only did I lack the preparation for the college experience but also the environment seemed foreign to me.

Our rooming situation was great in comparison to those of other students. There were rooming arrangements that were volatile. When you have people who come from different races, cultures and socio-economic backgrounds, you can expect differences in personalities and beliefs. I can remember visiting a student's room and they would say to me, "Just ignore her. She is only my roommate." Some students were able to find compatible roommates during orientation. Others may have attended high school together and they also became roommates.

The campus activities at Northwood University were worth the tuition. In the student union, there was the grill that prepared edible food at reasonable prices and also accepted checks that occasionally bounced. There were also pool tables, ping-pong tables, video games, and a lounge area where you could relax. Then we had accessibility to the basketball courts, swimming pools, tennis courts, and all the other facilities that were on campus. Even though Northwood was a small campus at the time, it provided everything necessary to make the atmosphere conducive for learning.

No matter where Black people are, we always have a tendency to come together. The Black social life was special. We had our own world on campus. Every weekend there was a party in one of the upper-class student's apartment. Most of the Black students were from Inkster, Michigan, and they socialized together. These students seemed to congregate in their own cliques with their own manner of being hip and trendy as they represented the Black culture on campus. If you were from Detroit, Flint or another Black city, you were easily accepted into the Inkster group. If you were Black, you were accepted. Being outnumbered 20 to 1, we had no choice but to stick together.

During my freshman year of college, I was what you would consider a "Nerd", "Square", "School Boy Roy", or any other name associated with a person who was considered "uncool." I hung with a brother from Detroit, who had the reputation of being the only Black person who could not play basketball. We were not heavily into the social life. There were cool brothers and athletes who were so cool, that by today's standards, they would be considered, "True Players." I was definitely not one of them.

The social atmosphere at Northwood was different from reality. There was no problem or stigma placed on Black and White students socializing together. Most of the friendships were based on personalities and what you were raised to believe. One of my roommates was a good basketball player and we played basketball at the gym continuously. The brother who could not play basketball to save his life, my roommates, and I hung together regularly without any repercussions of us being considered different.

Academics and Instructors

During orientation, I realized that my tenure at Northwood was going to be short. In order to be placed into a curriculum, all incoming freshmen had to take various academic aptitude tests. To the best of my knowledge, English was my strongest subject and my grades in high school reflected it. After the results of my English Grammar Proficiency Exam, my command of the English language indicated that I had no command of it. To my surprise and disappointment, I was placed into a remedial English Course. This was a shock to my ego. According to a Manhattan Institute study, only 32 percent of public high school students leave qualified enough to attend a four-year college.[1] Many high school students are not prepared for the challenge and high demands of college coursework so it tends to be quite a shock and causes them to fail.

Like most college freshmen, I was unaware of what career path I wanted to pursue. I enrolled in the Hotel and Restaurant and Resort/Management curriculum. Since I was only there two semesters, it is difficult to determine if I would have successfully completed the curriculum. In my Business Food Management course, the instructor told us something that was branded into my mind and even today, it remains. Since there were not many Black students in the course, his statement was specifically for us. He said that there were certain hotels, restaurants, and clubs that would not allow certain people to be in the position of management or authority. In addition, he stated that whomever you married would determine if you received a job or if you would be able to keep it. For White people, if they married a person of the wrong race or ethnic group, it would basically prevent them from receiving certain jobs. The instructor was clearly stating that in the "real world" regardless of what Black students achieved academically, there were companies in America that would prohibit Black people from having a position of authority. At the time, discrimination based on color was not even in my thought process. It did not take several years for reality to remove my ignorance of what America was truly built on.

The elective courses at Northwood were academically challenging. One course that stood out was Philosophy of American Life Business. It was held in a large auditorium with approximately 100 students. The professor would request input from the class each day of the course. Most of the time, I would answer and give my opinion based on my life experiences and how I interpreted the reading assignment. Never, was my answer in line with the answer the professor was seeking. I received a "C" in the class. After the class was over, the professor thanked me for my input, because it stimulated class discussion and I was adamant about my opinion. For most of the White students, that course and others at Northwood were the first times, they had Black students as classmates. As I was creating this chapter, I just realized that I was a diplomat for Black people everywhere. The White students at Northwood perceived me the same way they would perceive all Black people. It was my opportunity to represent. Since grades were kept confidential, only the instructors knew how other Black students and myself matched up with our White peers.

The instructors at Northwood University were second to none. Even though the number of courses I enrolled in were limited, it was not difficult to notice the instructors who were knowledgeable in their field. Most of them taught courses where they had first-hand experience in corporate America. The best persons for teaching you about the rules of corporate America are the people who created the rules.

The school year at Northwood was composed of tri-semesters that lasted for ten weeks. At the end of the first tri-semester, my G.P.A. was 2.24. I earned a "C" in four courses and a "B" in another. During the second tri-semester, my lack of preparation for the intense academic demands of Northwood was manifesting itself. Because of limited finances, I had to work on the weekends. On Friday and Saturday nights, I worked from 9:00P.M. to 6:00A.M., in the morning. This affected my non-existent study habits. My study habits consisted of taking No-Doze tablets and cramming for tests the night before each test. I learned that method of studying from my roommates who did not work themselves. While I should have been studying, I was playing basketball, hanging at the student union, or in other students' dorm rooms. For some reason, something possessed me to take an 8:00A.M., Introduction to American Government course, which I conveniently failed.

By the end of the second semester, reality had finally set in. The transition from high school to a private college was too difficult for me. My G.P.A. at the end of the semester was a disappointing 1.67. I earned four "C's," one "B," and an "F" in my Introduction to American Government course. It did not take another ten-week semester for me to wake up. Every man or woman should know his or her limitations and I knew mine. For me to continue to waste my time, money and accumulate college loans just to struggle academically would have been irrational. Just because I did not have the maturity to discipline myself to study, did not mean I did not have common sense. My inability to excel academically at the college level could not be contributed to my high school or Northwood University itself. Northwood University was an enjoyable experience for me. It gave me the opportunity to leave my community and find out how other people lived; others such as those in higher income brackets and those in a non-Black culture. This was not my intention or reason for attending Northwood. In reviewing my high school transcript and reminiscing on my high school years, I realized that I never gave a 100 percent effort to studying. Even though some of the reasons for my mediocre study habits and discipline were out of my control, it was still my responsibility as a young man to rise to the challenge.

From my experience at Northwood, I was given the same opportunity to learn on the same level playing field as my White peers. We were all given the same syllabus, which stated the course textbooks, assignments, and due dates for the duration of the course. Even if some instructors were biased towards White students, this did not prevent Black students from acquiring the same knowledge. Since we were all in the same classroom, the instructors were not able to teach the White students differently from the Black students. There were times in some of my courses that I knew I earned a higher grade but did not receive it. I knew a letter grade did not determine the amount of knowledge that I retained in my mind and would be available for future application.

On the last day of class in March of 1983, I decided that it was time to say good-bye to Northwood University and Midland, Michigan. My dream of one day earning a college degree to make a better living for myself was not over. It was just placed on hold temporarily while I devised a plan to approach higher education successfully the next time. There was going to be a next time!

Advice

Higher education is still one of the best investments for Black people to earn a decent living in this country, even though it's not fail-proof. Today, there are over 2,600 colleges and universities in the United States.[5] This would include private, public, and community colleges along with the universities. In Michigan alone there are: 44 private colleges/universities; 15 public colleges/universities; 29 community colleges.[6] Some students are not informed about the numerous options they have in selecting a college to attend. I made the mistake of selecting Northwood University because it gave me an opportunity to get away from home and the only college recruiter I spoke with was the one from Northwood. I did not take advantage of the information that was available at my high school college fairs nor did I conduct my own research into the various colleges. These are things I would strongly advise anyone who is interested in attending college to do. There is still the underlying factor of the extreme costs associated with better schools that may even be outside of a student's state of residency. Issues such as costs and location are factors that can possibly limit the choices some students, especially Black students, have in selecting a college.

I recommend that anyone who wants to attend college research their college choice(s) thoroughly. Make sure you seek advice from guidance counselors and people that have graduated from college. Visiting college campuses and talking with actual students there can also familiarize you with the college and campus life. With all the information that is available on the Internet, there is no reason why a student would make an unwise decision. If for some reason, a wrong choice is made, do not be afraid to transfer to a different college as opposed to quitting.

The expense of higher education rises every year. If you are not fortunate enough to earn a "full ride" scholarship or an athletic scholarship, there are other options available. There are countless grants and scholarships available for students who search for them in a timely manner. Almost every college has a financial assistance office that can help in securing funds for higher education. Searching for financial assistance should be done as early as the junior year in high school. Most scholarships have deadline dates and application periods that students need to be aware of in advance. If you are applying for scholarships, it is best to apply for as many scholarships as you can.

Other sources of financial aid include grants (state and federal), loans, and college work-study employment. The work-study employment allows you to receive a job on-campus for usually about 20 hours per week and your earnings from that job go toward your tuition cost. The opportunity to attend college is not solely about having the financial means, so this should not be an excuse for anyone to neglect obtaining a higher education if that is what you want to do. College is not a joke or a place where you go to have fun. Yes, college can be an enjoyable experience. For most students it is a chance to get away from the home for the first time and make a gradual transition into adulthood. It is also an opportunity to get away from negative people and unpleasant living environments that are not conducive to you having a positive and productive life. Many students have problems transitioning from high school life to college life. This was a shortcoming for me. Another one of my mistakes was getting caught up in the social aspects of college life rather than focusing on my purpose for being there. You must realize that it cost money to attend college. Whether you are receiving loans, government assistance, a scholarship, or your parents' hard earned money, the primary purpose is to learn and not to have fun.

Please do not waste other people's money or your time attending college just to have fun. If all you want to do is party, drink and have sex, you could do that at home for free. Another thing, college is not a place where you take a four-year vacation from reality and approach your studies with a nonchalant and mediocre attitude. The purpose of college is to prepare you for the extremely challenging workforce where the playing field is not level for Black people.

It is not on the first day of college that you decide to be serious about learning. Your focus should begin in high school. If you wait until the first day of college to become focused and choose your path for success, then it may already be too late. Realistically, if you are not prepared for college, you will end up back on the block in two semesters like I was. You need to prepare academically and mentally for the challenge now!

Chapter 2

UNITED STATES ARMY

"The way of a fool is right in his own eyes:
but he that hearkeneth unto counsel is wise."

—*Prov 12:15*

After leaving Northwood University, the only place for me to go was back home to Royal Oak Township, which is in Oakland County, Michigan. The famous "8 Mile Road" separates Detroit from Oakland County and Royal Oak Township. Please don't confuse Royal Oak Township with the city of Royal Oak. The "township" in 1982 had an exclusively Black population, except for a small area located one mile north. The city of Royal Oak, which is located approximately 15 miles farther north in Oakland County, has a predominantly White population.

I returned to the "township" to decide what I would do with my life. Employment opportunities were extremely limited in the Metropolitan Detroit area for people without a college degree. The Big 3 automobile manufacturers—Ford, Chrysler, and General Motors—were probably hiring at the time, but I did not have any connections to get a job with any of them. The other available employment opportunities only paid minimum wage. As comedian Chris Rock said, "Minimum wage is the minimum they can pay you, but if they could, they would pay you less." Minimum wage was $3.35 an hour in 1983 in Michigan. Saving money for college would have been impossible on such meager wages.

It was during this time that a new career opportunity became available for young Black men who were tired of being poor, attending school, or working at "dead-end" jobs with no chance for advancement. The position was (Street) Pharmaceutical Sales Representative. I qualified for the position, but I passed on it because the "fast life" was not for me. It was rumored that the pay and fringe benefits were excellent, but your career was usually short. Instead, I thought it would be more advantageous to work for one of our relatives: Yes, our *Uncle Sam*.

I went to the U.S. Army Recruitment Office in Ferndale, Michigan. One of the incentives the Army used to lure young people was the Veteran Education Assistance Program (VEAP). For every dollar you saved towards your college education, the Army would give you two dollars. Since I was not completely convinced that the Army was for me, I was able to sign up for a two-year tour of duty. As with all Armed Forces, I had to take the Armed Services Vocational Aptitude Battery Test (ASVABT). This test determined what occupations I was qualified for based on my test results. After the recruiter informed me of my choices of jobs, I selected the Military Occupational Specialty (MOS)—76P, which was the position of a Supply Clerk. At the time, it did not sound very challenging, but I could deal with it for two years. There were other jobs that offered more money for college, and even a signing bonus, but they were the difficult "grunt" jobs. These jobs were infantry, field artillery, tanker, and other jobs that trained you to be proficient at killing people. If I selected one of those jobs, I would have been on the front line during the time of war. The reason I joined the Army was to earn money for college and possibly learn a trade to increase my marketability after I got out of the Army, not to have a flag presented to my mother at my funeral.

Once I decided to join, I attempted to get some of my friends to join also, but they did not want any part of the Army. I assume that some of them were afraid to leave the "township". I was not afraid to attend college away from home or join the Army. As a young man, I was anxious to see what the world had to offer me, and it was important for me to have something to compare to the "township". If I returned home after my Army enlistment was over, at least it would have been by choice. Some people have never left the community where they grew up. I was not going to allow the fear of the unknown or the institutionalized racism in the United States to prevent me from "being all that I could be".

Basic Training

On May 26, 1983, I reported to Fort Dix, New Jersey, which was a place I would never forget. For eight weeks, this is where I was transformed temporarily, from being an individual to becoming the property of the United States Government. Now that I think about it, it almost sounds like someone owned me. That is a scary thought. Nonetheless, basic training was what a person made of it. For some, it was hell on earth. For others, it was fun. For me, it was tolerable. Can you imagine a job where you earn a decent salary, receive three meals a day, and are trained in combat? The Army gave me this opportunity.

In basic training, you were taught how to be a soldier and a member of a team. The living arrangements were "different." We lived in barracks, which were two-story buildings with none of the luxuries of home. There were ten men assigned to a large room, and fifty soldiers had to share the same bathroom, as the Army refers to it, the "latrine." The female soldiers lived in separate barracks. I wondered, "Why?" The cafeteria or, as it is referred to in the Army, "Mess Hall" was similar to an all-you-can-eat restaurant or a cafeteria at any large college or university, "in the world." "In the world" is what we referred to as civilian life. During basic training, there was no fraternizing between the male and female soldiers. When we ate our meals, the women sat on one side of the mess hall and we sat on the other side. If you were caught socializing with the opposite sex, the penalty was severe.

Before the break of dawn, basic training was extremely regimented and repetitious. Male and female soldiers were subjected to the same conditions and treatment during basic training. The only difference was that we were tormented separately. Every morning, we were forced to get up; I said "forced" because I would not voluntarily get up that early, unless I thought it was necessary. It did not take me very long to figure out that no one cared about what I thought. Some of you might remember the commercial, "We do more before 9 o'clock in the morning than most people do all day." They never lied. My day went as follows:

3:30A.M.:	The sound of "Taps" (a traditional song for the Armed Forces, played by bugle) over the sound system would wake us up. Every morning, all of us would rush to the latrine to wash up, and rush back to the room to make our beds. If you were late to formation, you had to do push-ups.
4:30A.M.:	We reported for formation for roll call and morning physical training.
5:30A.M.:	We ate breakfast fast because the day was filled with fun activities.
6:30A.M.:	By this time, all of us had to be in our fatigues and in formation. This is really when basic training began. My day
5:00P.M	consisted of exercising, training, and marching.
5:15P.M	Dinner
6:00P.M.	Free time.
9:00P.M.:	Lights out!

Allow me to give a more detailed description of a typical day for a male or female soldier during basic training. An important part of being a soldier is being in good physical shape. The Army used physical training (PT) to obtain its objective. PT consisted primarily of push-ups, sit-ups and running, and running, and running, and more running. My thought was: If you're going to give me a weapon, why do I need to run? We would run all over Fort Dix. The only time I can remember running on a track was during our competition. Everyday, sometimes twice a day, we endured the same routine. The fun part about PT was that there were soldiers from all over the United States competing to be the best in doing push-ups, sit-ups, and running. No matter what exercise, I usually finished in the top five. Some soldiers could not take the physical demands of PT and basic training. Unfortunately, those soldiers were kicked out of the Army. If you ever see an out-of-shape soldier, he or she became that way after basic training, certainly not during it.

An interesting part of basic training was when we had to march to a location on post for Tactical Training. This is when we were trained to properly operate the M-16A1 Rifle, M60 Machine Gun, Light Anti-tank Weapon and the Grenade Launcher. Everyday, we practiced shooting and thoroughly cleaning the M-16A1 Rifle. We were taught that, during combat, your weapon was your best friend so you had better know how to take care of it. Target practice was challenging. We were taught how to hit a target up to 100 yards away, using our M-16A1, without a scope. On the final day of Tactical Training, we were tested for accuracy and our ability to perform under pressure. Expert is the highest badge you could earn, followed by Sharpshooter and then Marksman. I earned the Marksman badge. For me, that meant that on a good day, the enemy would be shipped home in a body bag. On a bad day, I would be shipped home in a body bag. If you ever go into combat, make sure the person who shares a foxhole with you earned an Expert badge.

The most stressful training was learning how to throw a hand grenade. In the movies, they make it look easy, but in real life, it is scary. Every time we were trained in the use of a particular weapon, a trained, experienced sergeant was the instructor. One at a time, we had to climb into a foxhole while wearing a flack jacket, a.k.a., a "bulletproof vest" and helmet. The sergeant would instruct us on how to correctly position the hand grenade against our chest, pull the pin and throw it. If you dropped it in the foxhole, you had better pray that you were able to get out of there before it exploded. When we were going through our Tactical Training exercises, the weather conditions did not matter. We trained in the blazing sun, and in the rain. It is safe to assume that when you are in war, the enemy does not wait for a sunny day.

Basic training was not all misery and no fun. The obstacle course was challenging. If you ever watched the movie, "Stripes" with Bill Murray, a real obstacle course is similar to the one seen in that movie. All of us had to race against the clock, and each other, through various obstacles. Since I had always participated in sports, anything that was physically challenging kept my interest.

One unforgettable and unpleasant experience of basic training was when we were trained in the proper use of our gas masks. During war, some countries use chemical and biological weapons that can kill you slowly or instantly. Being able to put on a gas mask properly could be the difference between life and death. At the end of training one day, a group of us was led into a room where we were informed that we had thirty seconds to put on our masks with a secure seal. You would know that it was not sealed properly if you started choking and gasping for air. After the gas was released, we were instructed to remove our gas masks and recite our name, rank, and social security number. As soon as I removed my mask and inhaled the gas, which is similar to the gas that police release during riots, I tried to run through the wall to get out. The gas caused an unimaginable burning sensation in my eyes and throat, which caused me to cough uncontrollably. Some of my fellow soldiers were able to inhale it and it did not affect them at all. Other soldiers ran out of the room and vomited. I told myself—never again.

The worst parts of basic training were the drilling and marching exercises. To practice drilling and marching, two to four hours a day, was excessive in my opinion. Although I hated marching, I understood the need to learn how to march effectively. In all honesty, if the Army did not teach us how to march, most of the brothers would have been marching cool, as if they were back home on the block. The cadences that we marched to were humorous. The only cadence song I can remember is, "Jodie got your girl and gone . . . Your left, your left, your left, right, left. Pick up your left, your left, your left, right, left." Listening to a drill sergeant, or another soldier lead a good cadence song made marching halfway enjoyable. Can you imagine marching in the hot blazing sun with fatigues on, wearing a backpack filled with survival gear, and carrying an M-16A1 Rifle? I don't think so.

When we were not marching, for what seemed like countless miles on some days, we were in drill practice. During drill practice, we were taught basic maneuvers such as: How to pivot on your opposite foot when you made left and right turns; How to do an "about face" (a 180 degree turn); How to perform maneuvers with our rifles as we marched. The drills looked impressive when all of us performed them with precision. The drills we practiced were for the battalion competition and we had to be inspected by the Battalion Commander. We had to stand at the parade rest position, where our arms were folded behind our backs for one half-hour in the blazing, hot sun. One soldier had fainted. Later, he claimed it was from heat stroke. I think it was because his I.Q was higher than the rest of ours. The rest of us were stupid for not coming up with that brilliant idea before he did. Fortunately, I decided to join the Army in May and was assigned to basic training in New Jersey. It would have been difficult to learn to march in the dead of winter in New Jersey or in the middle of summer in Georgia, Alabama, or any other hot state where basic training was held.

When training was finally over for the day, we were allowed three hours of free time, from 6:00P.M. to 9:00P.M., which was when the lights went out. Just before we were released from the final formation at 6:00P.M., we had mail call. Some soldiers received letters and others did not. Some received a "Dear John" letter. A "Dear John" letter is a letter from your mate back home stating that he or she was leaving you for someone else. It was devastating and a total heartbreak for the soldier who received that type of letter. If you told anyone about it, you would be teased throughout basic training.

After mail call, all of us went our separate ways for three hours. We could use most of the facilities on post. Since most military posts are similar to large college campuses and comparable to a small city, a number of activities were available. Although we were not supposed to fraternize with soldiers of the opposite sex, as always, the cool brothers found a way to get the women. I was not one of the cool brothers. Most of my time was spent writing letters back home or playing basketball. When I was not doing that, I was performing extra duty for my inability to repress the desire to tell a certain drill sergeant where he could go and who he could take with him.

As I mentioned in the introduction, either you "manned up" or were harassed constantly in the "township." Well, I got harassed regularly during basic training. Not by other soldiers, but by Drill Sergeant "Pain" (Think of the meanest, toughest person you ever loved to hate, and this sergeant fit the description). Upon my arrival at basic training, our drill sergeant assigned me the position of Platoon Leader because the other drill sergeant for our company had not arrived. As a Platoon Leader, it was my responsibility to ensure that all of the soldiers were in formation and not getting into trouble. To make a long story short, I did not have this position long. When Drill Sergeant "Pain" arrived, I was relieved of my position after only one week.

For the next seven weeks, my life in the Army was miserable because of that man. I could not stand him! Every time he got the opportunity to make life miserable for me, he did, and it happened every day. Always remember that regardless of how bad you think you are on your block, in your school, or in your neighborhood, there is always someone bigger and tougher. You probably have not met that person yet, but if you live long enough, you will meet him or her.

Drill Sergeant "Pain" was my worst nightmare. I don't think he had anything personal against me. It was his responsibility to break any soldier that thought they could not be broken, and I was one of those soldiers. In order for a soldier to be effective during the time of combat, he or she had to be able to follow orders without questioning those orders. I have always wanted to be the leader and follow no one. There were numerous methods for a drill sergeant to attempt to break a soldier. Drill Sergeant "Pain" attempted a variety of ways to alter my "I fear no one" mentality. His first method was kitchen police, a.k.a. "KP duty". That is when you are assigned to clean the mess hall after hundreds of soldiers have been served one of the three meals a day. Can you imagine washing an infinite number of dishes, pots, and pans? "KP duty" did not motivate me to change my behavior. To me, it was a fringe benefit because I was able to eat all of the leftover food I wanted. Please do not believe the lies. The food we were served during basic training was delicious. Another reason I liked "KP duty" was because it got me out of daily marching drills. I hated marching in the sun and rain. The bottom line is, I hated marching. Period!!!

One day, after all other methods of breaking me had failed Drill Sergeant "Pain" did the ultimate. He ordered me to come out, front and center of the formation, because he did not like a remark that I made. I was told to "drop and give him twenty." That meant I had to get on the ground and do twenty push-ups. I finished and got up with a look like, "Is that all you got?" Drill Sergeant "Pain" was furious. He walked up to me and got right in my face. Our noses were almost touching. He yelled, "DO YOU WANT TO HIT ME, PRIVATE PROPHET?" I yelled, "YES DRILL SERGEANT!" He took off his hat and yelled, "DO IT, PRIVATE!" I balled up my fists as tight as I could, as tears rolled down my cheeks. Now, Drill Sergeant "Pain" was about 5'9, 200 pounds, and built like a cross between the "Rock" and an NFL linebacker. If I would have hit him, he would have beat me senseless.

Then I would have received an Article 15, a form of non-judicial punishment. I could not imagine having to forfeit half of my check every month, for a specific period of time, not being able to leave the barracks for thirty days, getting extra duty, and being demoted in rank. Those were the specific conditions of an Article 15. It provided commanders with an essential and prompt means of maintaining good order and discipline, and promoted positive behavior changes in service members, without the stigma of a court-martial.[1] It allowed the unit commander to do almost whatever he or she felt was necessary to make you conduct yourself as a respectable soldier. This would have been enforced against me, and I probably would have been kicked out of the Army since I was still in basic training. I did not want to be kicked out of the Army on a dishonorable discharge. It is difficult enough getting a job just by being Black. Add a dishonorable discharge to that, and it would almost be like having a criminal record. With one swing, my life could have become far worse than it already was.

I learned early in life, to think about the consequences of my words and actions before I act. After I thought about the consequences, most of the time, I did or said the same thing anyway. However, I decided to be both safe and smart this time. When I declined the offer to hit him, he laughed and said, "Look at you, crying like a girl." Well, like they always say, there is a first time for everything. That was the first time I could remember being verbally humiliated in public.

In life, you have to learn not to allow what someone says to you, to provoke you to say or do something that you will regret for the rest of your life. It takes more of a man to remain quiet and not react. It takes a fool to do or say something stupid. Later that evening, I was assigned to clean up a storage area in our barracks. From that day on, I was Drill Sergeant "Pain's" verbal punching bag.

I wrote my oldest brother and explained to him what happened. He wrote back and gave me the following advice: "Military is all about discipline, especially in basic training. Take my advice—STRAIGHTEN UP! Having an attitude is detrimental to getting ahead or getting what you want out of the service. It's recorded and will be considered in your evaluation. That could hamper you in promotions, special training, etc. Now don't get me wrong. There are a lot of things they do that are unnecessary, but there is nothing, or not too much, you can do about it. The more you verbalize your feelings, the worse it will get for you. Then, it will seem like you're being picked on, and you will be right. Just be cool and hang in there. It will all be better once you get out of basic training."

After I read the advice from my wise, older brother, Drill Sergeant "Pain" did not have any more problems out of me, although his efforts to demoralize me lasted for seven more weeks. I added the advice that my brother gave me about basic training because a number of young people are going to join the Armed Forces, and they may not have the opportunity to receive good advice from an older brother or sister who was also in the Armed Forces. As I have matured and experienced more in life, the same advice still holds true today— The more you verbalize your feelings, the worse it will get for you. It will become apparent, as you continue to read, that I did not follow my brother's wise advice completely.

Finally, after enduring eight weeks of intense training and ego deflating experiences, I graduated from basic training on July 22,

1983. Not with flying colors, but definitely more of a man than I was when, I first arrived at basic training.

Advanced Initial Training—(AIT)

The bus left Fort Dix, New Jersey on Friday at 4:00P.M. and arrived at Fort Lee, Virginia at 2:00A.M. on Saturday morning. I did not get to bed until 3:00A.M. When I woke up, it was around lunchtime. After I ate, I toured the base. Fort Lee was nothing like Fort Dix. This was primarily a training base for certain job classifications, although I don't think there was any basic training conducted there at that time.

Advanced Initial Training (AIT) is for soldiers to learn the academic application of their Military Occupational Specialty (MOS). It was similar to a short training course that a person would enroll in at college or training that is provided at work for employees. AIT is designed to prepare the soldier for work once he or she is assigned to a permanent duty location. When not in combat, every soldier is assigned to a regular job like in the civilian world.

When I entered the Army, my job classification was a 76P, which was a Material Control and Accounting Specialist. I was enrolled in courses that provided basic bookkeeping and accounting principles. And just like in basic training, we had to get up at 4:00A.M., clean up, eat breakfast, do police call and march to class. We attended classes from 7:00A.M. to 1:00P.M., Monday through Friday, for eight weeks.

After we ate lunch, we all participated in "Fort Lee Beautification." We would march around the entire base, picking up paper and debris for three hours, supposedly. I am sure that I eventually figured out a way to get out of it. After the beautification assignment was finished for the day, we marched to the mess hall for dinner. Again, the food was delicious.

In AIT, leaders placed a great emphasis on order and cleanliness. From 5:00P.M. to 8:00P.M., we had "G.I. Parties." No, this was not a party with music, food, drinks, and ladies. This was a party with mops, brooms, sponges, toilet brushes, soap, and elbow grease. We had to clean every square inch of the barracks. Our rooms had to be immaculate. The barracks were similar to the one I lived in during basic training but more modern. There was a specific layout for our locker, and it had to be set up accordingly, without any deviations. The brass that we wore on our Class-A uniform, our belt buckles, boots, and dress shoes had to shine. The beds had to be made so tight that you could bounce a quarter off of them. During AIT, we were taught how to be disciplined soldiers, whether we liked it or not. At 8:00P.M., the unit commander would come through for an inspection. We had to stand at parade rest while he inspected our locker and asked us questions. If he found something wrong, it had to be corrected, immediately after he left.

When it came to military discipline, our unit commander was no joke. During the week, we had to be in bed by 10:30P.M. If it was discovered that you were not in bed on time, you were assigned to extra duty. If you left your locker unlocked and you were not in the room, you could be subjected to an Article 15. You also had to maintain a clean-cut appearance. Your hair had to be cut short and you could only wear beard if you had a shaving profile. A shaving profile is authorization from a physician, confirming that shaving causes hair bumps to develop on the face and neck. This skin problem only occurs with some Black men. If a soldier has a shaving profile, he does not have to shave, but he must still maintain a neat beard, that does not exceed the regulated length.

At 5:00P.M., every Friday, we were released until 7:00A.M. on Monday morning. During most weekends, I would get together with some other soldiers and go to Washington, D.C. or visit some other cities in Virginia. If I stayed on base, I would hang out at the gym or go to the movies. Compared to basic training at Fort Dix, AIT at Fort Lee, Virginia was marvelous.

One week before my graduation, I signed up for Airborne Training. I was going to learn how to jump out of an airplane without breaking every bone in my body. The waiting list to enroll in Airborne Training was so long that I would have had to stay at Fort Lee for another two weeks. I decided that trying to become a successful Black man in America was challenging enough. When my orders came, I said good-bye to Fort Lee without hesitation.

Tour of Duty—Fulda, Germany

After flying on a 747 over the Atlantic Ocean for what seemed like 24 hours, I arrived in Frankfurt, Germany. It was my first time leaving the United States. Another thing I can give the Army credit for is providing the opportunity for me to see the world. I had to remain at a processing center in Frankfurt with some other soldiers before we were transferred to Fulda, Germany.

Fulda, Germany was located in the eastern corner of West Germany, before the reunification of Germany. The bordering country was East Germany. In 1983, Fulda would play an important role if West Germany or the United States went to war with Russia. This was the place where Russia would have initiated its attack, through the Fulda Gap. I was extremely glad to hear that. Yeah, right! If WWIII began as soon as I arrived in Fulda, I would have been on the frontline. In order to prepare for such an attack, the Army had a tank division and an air cavalry division, which was on the airfield.

Throughout my military career, I was blessed to be stationed at what I considered to be the best duty posts, and I had the easiest jobs. The airfield was located approximately two miles up the hill and through a small village from the lower barracks, which was where the tank division was located. The soldiers who lived on the airfield were primarily helicopter mechanics, small vehicle mechanics, cooks, supply technicians, and all of the other occupations that were necessary for a division to operate efficiently.

In comparison to the lower barracks, life on the airfield was paradise, in part, because of our living accommodations. I lived in one of the Army barracks that looked like a modern apartment building. Unlike basic training, only two people shared a room. In addition, we had our own bathroom in the room. It was like a large one-bedroom apartment. Our cafeteria was located not more than 50 yards from our barracks. The living conditions were great compared to those of the lower barracks.

The soldiers who lived in the lower barracks stayed in buildings that were probably built right after WWII. There was no real comparison between the airfield barracks and the lower barracks, as the only advantage we had on the airfield was better living arrangements. The soldiers in the lower barracks had everything you would expect to find in a small city in the United States. The lower barracks had a grocery market, post exchange (PX), post office, gym, hospital, movie theatre, schools, athlete fields, and nightclub. The Post Exchange (PX) is similar to Target, Walmart, JC Penney, or any other department store but not as large. Another advantage the lower barracks had that we did not have was female soldiers. Female soldiers or civilians were not allowed on the airfield. There were female helicopter pilots, but they stayed off post. If I wanted to do anything other than eat and sleep, I had to walk two miles to the lower barracks. As I reminisce, I think the soldiers in the lower barracks had the advantage.

One of the first things I learned about the Army is that people from all over the United States joined for different reasons. A number of soldiers in my unit came in to earn money for college, just as I had. Many of them came from impoverished areas all over the United States. The Army provided an opportunity for them to have a stable life for the first time. Some joined to develop a career and support their families. All I wanted was to do my time and move on after completing my two years.

On the airfield, we were in our own world. The airfield was one place where your nationality did not matter. There were Blacks, Whites, Mexicans, Puerto Ricans, and Hawaiians. Most of the Black soldiers were from southern states—Louisiana, Georgia, South Carolina, and Mississippi. The accents of some of those brothers were hilarious. There was a guy from South Carolina with such a strong accent that I had to ask him to repeat himself three times before I could understand him. After I got used to their southern accents, I discovered they were regular people, like myself.

The brothers from Detroit, Cleveland, and certain cities in New York were no joke. The slightest word or action would provoke them to fight. It was easy to guess where the Black soldiers were from. Most of the Black soldiers from the northern cities were cool. There were some brothers from Detroit who did not have the hard mentality that was associated with Detroit. Then there were the soldiers who probably had only two choices—go to the military or go to jail. Last but not least, there were soldiers who joined to stay alive because they were trying to get away from someone who was out to get them.

For the first time, I observed that not all White people are alike. On the airfield, there were educated White soldiers who came from affluent families, as well as White soldiers from the southern states who were "country." There were also White soldiers who came from the poorest White communities in America. Please do not believe that Black people have a monopoly on being poor in America.

Once you are in the Army for the most part, you are not recognized by your color but by your rank. I came in as an E-3, Private First Class (PFC), because of my college credits, and therefore, was not the lowest ranking private. Being a PFC is not something to write home about, but it does give you more money and a little advantage over an E-1 and E-2. For an E-3 to try to pull rank on an E-1 or E-2 is like a third grader trying to bully a second grader. It is not worth it. All enlisted soldiers are under the ranking system of noncommissioned officers (NCO). If I entered the Army as an E-1 Private, I could have conceivably moved up to the rank of E-9, Sergeant Major. The chances would have been better for me to become the President of the United States than becoming an E-9. The ranks of the enlisted soldiers that lived on the airfield were from E-1, Private to E-5, Sergeant. Officers, NCO E-6 and above were not permitted to live on the airfield. They lived either in Army housing off post, or on the German economy, along with their families, if they came with them. The Germany economy was considered any place that was not located on the military post.

When it came to socializing on the airfield, rank and color did not matter. Most of the time, I socialized with eight other soldiers. We all ate together in the mess hall, played basketball, and hung out together after duty. Since nine out of ten privates were between the ages of 18 and 21, most acted their age. After we were released from duty, or after we came back from a field exercise, it was all about women, beer, and having a good time. The behavior of most of the lower ranking soldiers on the airfield was equivalent to the behavior of any young person on a college campus or "in the world." For example, my roommate, who was from Atlanta, was something else. For some reason, trouble would follow him. Every week he would be in trouble. One night, he fell out of the second floor window of our room and broke his wrist. They charged him with destroying government property. He was the government property they were accusing him of destroying. Countless situations that my roommate and other soldiers got themselves into were just as bad, or even worse than that incident.

The Army is an excellent place for young men and women to mature. The policies and procedures give you just enough rope to hang yourself, but the military laws and consequences stop you before you go too far. One such military law is an Article 15 as I explained earlier. As for me, I was determined not to receive an Article 15 after my experience in basic training. My primary goal for joining the Army was to save money to cover the cost of college, purchase a car, and do my two years without getting into any trouble. Because I joined the Army with a goal, I was able to remain focused and not allow the immature behavior of other soldiers deter me from my goals. Just like "in the world" or what is commonly referred to as "civilian life," you must always be careful of the people you associate with.

Initially, my job on the airfield was easy and boring. I was assigned to the supply room in the hangar. My responsibility was to fill orders for helicopter parts and maintain inventory in the stockroom. Two days a week, I had to drive a 2½ ton Army truck to a city, 50 miles from Fulda, to pick up helicopter parts. Of course, the reason it was called "the airfield" was that the Army Air Division was located there. For security purposes, I will not describe the helicopters. The same helicopters you have seen in war movies were located on the airfield. It was my job to provide all of the parts that the mechanics needed to ensure that the helicopters were ready for combat.

Just when I thought Army life could not get any easier, it did. On March 13, 1984, the Company Commander of the airfield reassigned me to the Unit Arms room. My job as the Unit armorer was to issue weapons to the guards. When we went on field exercises, or if we went to war, it was my responsibility to issue weapons to all of the soldiers. Most of the weapons in the arms room were M-16A1 rifles, M-60 machine guns, and .38 caliber revolvers, which were issued to the officers. Before I received the armorer position, I was required to be present at the 7:00A.M. company formation and pull guard duty. After I was given the position, I did not have to do anything. At 7:00A.M., I would open the arms room that was located near the main office. From 7:00A.M. to 11:00A.M., I cleaned and issued weapons. Then I went to lunch. After lunch, I returned to the arms room and chilled out until I got off at 3:30P.M. I was assigned to one of the easiest jobs on the airfield, and the other soldiers hated it.

I assume that the Company Commander assigned me to the arms room because of my former job title, as well as my level of mental competence. From the first day that I arrived on the airfield, I conducted myself professionally and courteously. Since I did not drink alcohol or associate with soldiers who had documented behavior problems, it was easy for me to develop a good reputation.

When I joined the Army, soldiers were not given psychological exams to determine their mindset. Some of the soldiers on the airfield were not playing with a full deck! I wouldn't have trusted most of them with a water gun, much less in an arms room full of weapons and ammunition. It was a job of great responsibility. In my mind, this was a classic case of "you never know when someone is watching you," so I was glad I always conducted myself in a mature, responsible, and professional manner, on a 24/7 basis. There is no way that the Company Commander would have entrusted weapons and live ammunition to an irresponsible or immature person.

Once a year, our unit had a major training exercise in a secret location in Germany. Army divisions from all over Germany would come together and train for war. I had to go to the field with our unit for one month. It was rough. We had to set up large tents with a heater in the middle of it to keep us warm in the dead of winter. Between 10 and 15 soldiers slept in one tent. It seemed a lot worse than it was. It's been said that misery loves company. I had a lot of friends to be miserable with. My job classification was primarily a support position. There was not much work for me to do, so I read and wrote letters everyday. The soldiers in the field infantry, tank division, and air division had to go to various firing ranges to practice engaging tanks, helicopters, and other confidential training activities that I cannot discuss. I was given the opportunity to fire live rounds out of a Huey helicopter during one of the training exercises. Other than almost shooting a deer because we were so far up in the air I could not see what was on the ground and being cold, the experience was fun. After we were relieved of duty for the day, I was able to lift weights in the gym or play basketball. Life in the field was not a bad experience, but everyone was happy when we finally made it back to the comfort of the airfield.

After we returned to the airfield, I kicked back and chilled out while other soldiers celebrated and had a good time. For the next eight months, my life was easy: Go to the arms room, Monday thru Friday, from 7:00A.M. to 3:30P.M.; after work, stay out of trouble; enjoy life and remain focused. Some time in October 1984, I received orders that I was going to be transferred to another unit in Frankfurt, Germany.

It came as a shock and a disappointment to me. I had finally established myself in the job as armorer and had developed camaraderie with the other soldiers. All of us on the airfield had come to terms with our assignment in Fulda, Germany. We were the first line of defense! Although we did not volunteer to be on the frontline, we knew what was expected of us. We were expected to fight valiantly to the death, if necessary.

The camaraderie not only existed among enlisted members but also among officers. Although enlisted members were not permitted to fraternize with officers after duty hours, we did work with them. Most of the officers who flew helicopters were Chief Warrant Officers (CWO). They were officers, but they were not into all of the head games like the regular officers. Most of the Chief Warrant Officers joined the Army because they wanted to be helicopter pilots and could care less about telling other soldiers what to do. The chemistry that I developed on the airfield with soldiers of different races, religious beliefs, economic backgrounds, ranks, and reasons for coming into the Army had finally become clear. If I had to go to war and die fighting for something, it would have been to fight to keep my fellow soldiers and myself alive. I would not have been fighting for the United States and the American way of life.

Frankfurt, Germany

I reported to a military post in Frankfurt, Germany on October 19, 1984. Frankfurt was to Fulda, what New York or Chicago is to any small city in the United States. There was no comparison. Fulda was a small farming community. The public transportation system in Frankfurt was the best that I had ever experienced. You could catch a train or subway anywhere, and it would arrive on time and depart on time. Anything you wanted to purchase was obtainable at the post exchange (PX) or on the German economy. Most Armed Forces posts in Germany and other countries are self-contained, which means that everything that military personnel needed was located on the post. One advantage for military personnel to shop on the German economy was the high conversion rate of the American dollar to the German Deutsche Mark. During 1984, for every American dollar, you would receive 3.20 German Deutsche Mark. That was an excellent conversion rate.

Frankfurt was where all of the military personnel from all over Germany came to have a good time on the weekends. The variety of clubs, entertainment, and nightlife activities was endless. Frankfurt was a present-day Sodom and Gomorrah. For those of you who may not know it, prostitution is legal in Germany and other countries in Europe. What do you get when you have legalized prostitution, cheap beer, and immature soldiers in the same place? Hell on earth!

I was stationed at a post so far from the frontline, it did not seem to be a part of the Army. Most of the military posts in Frankfurt were processing and support units. All of the military positions were administrative and non-combative. I think the military police had the most difficult job—to keep disorderly soldiers in line. I was assigned to a logistic unit that prepared . . . Again, due to confidentiality I cannot divulge any specific information. You are probably thinking that I was some kind of spy for the government. Not! My job was so easy that I can't remember what I did. All I can remember is that I worked in a unit for a Sergeant First Class (SFC), and that he was the most down-to-earth man in the Army. Some sergeants, and most officers, took their rank and job too seriously. The sergeant I worked for kept everything in perspective, and made the remaining seven months of my military career as tolerable as possible. As long as I was on duty, everything was orderly and in control. The hours after work, in the barracks, was when the Army life became intolerable. Unlike the apartments I lived in, on the airfield in Fulda, Frankfurt had large, 3-story buildings. My building was co-ed with four men to a room. There was one large latrine on each floor. For seven months, I had to co-exist with the most immature, alcoholic, partying, fighting, and irresponsible people that had ever been assembled in one place. Some of their behavior on the weekends was almost identical to a weekend party at a college fraternity house.

As most of you probably know, in the Armed Forces the people who give the soldiers orders are officers. The officers in my unit in Fulda were excellent. I would not have had any trouble going to battle and following their orders. The officers in my unit in Frankfurt were a different story. I did not respect most of them. The unit commanders were "straight." While in Frankfurt, we initially had a male commander, who left and was replaced by a female commander. There were other officers in the unit ranging from first lieutenant to captain. An officer has the authority to delegate orders to enlisted soldiers, ranked from E-1 to E-9. A low ranking officer would have to have some enormous testicles to tell an E-8 or E-9 what to do.

Some officers in the Army come from prestigious military schools like West Point, but I doubt that any of those officers were in my unit. Those officers were assigned to higher priority units. The officers we had were regular people with undergraduate degrees. A Bachelors' Degree was one of the requirements to become an officer in the United States Army. I think some officers came into the Army to get the respect that they could not get "in the world." I never respected the rank. If you want to be respected as a man, you have to earn that respect. You have to either be mentally or physically superior to me, or conduct yourself in a manner that I consider worthy to lead me. In Royal Oak Township, we did not acknowledge rank. We respected knowledge, courage and a "street mentality." Either you were respected as a man or you were considered weak. I believe in leading by example, and the officers in my unit were not worthy to lead anyone. Thank God, we did not go to war while I was in that unit. Not only did I not have respect for the officers, but I also had no respect for some of my fellow soldiers who were stationed with me in Frankfurt.

When you are in the Army, you are supposed to conduct yourself as a soldier, 24/7. I assume that leadership was more relaxed since we were nowhere near the frontline. In the barracks, we were all treated like adults, although the behavior of most of the soldiers was that of high school students. The behavior and actions of some soldiers in the barracks were too embarrassing to mention, but I will explain how the Army dealt with such problems.

"In the world," we have to answer to the laws of the city, state, and federal government. There are a number of criminal activities that people engage in that are not brought to the attention of the police or a higher authority. One reason is because people do not care, and another reason is that the police and people in higher authority are, oftentimes, committing the same crimes. Since there is a system of rank in the Army, there is always someone with a higher rank who will turn you in. Some of the acts of the soldiers in my unit were so blatant that the military police had to get involved. The chance of getting caught and reported to your unit commander in the Army is far greater than the chance of a civilian being reported.

Previously, I mentioned an Article 15 was a very effective deterrent. For the immature and irresponsible soldiers who came into the Army without any respect for authority or government property, an Article 15 could certainly get them back on the road to being a good soldier.

As my final days in the Army drew near, I was becoming a "short-timer." In the Army, soldiers would count their final one hundred days on a calendar. The closer you got to leaving, the "shorter" you became. If you were only a "good" soldier throughout your Army career, you became an exceptional soldier during the final 100 days.

Reasons For Leaving

Two months prior to the end of my two-year contract, an Army recruiter asked me if I wanted to "re-up," which means to sign up for another tour of duty. I am sure you can guess what I wanted to tell them. The United States Army and I had honored the two-year contract we made with each other.

I had accomplished my goals of saving money for college through the Veteran Education Assistance Program (VEAP), and the money I had saved for a car was more than enough. Saving money was easy for me. Especially since the Army provides a free furnished place to live and three meals a day. The only things I spent money on were items I needed for everyday living, a color television, a VCR, and some casual/dress clothes. Since I did not hang out at the clubs, drink alcohol, or participate in other activities that cost money, there was nothing for me to do but save my money. For two years, I remained focused and did not allow anything to distract me from my goal.

In my opinion, the Army had too much control over my life. The only person I want to have that much control over my life, other than God, is me. The Army controlled where I lived, how long I would live there, what I ate, what time I woke up, and who my friends were during the time I was under its authority. For instance, if I awoke one morning and decided that I was tired of being a soldier and wanted to quit, I would be court-martialed and most likely sent to military jail. In the Army, you cannot be tired of being a soldier until your contractual obligation has been fulfilled.

Throughout this reflection of my Army experience, I never mentioned racism. When you are dealing with a system of rank, racism can be easily disguised. If I was the victim of racism during my short military career, I was oblivious to it. I always received the easy job assignments and, apparently, as an E-3, I did not pose a threat to the higher-ranking NCOs and officers.

Although I did not experience blatant racism, I am sure racism existed. What if a White sergeant or officer thought that all Black people were inferior to White people? How would that White sergeant or officer treat lower ranking Black soldiers? It is my opinion that they would make the Black soldier's Army experience a living hell. A person's rank or title does not change the way he or she feels about something. Depending on that person's rank or title, it only gives them more power to practice their beliefs on others. If Hitler were only a private in the German Army, he would not have been able to wreak havoc the way he did. Therefore, it is important that the wrong people are not allowed to have power, because rank does have its privileges.

While I was stationed in Fulda, Germany, a White Chief Warrant Officer (CWO) told me to get out of the Army. I don't remember the conversation that we had that caused him to offer me that advice. However, his suggestion just reaffirmed something I already knew. A year later when I was stationed in Frankfurt, I had to attend a meeting with the Sergeant First Class (E-7) that I worked for. During this meeting, I was introduced to a Black General. I immediately respected him for his ability to move up through the ranks to such a high position. That was a monumental accomplishment for a Black man in the Army in the eighties. This general also told me to get out of the Army. Even though I had already decided to leave the Army, this general's recommendation only reaffirmed that my decision was the correct one.

Advice

I would highly recommend the Army to any young person who has graduated from high school or college. The Army can provide young people with a valuable experience that they can benefit from for the rest of their lives. In today's difficult economic times, the Army can provide greater career growth for minorities than most corporations. With the high unemployment rate for Black people, particularly Black men, the Army is a viable option. Today, young Black men do have a number of choices, but they are not choices that I would recommend. They can live off their parents, work at a "dead-end" job, hope that a woman will take care of them, sell drugs or commit a crime and become a member of the penal system. The options for young Black women are not much better. They can get a "dead-end" job, have children and get on welfare, have a drug dealer support them, or also become a member of the penal system. Life is about establishing a decent standard of living for yourself, and your family, if you have one.

In 2004, the monthly salary for an E-1 (Private) with less than four months of service is $1,104.00. After four months, it increases to $1,193.40.[2] That might not sound like a lot, but consider that you have no overhead or expenses. You will not have to pay for rent, food, medical, dental, transportation, or anything else that is necessary to live. If you wanted, you could probably save $800.00 a month.

If you are seriously considering joining any branch of the Armed Forces, you should take the time and research them, just as you would in selecting a college. To be eligible for any of the Armed Forces, you have to score a minimum of 31 on the Armed Services Vocational Aptitude Battery Test (ASVABT). The higher your score, the wider selection of jobs you may qualify for. If one branch of the Armed Forces offers a better fringe benefit package based on your test score, I suggest that you sign up with that branch.

The Army and the other branches of the Armed Forces, will always need good Black soldiers and officers, both men and women. We, as a people, cannot avoid certain occupations, schools, careers, and other opportunities just because we fear the unknown. If we did, we would never leave our homes. Those of you who are completing your college education should consider a career in the military. Young Black men and women need good role models as officers.

The most important thing that I remembered throughout my Army career was to remain focused on the reason I joined. My goal was to save money for college and a car. A lot of soldiers joined the Army without a goal or plan. I saw a number of soldiers spend their entire check every month, on partying and buying material possessions that would be obsolete before they finished their tour of duty. If you go into the Army without a plan, you will not benefit very much from your time there.

When you talk to your recruiter about career possibilities, select an occupation that will be transferable to a civilian job. For example, most military police get out of the Army and easily make the transition to becoming a police officer. Plan to learn a trade or skill that will make you marketable when you get out of the service. If you select an occupation that is not in high demand "in the world," you may find yourself unemployed.

If the main reason you are considering the Armed Forces is to receive money for college, get a head start on college. Some military bases offer college courses. You can start taking courses part-time. You can also start disciplining yourself by reading and becoming proficient with computers and the current software programs that are available.

Another major consideration is the length of your military career. You would need to decide the following: How long you want to stay?; You are planning on re-enlisting?; Are you going to make a career of the service? It was easy for me to decide because I had already determined that I was not going to do more than two years. If I had re-enlisted and completed four or more years, I probably would have made a career out of the Army. I think it might be difficult to acclimate to civilian life after an extended period in the Armed Forces. Also, consider that there is a chance that you would not obtain a job with comparable pay and benefits when you return to civilian life. If you start a family while in the military, the transition back to civilian life would be much more difficult financially. In my opinion, once you do eight years, you might as well do twenty years and then retire.

The worst thing about the Army or any branch of the Armed Forces is the possibility of war. The role of all United States Armed Forces members is to protect and serve this country, and whomever else your commander-in-chief, President of the United States, commands you. Dying in a battle is not something anyone wants to think about, but it is a reality that all soldiers have to face. One thing you can do to possibly decrease your chances of being killed in battle is to vote for the correct presidential candidate in the United States of America.

Reflection

The two years that I served in the United States Army were the most carefree, relaxing and fun period of my life, so far. It gave me the opportunity to get away from the "township" and see what else the world had to offer. Having the chance to visit different states, different countries, and meet different people made it worthwhile. The military service is like a parent. All you have to do is follow the rules and you can live an easy life. For me, that life was too easy. I live for excitement and challenges. When life gets too boring for me, I usually do, say, or write something that will force me to change the course of my life.

Nevertheless, if I was graduating from high school today and did not have the money to go to college, I would definitely go to the Army, without question.

Chapter 3

SAGINAW VALLEY
STATE UNIVERSITY

*"But let every man prove his own work . . . For whatsoever a man
soweth, that shall he also reap."*

—Gal 6:4a, 7

Before I knew it, I was back in the old neighborhood again.
Those two years went by in no time. While I was still in the Army, I had
already made all the preparations necessary to attend Saginaw Valley
State University (SVSU), in September 1985. Since classes did not
start until September, I returned to Royal Oak Township. As soon as I
got out of the Army, I was able to apply for unemployment. All I had to
do was purchase a car, which I did, and wait for my unemployment
check to come every two weeks. I told myself that this was something I
could do. In 1985, the State of Michigan Unemployment Agency was
excellent compared to what is happening today, in 2004. When
summer ended, it was time to continue executing my plan.

Unlike Northwood University, where I lived on campus, I had the
opportunity to stay off campus with my brother in a city right outside
of Saginaw. For me, this living situation offered two major advantages.
First, it offered me the comforts of home and gave me a chance to get

away from my friends, family, adversaries, and other distractions that would have possibly taken my mind off of studying in my old neighborhood. Being in an unfamiliar city allows you to focus on your primary goals, because you do not know anyone and you do not know where to go. The second advantage of living off campus was that I did not have to pay for room and board. Room and board at most universities is equivalent to the cost of tuition for the full year. Tuition at SVSU for the fall semester of 1985 was $47.50 per credit hour. In comparison to other colleges and universities in 1985 and 2003, SVSU has always been affordable. This is when the Army's Veteran Education Assistance Program (VEAP) came into play. Every month, VEAP would send me a check to cover the cost of my tuition. The money I saved from the Army, VEAP, and the part-time job allowed me to pay for my tuition and focus attention on learning, without the pressures of how I would finance my education.

Academics

During my high school years, the brief stay at Northwood University and while I was in the Army, I never seriously thought about what career I would pursue. All I knew was that if I continued setting goals and trying to better myself, eventually I would discover my true calling. When I enrolled at SVSU, I decided to pursue a degree in Business Administration, majoring in Business Management. Since I knew I wanted to be a leader and that I was a people person, I thought Business Management would be an ideal career for me.

My core courses were not difficult, at least not the ones that I was able to pass the first time around. One of the most difficult courses for me was Cost Accounting. For as long as I could remember, I hated accounting. I believe this was because accounting deals with money and I never had any, so I didn't see a reason for becoming an expert on irrelevant issues. I learned about accounting the hard way. Accounting was a course that was progressive. As you went through the course, everything you learned in the previous chapter prepared you for the next chapter. If you did not grasp the concepts and accounting principles from day one, by day ten you were lost. By the third day, I was lost. This was mainly due to my failure to complete daily assignments. Now, for a little advice; it is not wise to procrastinate in college. Since most courses build on the knowledge you learn from previous course assignments, the completion of the first two assignments or failure to complete them, usually dictates your success or failure in the course.

In college, you have to keep track of the deadlines for dropping a course. If you drop a course before a certain day, you can receive fifty percent of your tuition back. If you withdraw before the next deadline date, you can get a "W" for the course and it will not affect your G.P.A. If you do not withdraw by that final deadline date, you will get an "F" and it will bring your G.P.A. down substantially. So even though I made the mistake of not applying myself enough to pass the class the first time, I was smart enough to withdraw before the deadline. The next semester, I took it again and received a grade of "C." The reason I did not say earn is because the instructor probably thought, "This young man helped pay my salary for two semesters, so the least I could do is give him a 'C.'" Who was I to argue with my instructor?

I considered the remaining courses in my management curriculum to be challenging but not difficult. The courses that permitted me to apply my natural strengths and abilities, such as rationalization, coercion, and persuasion, were my favorites, and my grades were indicative of it. Labor-Management Relations, Executive Strategies and Policies, Personnel Management, and Organizational Behavior were some of the courses that stimulated my interest, and I was enthusiastic about attending those classes.

The elective courses at SVSU were the ones that you took with your core courses to balance out your course schedule. You should make sure that your elective courses are not as demanding as your core courses. They usually are not that difficult if you select the correct courses with lighter coursework. This can also be helpful concerning your G.P.A. if you are diligent in performing above average in the elective courses, since we may not always do as well as we expect in the challenging core courses with heavy workloads. For me, it did not happen quite that way. Some of the elective courses that I thought were interesting were the following: Science of Life, General Psychology and Introduction to Political Science. While I was taking the other not-so-interesting elective courses, I continued to ask myself what relevant importance they had in connection with Business Management. After I graduated, I figured out the answer.

Instructors

After my first semester at SVSU, I discovered that the instructors came as a package deal. When I registered for the courses during my first semester, I selected courses based on convenience. For instance, I always attempted to have all my courses scheduled on Tuesdays, Wednesdays, and Thursdays and always in consecutive order. One class would be 9:00A.M. to 11:00A.M., 11:00A.M. to 1:00 P.M. or all of them at night. Since I did not live on campus, I did not want to drive 20 miles for one course. After I had a bad experience with one instructor, I decided to give greater consideration to the instructor who taught the course, instead of the day and time of the course.

I learned, very quickly, to ask about certain instructors. During my time at SVSU, I classified instructors in the following three categories; racists, realistic and overzealous. Instructors are only people, just like you and me. At most public and private universities throughout the United States, I would take an educated guess that 90 percent of the instructors are White, while 8 percent are other nationalities, and 2 percent are Black. In addition, at most large public and private universities, the enrollment of Black students is usually no greater than 10 percent. If you attend a Historically Black College or University, the percentages are the opposite.

As soon as you come to the realization that there are still many White people in the United States with racist views, the better you will be able to acclimate yourself to it. If your instructor was the grand wizard of the KKK, how many times do you think you would have to take that course if you are Black? During the fall semester of my sophomore year, I had to take a marketing course. For some reason, it was difficult for Black students to earn anything higher than a "C" in this course. I did not mind that I earned a "C." If a course did not keep my interest, I did not fully apply myself. This is true for many students in college. I can remember busting my butt in some courses, and I was satisfied with the "C" I earned because I knew I tried my best. Now, for the other Black students in the marketing course, who happened to be women, they also received "C's." Their class participation and ability to apply marketing principles on assignments was a definite indication that they deserved higher grades. However, if you know that your performance in the course warranted a higher grade, you should address this with the instructor.

As I stated earlier, instructors are people too so they make mistakes—knowingly and unknowingly. What I had to realize early in my college career was that there were going to be instructors who would not grade me by my efforts, participation, and test grades but by the color of my skin. Since the administration gives instructors carte blanche over their grading system, determining a student's grade is subjective. Other than this one instructor, I can honestly say that most of the instructors I had at SVSU appeared to grade students on their work and nothing else. Anytime a person is in a position of authority that person will be able to impose some degree of his or her beliefs on the people that are subject to that authority.

On the other end of the spectrum were the realistic instructors. These were the instructors who placed a college education in perspective. One of the most realistic instructors taught a statistics course. This particular instructor graded on a curve. When you know an instructor grades on a curve, it may not be different from regular grading, because it is based on the performance of the class, as a whole, before grades are distributed. Grading on a curve goes like this: The highest grade on a test, establishes the plateau. If the highest score was 80 percent that is where the "A" grade would begin. This meant that if a student received 60 percent on a test, instead of that grade being a "D," it would be a "C." I took this instructor for Statistics I & II. Both semesters I earned a "C." Statistics is about figuring out probability, and it is also considered a difficult course for many students. If the instructor based my grade in the course on one particular question: What is the probability of a Black person with a college degree receiving a job before a White person without a degree?

I would have earned an "A." The answer to that question is slim. Give me my "A."

I had another realistic instructor who taught a Social-Political-Legal Environment Business. This instructor reminded me of Don Johnson from "Miami Vice." He wore a ponytail, and all of the White women were infatuated with him. I am sure some of them earned extra credit. This instructor would randomly call on a student to answer a question and I was randomly selected quite often. Even if I did not know the answer, after I gave a convincing argument, it would have taken a genius to realize that I did not know what I was talking about. I guess he was a genius, because I earned a "C" in the course. To me, that "C" was equivalent to an "A" because I studied and did my best. As long as I give something a 110 percent effort, I do not mind failing. It did not have to be perceived as a failure, because it was an experience I could learn from. The only thing that mattered was that I gave it my all. That is the way I feel about life. I am going to put a 110 percent effort toward fulfilling my goals, and I am not going to stop giving my all until I stop breathing.

There were other instructors who were realistic in another away. I can remember some instructors in my core courses who gave most students, Black or White, the benefit of the doubt. As long as students applied themselves and tried their best, they would earn an "A" or "B." These instructors were previously employed in corporate America and they knew what was important and what was not.

Lastly, and the most irritating, were the overzealous instructors. These are the instructors who feel that the course they are teaching is vital to the survival of mankind and without it, mankind would cease to exist. Depending on what degree you are pursuing, most of the courses will not determine how well you will perform when begin your career. I will not go into detail about the obvious reasons for most of these courses. I remember taking a Production Management Course during one summer semester. During the summer, courses are accelerated because the semester is shorter. This one instructor gave this Black woman a "D" in a course that I felt would not have any significance once she entered the workforce. To make the situation worse, she only needed the credits from that course to graduate. I think she had to take another class in the Fall semester to graduate. Some instructors attempt to make what they deem as a high priority, your high priority also. However, it does boil down to selecting the courses you need as well as those required along with taking advantage of resources available to you such as tutoring, the instructor's assistance, and group studies.

The most important advice I can give future or current college students is to always respect your instructors. These instructors control your destiny while you are at that college or university. If you attempt to embarrass or disrespect an instructor in class, you better hope it is not too late to withdraw. You might as well transfer to another college if you develop a negative reputation and the instructors decide, collectively, to make your stay at the college long, challenging, and expensive. I was fortunate to have a pleasant personality and sense of humor throughout college. How an instructor feels about you personally can determine if you receive that extra point that could take you from a "B" to an "A," or from a "D" to a "C." Always make every effort to avoid committing any of the following acts of disrespect; disrupting class, tardiness, excessive absenteeism, or snoring in class.

Success Factors

From day one, it is imperative that you develop a rapport with a guidance counselor. They are there to assist you with selecting the correct courses at the correct time. Throughout my three years at SVSU, I do not recall seeking the advice of a guidance counselor. If I would have received advice, I'm sure that I would not have taken all of my core courses together in a semester, and all my easy elective courses in another. I should have taken two elective courses and two core courses each semester. One good decision I did make, without assistance, was to take independent study courses over the summer. For independent study courses, you usually meet with your instructor on the first day of class to get your assignments, and then meet at the end of the semester to turn in your assignments. Taking summer courses is advantageous because it allows you to earn the credits you need to graduate with a Bachelor's Degree in three years, instead of four. When I paid for my first course at SVSU, I officially became an adult and controlled my destiny. This was when my self-discipline was activated. When I attended Northwood University, I was not extremely disciplined. I was immature, irresponsible and probably did not understand the concept of college. I attended college using financial aid and a guaranteed student loan, and I probably rationalized that it was not my money, so who cares if I fail a class? This time around, I was concerned because I had sacrificed two years of my life to earn the money to attend college. I was not going to waste my hard earned money attending college to socialize, have fun, and flunk out. I did that at Northwood University. I could have saved myself some class time and money if I would have taken care of business the first time around.

When you are in college, you do not have your mother or father holding your hand and telling you to; get up and go to class, study hard, not to stay up too late, eat right, not to associate with the wrong people, etc. Similar to high school, I had to decide on my own to do the right thing. Not to mention that the only reason my brother allowed me to stay with him rent-free, was to give me the opportunity to earn my Bachelor's Degree. I did not have time to waste, and I could not afford to take classes over, two and three times. The only course I had to take twice was Cost Accounting.

The first day I set foot on the SVSU Campus, I was already focused and had formulated a plan. All I had to do was execute it expeditiously. You do not realize how much you learn from failing at something. I remember my time at Northwood University, when my roommates and I would schedule our courses around the soap opera, "All My Children." One day while I was attending SVSU, I did not have any classes, but I had to study for a test the next day. I got up that morning and wrote out a schedule. From 9:00A.M. to 12:00P.M., I would study, and then eat lunch. From 1:00P.M. to 2:00P.M., I was going to watch "All My Children," then continue to study from 2:00 P.M. to 5:00 P.M. When 1:00 P.M. arrived I thought to myself, Angie and Jessie on "All My Children" are already paid in full. It is time for me to get paid in full. From that day on, I have not allowed television, or any other irrelevant events or activities to take precedence over important responsibilities.

The last factor for success in college and life is self-motivation. A lot of people do not have dreams and aspirations. They are not going to encourage or push you to do your best. They may perceive that you think you are better than them. I earned my degree because I wanted to earn it and possibly provide a better standard of living for myself. There was a time when only one person in most Black families graduated from college, and other family members applauded their achievement.

Deep down inside some people cheer for you to fail because misery loves company. Guess what? I was not going to be misery's company when it came to graduating from college. A college degree did not guarantee me fame and fortune, but it did set the stage for other accomplishments throughout my life. In order to graduate, I had to combine determination, sacrifice, hard work, desire, financing, and the will to persevere. If everyone possessed all of those attributes, more people would graduate from college or be successful at whatever they chose to pursue in life. To keep it real, some people are afraid to dream. Then there are others who dream, but never wake up and do the things necessary to make that dream become a reality.

Self-Discovery

Self-discovery was the most important lesson of my college career. As I continued to strive to earn my degree at SVSU, I discovered a pattern about myself that also existed at Northwood University—my writing skills were extremely deficient. It was hard to believe that I could not construct a sentence properly. A number of my sentences would be poorly structured or run-on, or consist of fragments, incorrect subject-verb agreements, etc. This problem originated back in elementary school when I spent most of my school day in the principal's office instead of in the classroom. This was a weakness that I did not want to hide or deny. I was determined to one day turn this weakness into a strength.

The ability to communicate effectively, both in writing and verbally, is essential, not only in the Business Management Curriculum, but in everyday life. People observe the way you express yourself so they can form an opinion about you. My deficiency in English also had an adverse effect on my other courses. Grades on my assignments were lowered because of poor grammar, rather than problems with the content. By the time I enrolled in Advanced Composition, my English and grammar skills still had not improved considerably. My instructor would always give me a high rating for content and paragraph structure, but it was my grammar skills that always lowered my grade from an "A" to a high "C."

In this course, I discovered how poor my English usage was, but more importantly, I discovered my ability to communicate my thoughts in a way that was thought-provoking and at times, emotionally charged. In Advanced Composition, we were always given assignments where we had to do intensive research. During this course, I developed the ability to gather research information, analyze it, and utilize it in a way to bring the issues in society to life from my perspective.

Since the instructor allowed us to select our own topics for our essay papers, I would always select a topic of interest to me. I figured that if I had to do something, I might as well research something that I wanted to become more knowledgeable about. One topic of interest to me was the system of apartheid in South Africa. The information I learned from that research allowed me to realize some similarities between South Africa and the United States. I also did a term paper on welfare reform. This was a topic that I was able to identify with on a personal level. Again, it was my poor grammar usage that lowered the grade on an assignment that had the potential to be excellent.

The research assignment that catapulted me to a new realm of understanding was my essay on the exploitation of Black athletes. Throughout high school and college, I always wondered what motivated students to prioritize sports over academics. I remember that there were football players in some of my courses. At any given time, they would arrive to class late or leave early to attend practice. Athletic directors refer to them as student-athletes. It is difficult to just be a student at most universities, so it must be extremely difficult to be a so-called student-athlete. I was so concerned about how our young Black students were exploited because of their athletic abilities, and the information that I gathered on this subject was so compelling, that it later became the topic of one of the chapters in my novel, *Last Year Before Reality.*

Reflections

As I think about my learning experience at SVSU, it was a good one. The instructors there gave me the opportunity to reach my maximum potential. It was up to me to determine how well I performed. During my 3-year stay, I had a tendency to procrastinate. My instructors would give me a syllabus on the first day of class and I would wait until the day before the assignment was due to start and complete it. It was foolish of me to procrastinate, but it appeared that I excelled under pressure. Had I completed assignments more timely, I would have had the opportunity to have someone proofread them, and earn higher grades.

The most important lesson I learned by graduating from SVSU was that I could remain focused long enough to achieve this goal. This achievement gave me the confidence to reach for more challenging goals in the future and enabled me to learn about myself. I remember that I registered for five courses in the summer of 1986— a total of fourteen credit hours—and I passed all of them. Then there was my final semester when I registered for a total of twenty credit hours and earned a cumulative G.P.A. of 3.15. One reason I was able to do that was because I inadvertently saved most of my elective courses for last, and I was determined to graduate from college as soon as possible so I could continue with my life. Most of my peers thought I was crazy. I was not crazy, but determined.

If I knew then what I know now, I would have selected a different career path. My first choice would have been in a field that would have allowed me to assist young people in dealing with life. I think I would have been an excellent teacher, counselor, or principal. My next choice would have been a defense attorney. Any career where I could make a more positive difference in society would have been ideal.

At SVSU, I was taught how to think inside the box. After I graduated, I had to learn how to think outside the box, because you do not live your life in a classroom, but on the battlefield of life. College is similar to the Army, in a way. College administrators and instructors determine what courses are necessary for you to earn a particular degree. They develop the protocol for your participation in the process; registration, tuition costs; classroom/lecture hall location; scheduling and curriculum. All I was responsible for was acquiring the money.

The aforementioned preparation process was designed to ensure that I made a smooth transition into corporate America. One vital fact that I did not learn or failed to take the course in, was about the unwritten rules. The same rules of success that applied to White college graduates were not applicable for Black college graduates. I was never informed that a Black graduate with a degree did not have the same employment opportunities as a White graduate with a degree.

There were a number of pertinent facts that I did not learn at SVSU, but as soon as I graduated, I received a crash course in what my place would be in life. Earning an honest living in the United States, even with a college degree, has not been easy for me. There have been numerous challenges, and I have been knocked down more times than I care to remember. But the dust has not settled yet, and when it does, I am confident I will still be standing, because I know God is holding me up.

Advice For Today's Students

Higher education in 2003 is extremely different from when I graduated in 1988. Selecting the right college/university is vital to your future success. It is important to determine which college will offer the curriculum and/or academic opportunities that will be conducive for you to excel in your chosen career field and mature as an individual. Some people select a college because a friend is going there, or for some other irrelevant or trivial reason. Be sure you perform a thorough investigation of every aspect of the college, such as tuition costs, campus location, room and board costs (if you are staying on campus), the school's accreditation and ranking for your preferred area of study, degrees offered in your area of study, and costs for commuting. It is important to visit all the colleges you are interested in and make comparisons based on job placement of graduates as opposed to the number of parties they have a month or how good the football and basketball teams are. With today's advancement in technology and the Internet, all of the information you need to learn about any college is at your fingertips.

The cost of higher education increases every year. Private colleges/ universities are always more expensive than public colleges/ universities. If you are blessed to receive an academic scholarship to a particular college, then you can forego the college selection process. If you graduate from high school at a status of "Thank Ya Lawdy," like I did, instead of Magna or Summa Cum Laude, it might be more practical for you to attend a community college in your freshman year. Unless you are extremely confident in your ability to make the adjustment from high school to college and handle the increased challenge and intensity level of a college curriculum, community college offers advantages for freshman students.

The most significant reason for attending a community college your first year is that it will prepare you for the transition to a 4-year university. The cost per credit hour at most public and private colleges can range from $139 to $475, respectively. At community colleges, the cost per credit hour can range anywhere from $55 to $110, which is a substantial difference. With the dropout rate of freshman college students at approximately 30 percent, it would be more cost-effective and insightful to test the waters of higher education at a lower initial cost to you.

Selecting a career in the 1980's was easier than selecting a career in 2004. Advanced technology has created more career opportunities for individuals who are well prepared. If you are serious about making a career choice, you have to decide what is more important; a career that is motivated by the lure of money; or a career that will give you satisfaction and fulfillment because you are making a difference. There are millions of people who work at jobs with no personal satisfaction. The reason they go to work is to provide for the basic necessities in life and to pay the bills in an attempt to provide a decent quality of life for themselves and their family. On the other hand, there are the people who have careers that they feel good about and for which they have a passion; the type of career that they would do because they love what they do, even if they do not receive a large salary. One good example of a very fulfilling career is that of a teacher or youth counselor. The primary motivating factor for these two professions is the desire to help students. Just having the opportunity to make a positive difference in some child's life is more important than the money.

No one can decide which career you are best suited for or which will give you the greatest benefit. I would like to suggest that once you decide on the career you want to pursue, you should identify and read the autobiographies of people who have been successful in your chosen field. This will give you an enlightened perspective of what that career truly involves. If you are interested in law enforcement, I recommend that you read, *BLACK COP: The Real Deal*, by Richard Lewis. If you want to be an attorney for a prestigious law firm, I suggest that you read, *The Good Black*, by Paul M. Barrett. No matter what you want to be, there are books available that will let you experience that career through the eyes of another individual. To be successful in whatever career you select, it will take effort, determination, and preparation.

On the flip side, if you do not choose a career and pursue it passionately, you will end up with just a job. If you only remember one thing from this chapter, please remember this; If you do not live your own dream, you will live someone else's dream.

The job market today is saturated and extremely competitive. Throughout the United States, the unemployment rate grows daily. There are two major factors that cause this. The first one is global competition. Talented people from all over the world come to America to compete for jobs that were, at one time, reserved for United States citizens. This means, the odds of a Black person finding a job in corporate America becomes, even slimmer. There is even major competition for the lower paying jobs in America.

The other major factor that is causing the job market to be extremely competitive is the movement of large American corporations and their jobs to other countries. Corporations do this because the United States has labor laws and unions that prevent them from paying their workers wages so low that it is difficult to determine if it is a job or slavery. In developing countries, these laws do not exist. The less a corporation pays for labor, the more profit the stockholders and company executives receive.

To succeed in America, you will have to make the necessary sacrifices and preparations to get a piece of the American pie. A college degree gives you an advantage over another Black person without a degree, but it won't put you on equal footing with your White counterparts. You must use what you've learned in college and in life to make opportunities for yourself and others. When I decided to study Business Management, I should have been thinking about who would be working for me and not who was I going to work for. For those of you who have a degree in Business Management, or will be attending college for a degree in that field, consider this; How many Chaldeans or Asians are in your classes? When I attended SVSU, there was not one Chaldean or Asian person in any of my courses. Yet today, they own almost every party store, independent grocery store, gas station, cleaners, beauty supply store and strip mall in the metropolitan Detroit area. These two ethnic groups have achieved success by sacrificing a lot of time and effort and, most significantly, by uniting with their own people.

Sacrifice is a part of success. If you do not make sacrifices, you will not obtain anything of great value. If you are a future college student, you will have to sacrifice desires for material things, social or extracurricular interests, and some relationships in order to get to the next level. Remember: "No pain, no gain." It is up to you to decide what you will sacrifice to achieve individual success and position yourself to help someone else.

Chapter 4

UNITED PARCEL SERVICE ROUND 1

"We are troubled on every side, yet not distressed;
we are perplexed, but not in despair;"

—2 Cor 4:8

After getting re-acclimated to the responsibilities of being a full-time college at SVSU, I had to find employment. My first job in Saginaw was at a merchandise store that has since gone bankrupt. It was a store where customers selected merchandise that was on display and filled out an order slip. An order selector would then retrieve the merchandise and send it to the sales floor. The store had just been built when I applied for a job. There were approximately 20 of us who were hired at the same time, and the majority of us were Blacks and Mexicans. We were responsible for stocking the shelves with the trailer loads of merchandise that arrived daily. As soon as the store was about to open for business, I was laid off with the majority of the other Blacks and Mexicans. I assumed that we were good enough to almost break our backs to place merchandise on the shelves, but not good enough to assist customers on the sales floor.

It was two weeks before Thanksgiving when I was informed that United Parcel Service (UPS) was hiring for part-time seasonal help during the peak season, which begins the day after Thanksgiving and ends on Christmas Eve. I was hired in as a package unloader on the A.M. Shift. My duty was to unload the thousands of packages that were loaded in semi-trailers. I am sure that most people have seen a UPS tractor-trailer on the highway. These trailers were eight feet high and filled from the floor to the ceiling with packages. They had to be loaded on rollers and sent to the primary sorting area. The packages were then sorted to the correct conveyor belt, loaded onto a delivery truck by a preloader, and delivered to the customer by the driver. As an unloader, I had to work non-stop grabbing packages and placing them on the conveyor belt correctly until the trailer was empty. At the same time, I had to be alert and able to move quickly, as walls of packages fell regularly while I was unloading them. Almost daily, I was hit by packages, but fortunately, I was never injured. Remember, I am an Army veteran, so I was trained to take pain and laugh. It would take anywhere from two to three hours for one person to unload a trailer. The job of an unloader was all about physical labor, and nothing else. Since this was an A.M. Shift, I had to be at work at 4:00A.M., in the morning. When my assigned trailers were unloaded, I was able to punch out for the day.

The starting pay for an unloader in 1985 was $8.50 an hour, and $9.00 an hour for a preloader. That was pretty good money for a college student without a car note and no rent to pay. Since the Army took care of my tuition, UPS and the generous hospitality of my brother permitted me to have a comfortable standard of living while I attended SVSU. By working the A.M. Shift from 4:00A.M. to 8:00A.M., I was able to schedule my classes after 9:00A.M. Working did not interfere with college or studying.

The health benefits for part-time workers at UPS were better than some companies offered their full-time workers. I received excellent medical, dental, and vision coverage. For some part-time workers, the benefits were their sole reason for working there. My reason was the pay and the work schedule. The reason for the excellent benefit package at UPS was the union. All part-time unloaders, preloaders, sorters, and drivers were represented by the Teamsters Union. Because of the physical demands of the job, medical benefits were definitely needed.

Unbeknownst to me, UPS was my introduction to corporate America and labor unions. I just saw UPS as a job until I graduated from college. In America, we live in a capitalistic society. People invest money in people, services, products, stocks and etc. in order to earn more money. UPS provides a service of delivering packages to customers as quickly and cost-efficient as possible and at a lower price than its competition. UPS is also responsible for providing a return on stockholders investments. UPS stock is privately owned by management and hourly workers. I technically worked for myself to a degree, because I was able to purchase stock. Before this chapter is over, I will re-visit this thought.

Work Environment

Some years ago, UPS had the slogan, "We run the tightest ship in the shipping business." They never lied. From the moment I punched in until the moment I punched out, I worked continuously. My arms and legs were moving every second. The pace that we had to work at was borderline insane. The unloaders performed the job that was the first phase of getting packages delivered to the customers. The quicker we performed our job, the quicker the sorter had to sort and preloader had to load. During a 4-hour shift, I only received a 15 minute break, and I needed it. Because of my physical conditioning and age, the physical demand of an unloader was more repetitious than physically challenging. Working at UPS was comparable to working at a factory. I was actually a part of a human assembly line, where my body was used for moving packages from Point A to Point B as quickly as possible. The quicker and more efficient I became, the less I got paid because being efficient meant I would punch out sooner.

UPS had the most advanced system of utilizing the body of its workers to achieve maximum productivity. They would have scientific management studies performed to determine if we were being used to our optimum level of productivity. If a study determined that elevation of a conveyor belt by four inches would allow a preloader to grab a package three seconds quicker, then the conveyor would be elevated. It would not matter if the adjustment in the conveyor belt cost a million dollars. Over time, that minor elevation of the conveyor belt would pay for itself. Just imagine how this adjustment, at just one facility, would allow preloaders to complete their shift in three hours and forty-five minutes instead of four hours. Because of that adjustment, UPS would recognize a savings on labor of $2.50 a day from a preloader that was earning $10.00 an hour. The savings of $2.50 a day from each preloader at a facility with 50 preloaders, would result in a total savings $125.00 a day for that facility. If you continue to do the math, you will get the picture.

Throughout my UPS work experience, there were policies and procedures that I opposed, but I could never accused UPS of discriminating. Regardless of your age, race, sex, religious beliefs or education, you were treated the same. You were worked like a dog! It did not matter what your position was. It was expected and required that all unloaders, preloaders, sorters, drivers, supervisors, and managers give a 150 percent effort, once they entered the facility. There were no double standards for women. If you could not handle the work, you were fired. The women I worked with put me and other men to shame. If you were 60 years old and could handle the physical demands and performed according to UPS expectations, you had a job. UPS was no joke. The philosophy at UPS was to make sure they provided the best service possible to their customers. If it took the blood, sweat, tears, and the broken backs of every person that worked there, so be it.

I would like to reiterate that there never appeared to be any institutionalized racism at UPS. When a corporation focuses attention on being the best, the only criteria that matters is performance, not color. There may have been some racist managers who, in their delusional minds, believed that they were superior to Blacks, Mexicans, and women. If a White manager thought this way and was actually attempting to incorporate this belief into the performance of his job, it was disguised, because all workers, regardless of race or position, were working at the same neck-breaking pace to make UPS "number one" in the package delivery business. Any personal differences I may have had with managers were not because of my color. They could be attributed to my refusal to buy into the hype of working myself to death so others could benefit more than I did.

As stated previously, I received my introduction to the operations of the labor union at UPS. In life, I have learned not to do certain things. These things include not blaspheming God or upsetting the Teamsters Union. The unions in America have helped facilitate a higher standard of living for millions of workers. If not for unions, corporations in America would exploit workers of all races, far worse than they are doing now. I am not stating that all unions and union representatives are perfect, but I believe that if it were not for unions, not only Black workers, but people of all races would be slaves to corporations in America.

The union at this particular facility was adequate, at best. When it came to securing contracts on the national level for all workers, the Teamsters Union represented UPS workers well. If you had an individual grievance against management at the local level, then you had a problem. We elected union stewards at our facility based on race, friendship and popularity; not on experience and/or negotiation skills. If you were not able to represent yourself at the local level, you were subject to mistreatment. At this facility, it was rumored that the union was "in bed" with management on a number of individual grievances. One of my co-workers saw a White union steward and White manager laughing and drinking coffee together just before he entered the conference room for a grievance hearing. If that manager and the union steward were that "buddy-buddy," what were the odds of my co-worker receiving fair representation?

One important fact that I learned at UPS was that regardless of what side of the fence a White person was on, whether it was union or management, when it came to disciplining a Black employee, the White men involved forgot their differences long enough to unite against a Black person. When it comes to keeping a Black person downtrodden in this country, most White people will come together.

My Black co-workers and I resented the union stewards because we paid union dues to be protected from management, and the stewards failed to protect us. We respected management more because it was their objective to ensure maximum productivity from every worker, and they usually achieved their objective.

Even in politics, regardless of the alleged hostilities between the Democratic Party and the Republican Party, a majority of White party members would put their differences aside to eliminate a threat from a Black person. To bring it home, even the Hatfields and McCoys would stop their feuding to lynch a Black man.

Management

Between 1985 and 1988, the full-time managers at this particular facility were unbelievable. Never before had I ever worked with managers who thrived on power and superiority. Most of the managers, who had been with UPS for over twenty years, possessed the same attitude and communication skills that they started with in the 1960's. Their demeanor and style was so similar that I thought they actually attended a class on how to verbally abuse workers in order to receive maximum productivity. Just like the drill sergeants in the Army, managers at UPS would try to use verbal intimidation to force workers into submission. Everyday, I would see a manager in a preloader's face, yelling and criticizing that worker for not performing the job to the manager's expectation. There was an apparent communication problem between management and workers, but most of the time it went unnoticed or ignored.

Most of the managers that I am referring to came up through the ranks when UPS first started delivering packages by horse and buggy. They were all White men, because Black men, Black women, and White women were not given high paying jobs in the 1950's and 1960's. The younger White managers were more compassionate with the workers. If I remember correctly, most of the managers started as drivers, and were then promoted into management. All of the part-time supervisors were cool. Since most of them were college students, it would not have been in their best interest to upset a preloader or unloader that attended classes with them at SVSU or Delta College, after work.

After about two months, a position as a preloader became available and because of my seniority, I was given a raise and the responsibility of sorting the conveyor belt on Line #3 and loading a delivery truck. It was my responsibility to ensure that the packages were sorted to the correct side of the conveyor belt. There were ten preloaders on my line, with five preloaders positioned on each side of the conveyor belt. If I did not sort the packages correctly, it would make my co-workers' jobs much more difficult. Since I was the belt sorter, I only had to load one delivery truck while my co-workers had to load anywhere from two to four trucks each. By performing my job efficiently, this meant that my co-workers were also able to perform their jobs efficiently. I was actually saving UPS money by getting us off the clock quicker.

Management at UPS had zero tolerance for absenteeism and tardiness.If I was late, it cost UPS money, because an inexperienced unloader had to do my job until I arrived. Regular tardiness was cause for verbal/written reprimands and if continued, tardiness resulted in termination. There were several times during my three years working at UPS that a manager or part-time supervisor would call me at home to wake me up. As a preloader, if you are more than thirty minutes late, you may as well miss work that day, because the packages would be so backed up, it would be difficult to catch up. I can remember calling in to work sick one morning. A manager called my house and told me that I was going to be fired if I did not come to work. Guess what? I was not sick anymore. There were several occasions when I would get up late and, to make it to work on time, I had to break every driving law that existed. Fortunately, my route from home to work was not heavily traveled between the times of 3:00A.M. and 3:30A.M.

Another intimidation tactic that management used to get us to perform our job as efficiently as possible was the "Black Hole." Before I elaborate on the "Black Hole," I will explain the importance of the job of a preloader. A preloader is responsible for correctly loading a driver's truck according to a load chart diagram. If the packages are loaded incorrectly or the stop count is off, it would cost UPS money. UPS, and no other corporation, will tolerate losing money. A stop count determines how long it will take a driver to deliver his or her packages during an 8-hour day. For example, if I recorded that a driver had 100 stops, and the driver had actually 80 stops, the driver would complete the route in seven hours, but would have to be paid for an 8-hour shift. Another example is if I said my driver had 100 stops and I actually loaded 115 stops, the driver would receive approximately one hour of overtime because of my error. In 1986, UPS drivers earned $18.00-$22.00 an hour. Failure to accurately record a driver's stops would have meant that the driver could have earned from $27.00-$33.00 overtime for one hour. According to UPS, what I did was the eleventh commandment: "Thou shall not give management and stockholders money to a driver."

The punishment for that sin was banishment to the "Black Hole", which was what we called the trailers where I was assigned when I first started with UPS. As you unloaded the packages and got closer to the nose of the trailer, it would become darker and darker. Being sent back to the "Black Hole" was dual punishment. First of all, unloading a trailer was twice as hard as preloading and, secondly, I lost money due to my shift being shorter since unloaders were the first workers finished. For a preloader, after you finished loading your truck, your supervisor would allow you to assist another preloader to work the balance of time on your shift. There is no question that the threat of being sent to the "Black Hole" made most of my co-workers work to the satisfaction of management.

The last intimidation tactic that was used by management to increase hourly workers' productivity was coercion. If management discovered that a worker was married, had children, or purchased a new car or home, they were able to apply more demands and pressure. UPS managers knew that if a worker had financial responsibilities, that worker was at their mercy. They used a worker's personal responsibilities as a bargaining tool to increase productivity. The worker knew his or her livelihood depended on remaining employed. I honestly believed that some managers at UPS would use any tactic possible to increase productivity.

Solidarity Among Brothers

From the first day I started my employment at UPS, until the day I left, there had always been a severe communication problem between the White managers and Black part-time workers. The managers' methods of communication and their motivation techniques were not conducive to high productivity and morale. At this particular facility, high morale was never the objective. Productivity was, first and foremost, the highest objective.

There were very few Black workers on the A.M. Shift, but some of the young Black workers that were there definitely represented Black people to the fullest of their ability. No matter where you work, people will challenge you to see what you are made of. If a manager thought you were weak, that manager would do everything in his/her power to coerce you into working up to his/her expectations. Some of the Black men who worked with me possessed a docile and timid demeanor. Management was able to force them to do whatever they wanted by using intimidation. Those same White managers would attempt to use the same methods on the rest of us, but it was not effective. This caused the work relationship between White managers and Black preloaders to become hostile, at times.

In retaliation of management's abusive ways, some preloaders intentionally worked slower, "milking the clock," thereby reducing their productivity and receiving the wrath of management. It was always the responsibility of the part-time supervisors to resolve any problems that were occurring with the preloaders. Since most of the part-time supervisors were young White men, the Black workers had even less respect for them. It became necessary for full-time managers to attempt to force the Black preloaders to conform to the work standards at UPS. In protest, one Black preloader would wear a chain symbolizing the slave-like working conditions that we thought we were subjected to. Another Black co-worker continued to write, "Free Mandela" on the white light fixtures. Both employees were reprimanded for their actions.

For me, UPS was a "coming out" party, so to speak. In the Army, my natural desire to express how I felt about various situations and treatment was suppressed by the threat of an Article 15. Since UPS was my first experience in corporate America as an adult, I did not have to suppress anything, or so I thought. The survival tactics that I used to survive in Royal Oak Township as a youth resurfaced. I observed how other workers at UPS were treated and was determined not to be treated in the same manner.

My first encounter with a full-time manager at UPS occurred because of my alleged inability to load a delivery truck correctly. Since most of the drivers were White, they had a tendency to blame the preloaders for their failure to deliver packages on time. These accusations occurred on several occasions. As a result, I was banished to the "Black Hole." When I went to the union to protest, the situation was not resolved. Instead of waiting for a union steward to file a protest for me, I wrote my own protest and gave it to the union steward to file for me. While I slaved in the "Black Hole," waiting for my freedom, I continued to protest. My co-workers started calling me, "Black Rambo" because I started wearing my Army fatigues and combat boots to work, and I was in excellent physical shape due to my Army training and personal workout regimen.

I was labeled as a radical, rebel, and militant. The White managers developed this opinion of me because I was big, Black, bald, outspoken, and possessed an intimidating demeanor. It appeared that every time a Black man exhibited assertiveness, principles, and beliefs that were different from those of the White power structure, that Black person was considered a troublemaker and had to be taught a lesson. What the managers at UPS did not know was that I was not the average young Black man. Being a preloader at UPS was just a job to me, and I never considered it as a career possibility. I was not going to allow their head games and verbal intimidation to brainwash or force me to conform to their philosophies.

Once I was emancipated from the "Black Hole," I declared war on UPS management. I loved challenges and thrived on conflict, controversy, and verbal confrontations. Since the managers at UPS took pride in intimidating and verbally abusing part-time workers, the battle line was set. It was me against management. Unfortunately, because of my ignorance and over-confidence, I was unaware of the strength of my enemy.

I was transferred back to Line #3 as a preloader. One thing I would give UPS management credit for was ensuring that they separated the allegedly rebellious Black preloaders from the docile and timid Black preloaders. They did not want me to influence other Black workers and cause them to "develop a backbone." The first week after my emancipation, management continued to try to convert me into a true UPS employee. The bottom line with UPS is that you have to have brown blood (UPS signature color). If you do not eat, drink, sleep, and dream UPS that is a problem for management. Like I said, UPS was just a job to me.

Management's first complaint was that I did not work fast enough. How fast did they think I could move while wearing Army combat boots and a heavy fatigue jacket? The first thing my mentor who worked across from me told me was, "Don't let them see you sweat." The part-time supervisors did not attempt to confront me. When they had a problem with me, they would have the facility manager come talk to me. He would ask me, "Why don't you work faster?" I told him, "I only sweat playing basketball." He would walk away with a red face, as I continued to work at my own leisurely pace.

The facility manager plotted to have me fired. While he was doing that, I was plotting my next protest. One advantage of having union representation was that management could not fire you, "just because." Just because you were Black was not an acceptable reason! As long as I came to work on time, tried my best, and did not threaten to cause bodily harm to anyone, they could not fire me. The money and benefits at UPS were too good to jeopardize it for some egotistical beliefs that I might have had. When I master a job and it becomes boring, I have a tendency to lose interest. Loading packages everyday for four hours straight was not the most exciting and mentally challenging job in the world. The things I enjoyed most about UPS were the pay, the camaraderie with other workers, and playing head games with management.

My next protest was during one of our 15-minute breaks. Every Friday, management would provide doughnuts for us. Supposedly, it was a reward for our hard work. I would tell all of the preloaders who would listen that management was providing us with sugar to boost our energy level so we would finish loading our trucks quicker and, therefore, save them money. The manager of the facility invited me to have a doughnut, and I told him that the same thing happened to the Native Americans. The White man gave them trinkets, and the Native Americans sold them New York. He just shook his head and walked away. There was no way someone was going to use food to entice me to work faster. The faster you worked, the less money you earned. I could buy my own doughnuts. Of course, some of the preloaders ate the doughnuts and still worked as slowly as I did. For me, it was all about principles. I would have felt remorseful if I ate their food and still worked at my own pace. This one-man protest lasted throughout my employment there.

Most of the young people who worked for UPS came from the Saginaw area. Their work ethics were excellent, and management easily exploited them. I would attempt to convince co-workers that it was ridiculous to kill themselves for $9.00 an hour. It was unbelievable how hard some of my co-workers worked to impress management. What they did not realize was that they were just a small part of a money-making system whose main objective was to make White stockholders rich. UPS stock was privately owned by current and retired employees. There was a maximum percentage of your pay that you could invest in stock. The amount of stock you could purchase was based on the amount of money you earned. Preloaders that were paid between $9.00-$10.00 an hour did not reap the great returns like full-time drivers, management, and retired UPS workers. Basically, management expected preloaders and unloaders to kill themselves to help White drivers, White managers and retired White people become richer. Between 1985 and 1988, there were not very many Black retirees or Black managers that were benefiting from the hard work of Black preloaders.

This is the same thing that happens to Blacks throughout corporate America. Black people do not own very much stock, but it is our labor at meager wages that makes the stockholder richer. In most instances, the stockholder is White. All they have to do is relax, while we work ourselves to death for their benefit. It is the same with Social Security. Young Black people pay into a system that benefits retired old racist White people. During their younger years these same racist White people prevented our parents from getting decent jobs, but now we are supporting them through the Social Security system. Since most Black people do not live to receive Social Security, we involuntarily pay into a system that supports White people who have hated us all of their lives.

In my opinion, unloaders and preloaders had the most physically demanding jobs that were integral to the package delivery system, but we were not getting paid accordingly. Delivery drivers also worked hard, but their pay rate was two to three times more than ours per hour. During the Christmas season, the full-time drivers received countless hours of overtime, so what was supposed to be my motivation to work harder and quicker, while getting paid less? There was no reason for us to worker faster, and I would share this insight with all of my co-workers, but they refused to listen. It was useless for me to attempt to explain some issues to co-workers, so after awhile, I left it alone.

During my three years of employment at UPS, I went back and forth with management. They would win some battles, and I would win some battles. Surprisingly, there was a time when management approached me about becoming a part-time supervisor. I thought about it for a minute and gave a resounding, "NO!" It was their attempt to get me in a position to fire me. Because of my attitude and candid demeanor, it was important that I had a job that was protected by the union.

All of management's tactics to make me conform continued to fail, until an event occurred that could have been extremely detrimental to my future. The facility manager, who had worked for UPS probably from its beginning, confronted me. This was not unusual because this White manager had the habit of trying to intimidate all workers of all ethnicities. I was loading my truck when he began shouting at me for something he felt was important, but I thought it was trivial. I started shouting back at him. It turned into a shouting match. At UPS, management did not give you respect, you had to take it. My mother very rarely raised her voice at me, so I knew that no White man, or any other man, was going to raise his voice at me without retaliation. In life, people will get away with anything you allow them to. I refused to allow anyone to disrespect me. Since the manager could not out-talk me, he slammed both of his hands down on the conveyor belt as hard as he could. I slammed mine down on the belt to prove to him that he was not the only one who could become angry. Being old with bad knees, he attempted to gracefully crawl across the conveyor belt that was three feet wide. I jumped across it with ease, right behind him.

It was apparent that this manager did not have a clue who he was dealing with, because he grabbed me by the upper arm and tried to force me into a truck. That was a cardinal sin. Nobody touches me. I gave him to the count of three to get his hand off me. Out of the corner of my eye, I saw a Black co-worker sneaking up behind the manager. Before I could count to two, he had his hand off me.

From that moment, I knew my days were numbered. In May of 1988, I took a one-week vacation and went out of town. When I got up Monday morning, I decided to quit. The next day, I went up to the facility and asked the manager for my job back. After a couple of days of deliberation, he said that I could start the following Monday. I thought about it, and decided not to return. It was apparent that management thought I was a good worker by giving me another chance, regardless of my outspokenness and refusal to pledge allegiance to UPS.

Overview

There is no question in my mind that because of UPS, I was able to earn my Bachelor's Degree from SVSU without any financial hardships. The hours that I worked were ideal for attending college on a full-time basis. If I had worked somewhere else, the hours would have been an inconvenience, and the pay would have been considerably lower. The health benefits were the best around. Working at UPS assisted me through college, and prepared me for corporate America.

In my prior work experiences, it was not always the job or pay, but the people I worked with that made the job a better place to work. There were three young men who I became friends with at UPS. One was a young Mexican who used to carpool to work with me. This guy was so nice that it was sickening. He was the kind of person that, no matter what someone did to him, he would never get upset. One of the things, that infuriates me is to see someone be exploited or manipulated. He and I would argue about his high tolerance level. If it was because he was emulating Christ, he did an excellent job, because nothing affected him. My other friend started at UPS the same week that I did. He was originally from Arkansas, and he was very laid back. Like my Mexican friend, he also had a high tolerance level. Eventually, he became a part-time supervisor at UPS, and was one of the best. Fortunately, he was not a supervisor on my line. We did not allow our different positions to affect our friendship. Over the years we became excellent friends and even to this day, we continue to be friends, although our lives have taken different paths.

One friendship was not more valuable than another, but this last friend that I met at UPS had the greatest impact on me because he educated me on the struggles of our people in America. The first two books he gave me were, *From Slavery to Freedom: A History of Negro Americans,* by John H. Franklin and *The Autobiography of Malcolm X,* by Alex Haley. Prior to working at UPS, I did not read very much Black literature. Reading those books opened up doors in my mind that I did not know existed. This particular co-worker became a friend and mentor. Although he was a couple of years younger than me, his knowledge about our people was unlimited. Sometimes in life, you are put in a certain place at a certain time, and it is not until years later that you discover why you were there. The combination of my experiences at UPS and my connections with this dear friend certainly prepared me for the challenges that were awaiting me.

Regardless of the arguments that I had with the managers at UPS during my three years of employment, I must admit that I respect their commitment to their jobs. They truly had the best interests of UPS in mind, and every decision they made was in an effort to make UPS the best in the package delivery business. I hope they respected me doing what was in my best interest. It was in my best interest to come to work and earn an honest day's pay for an honest day's work. I also expected to be respected as a man, and for others to be respected, regardless of their race, sex, or title. I was determined to get my respect or take it. At UPS, I had to earn my respect everyday.

As you continue to read this book, you will read other encounters that I have had with other White people, but those White people stood behind their titles, probably always praying that nothing ever escalated beyond a verbal encounter. The managers at this UPS facility were fearless like White NHL hockey players. They were not afraid to do whatever was necessary to get their point across. If it meant going to blows and bleeding "UPS brown blood" to prove a point, they would do it. I had to respect a manager who was willing to take a butt whipping for the brown team.

Interacting with the White managers at UPS certainly prepared me for my future, as I was able to realize my true identity. You never know how you will handle the fire until you have experienced it. My experiences gave me an introduction to a different mindset of what people will do to be successful and maintain a certain standard of living. By observing others, it also allowed me to determine what principles, morals, standards, and beliefs I was going to live by, to be successful and maintain a certain standard of living. The sooner in life you determine what you will stand for, the sooner you will arrive at your true calling.

For college students, or any young person who wants to get their foot in the door of an excellent corporation, I would still highly recommend UPS. You may have to endure some challenging and, possibly, unpleasant experiences, but you are going to experience that everywhere you work in corporate America. However, at least at UPS, you will be compensated for your troubles, and also receive an excellent health benefits package.

Career opportunities continue to become available at UPS as they continue to diversify in the package delivery business. In addition, UPS will continue to be one of the most powerful corporations in the future because of their management's ability to see an opportunity and take advantage of it. If you are willing to bleed brown blood, UPS is for you. As for me, I will continue to bleed red blood and remain Black.

Chapter 5

KMART CORPORATION

"Yea, though I walk through the valley of the shadow of death,
I will fear no evil: for thou art with me . . ."

—Ps 23:4

Introduction to Racism 101

Never before had I experienced the events that took place during the three years that I worked for Kmart. Royal Oak Township, Inkster, MI, Northwood University, the U.S. Army, UPS, nor Saginaw Valley State University (SVSU) had prepared me for an experience that would affect me so deeply that I would remember it for the rest of my life.

Growing up in an all Black community does not prepare you for dealing with racist mindsets. In the microcosm where I was raised, all men were born equal. It is true that some of my friends were born into more financially stable families than others, but no one was considered better than anyone else just because of their birthright. I came of age in the late 1970's, and my world had not expanded beyond the boundaries of my small community. Therefore, encounters with White people were almost nonexistent. I can remember that the insurance man was White, the Twin Pines milkman was White, and a White man owned a small grocery store in my neighborhood. Other than those three White men, all of the other businesses in Royal Oak Township were owned and operated by Black people. Even during my elementary school years, all of my teachers were Black until I reached the sixth grade. As a child, White people did not exist in my world. Interacting with White people did not become a norm until I attended junior high and high school. Even then, it was not a concern, because there were Black students at or above the same level as White students, both academically and athletically. The notion that White people were superior to Black people just because of the their skin color would have been impossible to prove then, and is still difficult to prove today. It was also never a notion I accepted then or now.

After successfully co-existing with White officers and enlisted men in the Army, being taught by White instructors with advanced degrees at SVSU, and having physical and verbal confrontations at UPS with White managers who earned my respect because of their toughness and willingness to fight for their beliefs, how in the world could I conceivably begin to fear any White person regardless of gender or title, at Kmart?

There was no question that it was inevitable that my motto of "I will get with you mentally, verbally, or physically" would clash with what I considered to be the racist mentality of the White managers and the higher chain of command at Kmart. My determination to challenge a belief system that was established in 1619 when the first African was brought in chains to the shores of this country as a slave was a lost cause even before I waged my one-man war. Since I was always outnumbered in what I considered to be my personal fight for justice, I was determined to establish my position by any means necessary. No matter what it took to earn respect as a Black man, I implemented and executed my strategy. Subconsciously, everything that I learned on the streets of Royal Oak Township and Inkster, MI resurfaced. If there are not any courses offered in colleges and universities today that teach Black students how to be successful, even in the face of racism, someone should create one.

It has been said, "All battles were not meant to be fought." If I laid down and did not fight my personal battle against racism, it would have only given the enemy more confidence to believe that they were superior to Black people, and made the battle for the next Black man that much more difficult. I could not change what the people at Kmart thought about Black people, but after the smoke cleared, I was still standing and ready to fight another day.

For my young brothers and sisters who have not encountered racism because you are still in high school and college, I would like to forewarn you. If you want to be successful in corporate America, please do the opposite of what you are about to read. For my other brothers and sisters who have already gone through the battles I am about to describe and who are still going through them, please keep your head up and continue to fight. Rest assured that you are not fighting alone.

The attitude, behavior, and conduct that I exhibited at Kmart on a number of occasions was not conducive to a financially successful and upwardly mobile career. My behavior was certainly not a reflection of the excellent display of professionalism that other Black people have shown in similar stressful situations. My conduct and behavior, at times, was best defined by the saying, "You can take the man out of the street, but you cannot take the street out of the man." Because of the emotional stress that I encountered on a daily basis at Kmart, I felt I had no other alternative for dealing with hostile situations aside from the manner that I did. I practiced the same behavior as I did "back in the day" when I was on the block in my neighborhood. Sometimes in order to survive in life, you have to forget what you learned in the classroom and remember where you came from.

As you read about this period in my life, I hope you learn from my experiences and choose not to duplicate them. The rule of the game is to "Do as I say, and not as I do." There will be some events you will read about will make you question my sanity. But until you have experienced the things that I have experienced in my life, please do not pass judgment. You do not know how you will respond until the fire of racism tests you. I am not condoning or condemning what transpired during my years at Kmart. Regardless of whether I was right or wrong, only God can judge me. It is my desire to tell my story. So this is my story, and I am sticking to it.

*   *   *

Always remember that you should never give up a "sure thing" for a possible. After returning from a 1-week vacation, my body and mind could not deal with another day of UPS. I can remember dreaming that packages were attacking me. There was one occasion when I abruptly got up, hurried and put on my clothes for work. Guess what? It was Saturday morning. Although I did not have a job and was offered the opportunity to return to UPS, I just could not take it any more.

The next day, I got a call that I thought was from heaven, but after what I later experienced, it was actually from hell. Since I had just graduated from SVSU and did not have a job, I accepted the first job that became available. When the district manager at Kmart hired me, he should have said, "Welcome to your new plantation, Toby." At least, then I would have known what to expect.

The district manager who hired me was extremely eccentric. This man was able to carry on a conversation on the telephone, talk with me, and talk out loud to himself without getting the conversations confused. During the interviewing process, I assume that my demeanor, my clean-cut appearance, the manner in which I answered the questions, and the references that he received from my instructors at SVSU influenced him to hire me. On one of the Scholastic Reference Requests, one of my professors gave me superior ratings in the following categories; general behavior, initiative, communication, potential leadership and ability to get along with others. Additional comments included; very hard worker, gets points across without causing ill will, tremendous capability, will excel in life. One interesting question is: What circumstances would prevent me from exhibiting all of the qualities that the professor believed I possessed? That question would soon be answered.

There is no question in my mind that Affirmative Action was a major contributing factor for me being hired by Kmart. White people, and some asinine Black people, think that Affirmative Action assists incompetent Black people in obtaining a job; and if it were not for Affirmative Action, we would not qualify for the job. That is true in one aspect. The only reason we would not get jobs on our own merit and ability is because racist White people would not hire us if it were not for Affirmative Action. In this racist society, even a college degree does not guarantee a Black person a job over a White person without a degree. A college degree only positions a Black person above a Black person without a degree, but still below a White person without one. Some White employees probably thought I received my job because of Affirmative Action and not because of my ability. They resented me for it. I assumed that I should have been happy that "Master" gave me a job. Of course, I did not look at it that way. The great Paul Robeson wrote the following:

"The Negro must never appear to be challenging white superiority. Climb up if you can, but don't act uppity. Always show that you are grateful. Even if what you have gained has been wrestled from unwilling powers, be sure to be grateful, lest they take it all away. Above all, do nothing to give them cause to fear you, for then the oppressing hand, which might at times ease up a little, will surely become a fist to knock you down again."[1]

It is unfortunate that I was not aware of Mr. Robeson's warning until I read his book in 1993. By that time, I had already endured several tumultuous situations. From day one, working for Kmart was a nightmare that I thought would never end. Yes, I could have quit at anytime, but like every other responsible adult, I needed money to pay my bills.

Garden City, MI

The first store that I was assigned to was in Garden City, Michigan. It was a little "hick town" outside of Detroit. In 1988, the population of Black people in this city was probably under two percent. I was an assistant manager in the apparel department. Immediately, I discovered that I hated working in retail. We had to work a minimum of 48 hours a week. Two days during the week, managers had to work a twelve-hour shift. I only had one weekend off a month, and I had to attend the Army Reserves during that weekend. My first job out of college definitely was not my proverbial "dream job."

In 1988, there were two Kmart Corporations within the same store. I was hired by Kmart Apparel Corporation, which consisted of all apparel—clothing for men, women and children; fashion accessories; baby furniture and accessories. The Kmart Corporation side of the store was referred to as hardlines. Hardlines merchandise consisted of everything else in the store—furniture, tools, jewelry, food and etc. Throughout this chapter I will just refer to Kmart Apparel, as Kmart. The same philosophies applied to both corporations anyway.

The White employees at this store did not like me from day one. Other than me, there was a Black supervisor on the hardlines section of Kmart. He was an older Black man with a wife and five children. Because of his responsibilities as a husband and father, he had no other choice but to have a peaceful and passive relationship with the White management staff and White employees. Since his position as supervisor was considered a glorified regular employee, the White employees did not feel they had to give him respect, and, therefore, they did not.

As for my position as an assistant manager, they had to show me respect and they hated it. Most of the employees were White women in their upper fifties, and some of them refused to address me as "Mr. Prophet." They would come up to me and just start a conversation, or just ask a question without acknowledging my title. I received worse treatment from the White men, both young and old. They simply refused to address me as "Mr. Prophet," nor would they take any orders from me without a hassle. All of the older White employees probably started there straight out of high school and worked their way up. It was difficult for some of them to accept the fact that a young Black man with a college degree was getting paid more money than they were, and they also had to actually show me some respect. I know they wished that the good old days in the South would return, where all Black men were considered or treated as boys.

My relationship with the Black employees at this store was excellent. All of the Black employees were young Black women who recently graduated from high school and some were attending college. Being from the same culture helped us to understand each other, so it was not difficult to get the Black employees to respect me and perform their assignments without resistance.

The first manager I had when I started was a White woman. She was down to earth and really could have cared less about Kmart or anything else. At the time I started, she was either about to become a district manager or about to resign. Since I do not remember very much about her, I am sure that we did not have many confrontations. But her replacement was an entirely different story.

This manager was a young, White male with blonde hair and blue eyes, of course. He was, as they say, "on a career track." Kmart was grooming him to become a district manager and to one day have a position high up on Kmart's chain of command. This manager's mindset was similar to that of the managers at UPS. He gave 200 percent to Kmart, worked more than the required amount of hours, and expected the same out of me. By now, you have learned enough about me to know what he got from me. This White manager and I were at different levels in our professional careers. He was on his way up and, unbeknownst to me, I was on my way out. Even though it took three years for my destiny to manifest, by the end of my first week, it was already determined.

One important fact you should know when you become a supervisor or manager at any company is that you are expected to take on the company's mentality/philosophy. That means that you are required to be ready to defend the company when it comes to its mission statement, philosophy, policies, goals, and all other company objectives, whether they be written or unwritten, spoken or unspoken. This was one of those unwritten rules that I was never informed of. I guess it was assumed that since I graduated from a university, it was a given that, by way of osmosis, I would know this. Apparently, this was an elective course that I did not take and it definitely was not taught in Royal Oak Township or Inkster, MI.

Personally, I think any position that a person is in where they are paid a salary is equivalent to being a slave, figuratively speaking. That is, depending on the corporation you work for, of course. People who are employed in salaried positions usually are not protected by a union. An employee in a salaried position must do what they are told, or risk the possibility of being fired. I could not work with that threat constantly in my mind. That is why I am pro-union. Sorry for the commercial break. Now back to the story.

Almost immediately, this White manager and I clashed. He would verbally reprimand me and continuously attempt to coerce me into assisting him in reaching the next rung of the career ladder. If he really thought I cared enough to assist him in reaching the top, he was sadly mistaken. I did not mind being reprimanded about my habits and inability to supervise the older White employees, because to them I was a Black boy, and to me, some of them were ignorant hillbillies. Tell me, what hillbilly is going to do anything to make a Black man's life easier? It was a lost cause from the beginning, so my attitude and enthusiasm was indicative of my feelings about the reality I had already accepted.

It was only a matter of time before my manager did or said something that would set me off. As I stated earlier, I had established an excellent working relationship with the Black employees. One day, my manager overheard me addressing a Black female employee as, "girl." I probably said something like, "Girl, come here." He called me into the office and reprimanded me for not communicating effectively with employees. There was probably some validity to his accusation, but I thought it was trivial. I did not feel it was necessary for me to communicate in a formal, professional manner on a continuous basis, and that was attributed to the good working relationship that I had established with some of the employees. My first thought was to tell him where he could go. Instead, I took out my faithful pen and played "the race card." I wrote a letter to the district manager, accusing this manager of being racist, and mentioned other incidents that substantiated my charges. After the manager read it, he did not say anything else to me about how I communicated with anyone. Although I did not send the letter, I did request a transfer, and received it immediately. Good-bye, Garden City. Hello, Oak Park, Michigan.

Oak Park, MI

The next stop on my, "Introduction to Racism 101 Tour," was in Oak Park, MI. This Kmart store was located three miles north of Detroit's northern border, 8 Mile Road on Greenfield Road. This was a newly-built model of Kmart stores of the future. It was supposedly designed in order to compete with Wal-Mart and Target, which were closing in fast on Kmart in retail sales in 1989.

In 1989, this Kmart store was located in a diverse city with a Black population of 34.3 percent[2]. The district manager ensured that the management staff reflected the same diversity. I was in the apparel department, which had a White female manager and five assistant managers—one Black woman, one White woman, one White man, one Black man and me. We were responsible for supervising a diverse staff of mostly young Black and White employees. Women employees worked primarily on the sales floor assisting customers and the young Black men were assigned to the stockroom and dock area.

Since we were a promotional store, regional managers and buyers from Kmart Headquarters in Troy and New Jersey would visit to tour the store every week. Our manager would follow behind them like a puppy, writing down everything they felt was necessary to change. I can remember being ordered to take down a wall of merchandise that took five employees four hours to put up, according to the specifications of the layout. After I instructed them to take it down, the next day the executives wanted it put back up, exactly as it was previously. Once a week, we were subjected to this type of indecisive management. As assistant managers, we were not allowed to share our opinions. All regional managers and buyers from New Jersey had expense accounts and they would periodically request that we go to lunch with them in an effort to impress us. I am not impressed with free food. When you show me more money on my paycheck and competent leadership, then I am impressed.

The other two Black assistant managers and myself usually worked together. We complained to each other daily about what was occurring and actually made a wager. The last one employed at Kmart had to take the other two assistant managers to dinner. None of us were feeling the Kmart spirit. The hours were long, and the rapport with our manager and some of the employees was only tolerable at best. For some reason that I did not understand at the time, some Black employees refused to give me and the other Black assistant managers respect. On the other hand, they would worship the ground a White assistant manager walked on. I find this slave mentality to be extremely humiliating and frustrating. On one occasion, I instructed a Black employee who was working in the dock area to perform a simple task. Instead of doing it, he told me he was not going to do it and then threatened to physically put me in my place. I could have taken the professional approach and had him written up and fired. Instead I went "back to the block" on him and told him we could go outside and I would beat him down. There was no way in the world I was going to be worked like a slave by management and disrespected by one of the Black employees who I always tried to protect. Other employees, and one of the other Black assistant managers, had to pull us apart. This employee had me by five inches in height and probably thirty pounds, but it did not matter. If I had to take my respect, I was going to get it. After that incident, I did not have any more problems out of him, nor anyone else.

The racism at this store was actually subtle compared to what I had experienced at the previous store, but definitely nowhere in comparison to the racism that awaited me at the next store. For example, the White female manager exercised favoritism because she usually assigned the easier assignments to the female assistant managers. One thing you will discover as you read this book is that it does not take long for excitement to occur.

Our manager was going on vacation and an assistant manager had to be appointed to the position of manager during her absence. The district manager assigned the White female assistant manager to the position, even though the Black male assistant manager had more seniority. He was furious, but he just blew the entire incident off. This Black assistant manager had aspirations of one day managing his own Kmart store, and it was displayed in his work ethics. In contrast, what was exhibited in my work habits was, if I get fired, can I still collect unemployment? Yes, out of all of the assistant managers, I had the lowest morale and work ethics. It was not because the other Black male assistant manager was a harder worker than I was. It was because I already knew he was laboring in vain. At Kmart it was easy to determine if you were on the right track for advancement. Neither he nor I was going to be advancing anytime soon. The consolation for me was that I did not care. I was trying to do enough to remain employed until another employment opportunity came along.

As for the Black assistant manager, it appeared that he was not in touch with reality when it concerned Kmart. One day, we learned of a Kmart store in another state that had an opening for an apparel manager. The brother thought that he would certainly be promoted to the position at that store. Surprisingly, to him, but not to me, the position was given to a White assistant manager with less seniority. When the brother inquired about why he did not get promoted to the store manager position, our district manager said that the store was a perfect match for the White assistant manager he selected. I could see the tears forming in the brother's eyes. We walked out to the trailers that Kmart used for stockrooms and discussed the situation. He was not crying because he was soft, but because he was angry. If we worked for a legitimate corporation that promoted assistant managers based on hard work and commitment, he would had been given the promotion.

Since we worked for Kmart, it was business as usual. I continued attempting to explain to him what had occurred, but he was not listening. Finally, I had to break it down in a vernacular that he could understand. Basically, I cursed him out. Although I was in the Army, I cursed like a sailor when I was younger. For some reason people did not always understand basic standard English, so I had no problem communicating in any dialect that would get my point across effectively. From that moment on, both of us were desperately trying to find other employment. Years later, I asked a co-worker what a slave thought about everyday? I told her, "Freedom." Yes, that was my goal. Like I said before, never give up a "sure thing" for a possible. Quitting is another word that is not in my vocabulary.

A month after this devastating incident for that assistant manager, I had the opportunity to interview for a district manager position with a distributor of a popular food item. Since I do not want to incriminate innocent people or company, I will not mention the company's name. The interview process consisted of three steps. The position was listed in the local newspaper, so close to a hundred people applied for the position. I was one of the two finalists for the position. As a district manager, you were given an office, your own sales territory and a starting wage, which was substantially higher than that of Kmart. The best thing was that I would not have to deal with incompetent upper management and trifling employees who did not want to take directives from a Black man in authority.

After the last interview, I was informed that they would make their final selection and call me the next day. I waited at home patiently for the call. When I received it, I was devastated by the answer. I had come in second place. The feeling was extremely eerie. I had never felt it before. I felt like Adam Sandler in the movie, "Wedding Singer" when he was left at the altar. The next day, he couldn't get out of bed. It felt like a part of my soul was snatched from my body. To this day, I have never felt that level of disappointment before. I guess the reason I felt so bad was because I hated working for Kmart. As with all disappointments in life, you have to shake it off and keep on fighting.

Soon after that, it did not take very long for my tour to end. The White female manager and I never got along. It was not because she was a White woman. I disliked her because she was one of those ego-tripping, power-hungry people who would try to make it to the top by any means necessary. Plus, throughout my entire Kmart career, she was the only apparel manager who never did any physical labor. All she did was delegate assignments while she sat in the snack bar area drinking coffee and chain-smoking cigarettes like an addict.

On a number of occasions, she and I would have heated discussions about assignments I received in comparison to assignments that were given to other assistant managers. She despised me for questioning her authority. One day, I was in the stockroom, close to the end of my shift when she assigned me a task that another assistant manager was assigned to do earlier. She initiated an argument by raising her voice and yelling at me. It took all the strength I had to keep from knocking her head off. That is what I hated about female managers and White male managers who hide behind their position. They already knew that no sane Black man was going to physically touch them. If this woman was anywhere else but inside Kmart, there is no way in the world she would confronted a Black man.

Fortunately, for her and me, I just took it like a man and left it. I went to my mother's house and cried like a baby. I cried because I was angry. I was never soft. What I experienced was more humiliating than when Drill Sergeant "Pain" confronted me, in the Army. At least he had the ability to defend himself if I decided to try to put my fist down his throat.

Again, I requested a transfer and my tour continued. I was just wondering when and where it would all end. There are some people in jail because they allowed their emotions to dictate their actions. Never allow anyone in an employment situation to get you so angry that it causes you to retaliate with physical violence. Not only will you get fired, but you will also be ineligible to receive unemployment compensation. In addition, you will probably do some jail time if you are a Black man, and may never receive legitimate employment again. Can you imagine interviewing for a job and the White interviewer asks you why you got fired from your previous position, and you say, "I gave my last boss a beat down." It is not worth it. It is hard enough for a Black person to get a job without a criminal record.

Southfield, MI

On November 1, 1989, I made the third stop on my, "Introduction to Racism 101 Tour." This store was located in Southfield, on 8 Mile Road and Beech Daly. Every time I thought it could not get any worse, it did. When I walked into the store, I had the displeasure of meeting all of the managers and supervisors who would work with me. Other than myself there was only one Black female assistant manager and a couple of Black supervisors that worked in the entire store. The other eleven managers and supervisors were White. Of course, the majority of the workers were Black women and men who made minimum wage, or maybe just a little more. The White employees were average, everyday White people.

It is ironic that the other Black assistant manager and I were the only managers who had college degrees among all of the managers and supervisors. The head store manager probably received his degree from KKK University. It is just amazing how White people can work their way up from stock boy, paperboy and any other boy to one day become a manager. If a hard working Black man started at Kmart as a stock boy, you could bet your last dollar that he would most likely be there ten years later in the same position.

Now prepare yourself to read about one of the most constant battles that has occurred in America's history. The battle I am referring to is the Black man versus the White man. Never in history have I ever witnessed the impact of the natural hatred of one man against another.

As some of you already know, knowledge is power. No matter what a person takes away from you, they cannot take away your knowledge. There was probably a time when I harbored great resentment against the White managers at Kmart. In a short period of time, they had earned my greatest dislike. The primary reason was because of the way they treated other Black employees and the way they attempted to treat me. The books I started reading made my dislike increase exponentially. Some of the books that I read from 1988-1990 were: *Black Like Me*, by John Griffin; *Kaffir Boy In America*, by Mark Mathabane; *Soul On Ice*, by Eldridge Cleaver; *Eight Men*, by Richard Wright; *100 Years of Lynching*, by Ralph Ginzburg; *The Autobiography of Malcolm X*, again; the Bible and several other books. That is the knowledge that consumed my mind. Since I first started working for Kmart, I was experiencing some of the events that the Black characters in the books I read had experienced.

Kaffir Boy In America, was the second book I read by one particular Black man from South Africa about his experiences in America. The author's first book was about apartheid in South Africa and was similar to what I saw at the store I was working in at the time. A majority of the menial laborers were Black, while the majority of those in supervisory positions were White. To add insult to injury, approximately 85 percent of the customers were Black. Basically, Black people were paying the salaries of the White management staff. It was only a matter of time before all of this great disdain I had for White men would surface.

Even though I also read the Bible, it did not have any relevant meaning to me during this period in my life. I could not love my enemy, like the Bible says. I could feel "an eye for an eye and a tooth for a tooth" though. At this time in my life, I was dealing with an internal rage resulting from racism, and made the mistake of placing the blame on every White person, instead of only the guilty ones.

Someone forgot to tell me that working in corporate America was a "Catch 22." In order to walk through the doors of opportunity I had to denounce my Blackness, assimilate and check my manhood at the door before I walked through. In my mind, that definitely was not happening. If they wanted a Black boy, they should have hired one. The last time I was a boy was at the age of five. At the two previous Kmart stores, I got treated like a slave, 24/7. As all of you know, the party was over. It was time to bring the pain. If these borderline hillbilly, trailer park White people thought they were superior to me just because of their skin color and thought they could disrespect me just because they outnumbered me, they thought wrong! The pain of all the Black people who suffered at the hands of White people in all the books I read and throughout our existence in America, now became my pain. I was determined that while I was in a position of authority at that Kmart store, no Black person would be oppressed. I was determined to be my brothers' and sisters' keeper!

From the beginning, the White apparel manager and I did not get along. He was probably one of the managers who worked his way up from a stock boy. I do not think he had anything personal against me. He was only concerned with keeping the store manager and district manager off his back. As I indicated above, I had several issues with the White managers at Kmart and I felt it was justifiable. Eventually, the apparel manager and I came to a mutual understanding. The less he said to me, the better.

The person I truly despised was the store manager. Our first confrontation was when he came up to me and placed his arm around my shoulders like we were buddies. The worst thing a person can do to me is to invade my personal space. Of course, I do not mind if people that are close to me enter my personal space, but definitely not someone, I despised. I immediately pulled away and told him not to ever touch me again. From that day forth, we battled back and forth. Any opportunity he had to make my day a living hell, he did. If I was not getting into it with the apparel manager, I was getting into it with the store manager. As you can tell, I hated working for people who I felt were incompetent. Day after day, the store manager would say something to me to provoke me to anger. It did not take very much to upset me. If he said, "Good morning," I would ask him, "What was so good about it?" My philosophy was: Let me come to work, do my job and go home, without going to jail. I know that is a terrible mindset to have, but the people I worked with in that store caused me to be that way.

When the store manager was not tormenting me, he was tormenting other Black employees who did not bow down to him. Unfortunately, most of the Black employees, young and old, gave him more respect than I thought he deserved. The way the store manager and the other White members of the management staff treated Black employees was disgraceful. All the best positions, shifts, promotions, and hours went to White employees. Black employees were treated like second-class citizens. As usual, I always attempted to come to the defense of the Black employees. The entire management staff hated me, and the feeling was mutual. It was only a matter of time before the problem escalated to uncontrollable levels. There was no doubt that this episode would not end happily unless I did something radical.

Organized Boycott

The harassment that I received from the White management staff was relentless. Some of the problems I was experiencing were initiated by me. And, just like a chess game, I always had to anticipate their next move and stay one step ahead of them. Thinking back on some of the successful strategies that were used by our people in the 1960's during the civil rights struggles, I decided to organize a boycott. I know it seems strange that an assistant manager would attempt to organize employees to protest against the employer who was paying their bills. I did not look at it that way. The title of assistant manager was given to me. I considered being born Black an honor and a privilege bestowed on me by God. Before I became an assistant manager, I was Black, and when they fired me, I would still be Black. There was no way I was going to allow a temporary position and salary to allow me to forget my first priority at this point in my life. My first priority was to my people; regardless of what position and responsibility a White man gave me. The position and responsibility I gave myself superceded any position someone else gave me. It was my responsibility to defend those who were unable to defend themselves. Throughout the history of our people in America, we have always been blessed with strong individuals to protect and lead others to a better day. Many are called, few are chosen, and some just go. I selected myself.

The attendees at the first meeting were eight people, two were family members, and the rest were Kmart employees. There was no question about the risks of staging a boycott, but that was of minor concern to me at that time. My greatest concern was how Black people were being exploited and treated at this particular store. Below is the "Blue Light Special Letter" that I wrote to be distributed to customers as they entered the store:

"Hello Kmart shoppers. I would like to take a couple minutes of your time to discuss a very important issue. As you walk through the doors of this Kmart store, you will be going back into the past. Yes, right here in Southfield, MI, this Kmart store practices beliefs that were standard in the 1960's and before. Afro-Americans in this store are blatantly discriminated against. As we start off the 1990's, here are some of the injustices that occur in this store: Afro-Americans are under surveillance because of race; Promotions are given based on race and not job performance; The store manager refers to Afro-Americans as 'you people' and 'those people'. These are just a few examples of discrimination that occur within these walls.

In the 1960's, numerous Afro-Americans died to secure our basic freedoms. Some of those individuals were Dr. Martin Luther King Jr., Malcolm X, Addie Mae Collins, Denise McNair and Carole Robertson. The last three individuals mentioned were the three innocent girls that died in a church bombing in Birmingham, Alabama on September 15, 1963. Are we going to allow these Afro-Americans deaths to be in vain? Now is the time for us to do the right thing. Until these injustices against our people stop, I ask that all Afro-Americans discontinue patronizing this Kmart store. What Kmart and other corporations have to realize is that Afro-Americans have tremendous buying power. If we, as a race, unite and boycott this store, eventually justice will be done. It is my hope that you will act accordingly and not allow these injustices to continue. My job is to make you aware of what time it is. Now it is your turn to act."

There was no question in my mind that it was going to be an extremely effective boycott. I probably would have been fired, but that was inevitable anyway. If I had a choice, I would rather go out on my terms than on another man's term. I was so shocked and disenfranchised about my first corporate America experience that the only thing that mattered to me was to eliminate all the pressure and stress that I was experiencing. Just like I got this job, I knew I would get another one.

Everything was finally coming into place. The people who were supporting the cause promised to deliver once the date was set. All the responsibilities were delegated to me. I organized the meeting, formulated the strategies and created the literature. It was a personal battle that was only affecting me at this time. A number of employees were wondering why I was so upset when I had a good paying job that paid twice as much as they were receiving. To me, it was not about the money. It was about being in a position of authority and utilizing that position to improve the lives of those who were not as fortunate as I was. Some of them assumed I had "arrived." I will never "arrive" until all our people who want the opportunity to have a better life are given one. Since that is my goal, I will never "arrive" because there is no way, in my lifetime, that all Black people in America will receive equal opportunities and justice. This reality did not disappoint me. It only meant that I had to be more diligent in my efforts to educate our people.

We were closely approaching the date of the boycott. The commitment and excitement of the others were still high. I felt now was the time to create a speech that would motivate our people even more. For some reason, expressing my thoughts on paper came easy to me. I always told myself that I was a writer-thinker, 24/7. To avoid going insane, I had to get thoughts off my mind at regular intervals. This is the speech that I hoped would propel those that read it to remain focused on our mission.

"What time is it? 'The Time is Now' to put up or shut up. You are either with me or against me. I am tired of everyone talking the talk, but when it is time to walk, everybody walks away. I was born alone, will die alone, and when the time comes, I will be judged alone! This is the opportunity for Black Brothers and Sisters to show unity and fight for a cause that is holding all of us down. This fight is not just for you and me. It is a fight for everybody. If they did it to me, they will do it to you. Now tell me what will stop them from doing it to our families? The struggle is not only for the present, but also for the future, and let's not forget about the past. Not so long ago, people died for us, and before that, people died for them. Now is the time to join together to end racism today, or it will never end.

Young Black people say that the fight is not theirs. Unless they turn White, it is their fight, too! They probably don't have to fight today, but when tomorrow comes, it will be their turn. Why put off tomorrow what we can do today? Wouldn't you rather fight alongside your brothers and sisters, than runaway? The choice is yours to turn your back on your people. When it's your turn to fight, don't be upset because you have to fight alone.

There was a time when we were strong, but tomorrow our strength will be gone! Everyday we lose more people to crack, jail and death. The 'Time is Now' to get it all started, and don't stop the fight until we have won. The battle we have to fight will be long and hard, but if we don't fight now, they will pull our holding card! When we go to battle, the odds will be against us, but if we were afraid of the odds, we would not play the lottery. We will fight this battle with dignity and pride, and always remember who is on our side. The only thing that beats a failure is a try, and if we fail the first time, let's just get up and try again. We all have come from the school of hard knocks. If you had the class before, why take it again? All of us have to do the right thing. That is not to forget about Dr. Martin Luther King Jr. and his famous, 'Dream.' Just like Dr. King, we all have dreams. In order to make them come true, this is what we must do; Wake up, straighten up and listen up. I am going to tell it slow and low. Only we know that we are tired of getting mistreated. Shhhh! I hear someone coming. It must be Mr. Charlie or a sellout at the back door. I got to run, but I certainly had fun. Don't worry, I will be back, if not me, there will be other brothers. Please remember what time it is. The 'Time is Now!!!'"

After that prepared speech, we all should have been ready to demand justice. Of course, the boycott never happened. Everybody became scared and decided against participating. Someone even told management of my plans. I was not mad about being abandoned because most of the employees were Black women with families and responsibilities. They were not in the position to be fighting for a cause that they were not prepared to pay the cost for. I was not even upset about the young Black men who sold me out. They thought this was a personal vendetta I had against management. I can almost guarantee that they will be confronted again with this problem before they leave this earth. The only way for a Black man to escape racism is either by "selling out" or dying. I always preferred to fight. Now, I had to execute Plan B.

Immediately, I began writing letters to the CEO of Kmart, EEOC and two Black organizations in the Detroit area. EEOC did an investigation, but did not discover any discrimination. Of course the CEO of Kmart never responded to my letters directly. I am sure he responded to me indirectly. Only one out of the two Black organizations responded to my letters. This battle was mine to fight alone. The cavalry was not coming.

Security Issues

At this Kmart store, it seemed like there was always something that kept me from performing my job as an assistant manager. Blatant injustice toward our people has always been something that I could not and would not ignore, especially if I was in a position to make a positive difference.

Starting in 1990, the media began bringing to the public attention the abuse of alleged shoplifters by store security personnel. At this particular Kmart store, the Loss Prevention Personnel, better known as "rent-a-cops" had a tendency to go beyond the call of duty when they apprehended alleged Black shoplifters. There were two White, plain clothes "rent-a-cops" who appeared to thrive on afflicting pain on any Black person they could. Most people do not want to accept that when some White people are in the position of authority they will use this power to make the lives of Black people a living hell at any opportunity they get. Examples of this are evident in numerous documented cases of White police officers across the United States violating the rights of alleged Black criminals. There have been several lawsuits against security personnel that work at malls and stores because of the injuries and deaths they have caused to alleged Black shoplifters. If you think about any incident involving a police officer or security guard, seldom are the victims White in any of these attacks. It makes you wonder, "Why?"

There is no question that when I become bored with a job it is usually because it does not challenge me mentally, and I find other ways to occupy my time. One of my greatest passions, next to writing, is defending the rights of our people and those who are not able to defend themselves. When it came to alleged shoplifters, I would make sure that the apprehension was not what I considered to be unreasonable force. White managers always questioned my involvement in security issues. When you are a Black man in America, you are always capable of being the next victim of unjustified abuse by White men, on any given day.

On several occasions, I would observe these two White "rent-a-cops" using what I considered to be excessive force when they were attempting to take alleged Black shoplifters into custody. It did not make a difference if the alleged shoplifter was a Black man or woman, excessive force was still used. There was one incident where one of the White "rent-a-cops" choked an alleged Black male shoplifter to the point of the man defecating on himself. What could that Black man possibly have stolen that he had to be restrained to the point of losing control of a bodily function? The answer is nothing. The punishment definitely did not fit the crime in this situation. Every time these two White "rent-a-cops" would apprehend an alleged Black shoplifter, I would be present to ensure that the person's human rights were not violated.

Almost everyday, a situation would occur between these two White men and alleged Black shoplifters. Never had I seen White shoplifters being apprehended. Is it safe to assume that White people do not steal? Or was it that while security were always watching Black people, White people were free to steal whatever they desired.

There were occasions when these two White men complained that I did not assist in the apprehension of Black people. They said I was not a team player. Newsflash: Never did I feel that I was a part of the Kmart Team. Just because I worked there, did not mean I condoned the treatment of Black employees, Black customers, or alleged Black shoplifters. Regardless of what a person is accused of stealing, that person does have protection under the law. They accused me of interfering with their job. If their job was to abuse Black people, my responsibility as a Black man and assistant manager was to ensure that every person who entered that store was treated with courtesy. You call that customer satisfaction.

One excellent example to show how overzealous these two White "rent-a-cops" were was when one of them chased an alleged Black shoplifter's car through the parking lot as it was speeding away. What could that person have stolen that was so valuable that security had to chase his car? These two young White men took their jobs too seriously and the management at this store basically condoned it.

The following incident is one that I will remember for the rest of my life. It was in the middle of January, when security chased an alleged Black shoplifter out of the store and into the parking lot. While they were attempting to apprehend him, they were wrestling with him on the ground, which was covered with a mixture of snow, water and ice. Other White employees and White customers helped security subdue the alleged shoplifter. Once I saw all of these White people on this Black man, I lost it. I was quoted as yelling, "Get the man off the ground before he catches pneumonia." This White woman supervisor told me to return to the store and it was all over. I yelled and asked who she thought she was talking to. It was probably 20 degrees outside, but I was so hot with rage that I was sweating. I kept shouting and demanding them to get the man off the ground before he got hurt. As usual, I was outnumbered. After about ten minutes of going ballistic, the Black female assistant manager was able to convince me to come back into the store.

When I saw the Black man on the ground, I was reminded of the pain and struggles of the people in the books that I had read over the years. Also, all of the newspaper articles and news stories of Black peoples' rights being violated everyday in America. There was no way I could just stand there and pretend like it was not happening, or that the actions of those White people were justifiable because the man allegedly stole something. That Black man could have easily been me, or someone close to any of us. Throughout our history in this country, thousands of our people have been killed at the hands of White people, and our people were too afraid or powerless to do anything about it. On this one occasion, I was not going to stand by quietly and allow a Black man to be killed. Am I exaggerating? If I am not mistaken, in 2002, there were two or three incidents in which "rent-a-cops" in the Detroit area killed alleged shoplifters. I made sure this was not going to occur that night.

The next day, the entire White management staff met in the conference room, without their white hoods, and wrote up statements about the incident. Even White people who were not outside during the incident, wrote statements. All of the statements were almost identical. It appeared that someone was telling everyone what to write. One thing I can give White people credit for is uniting when it is against a Black person. There were even statements from Black employees against me. I did not expect the Black employees to lie, but convenient amnesia is usually a good defense. It works for White people.

Two weeks later, the regional manager of Kmart, came to the store to meet with me. At the meeting, the district manager, two other White store mangers and I were present. The regional manager revealed six different incident reports where I had interfered with the Loss Prevention Personnel, I mean, White "rent-a-cops." We discussed all of them in-depth, and I gave him an explanation for all of them. In the interview summary, the regional manager stated the following:

"Mr. Prophet is being advised that he is to respond to 'Caroline Calls'. He is not to interfere with the Loss Prevention personnel in this store. He is not to question Loss Prevention Personnel in regard to their actions. If he has questions about Loss Prevention Personnel, or any other employee in the store, he should direct such questions to . . . ."

Of course, we totally disagreed on all of the above recommendations. The first one was how I was supposed to respond to a "Caroline call." A "Caroline" is when the "rent-a-cops" were having difficulty with an alleged shoplifter and all male employees were to hurry to assist them when someone said it over the loudspeaker. I informed him that apprehending shoplifters was a dangerous job and it was not worth me jeopardizing my life for. I also explained to him that it was not my responsibility to remove angry customers from anywhere. Even though I did not write it down in my summary, I am almost certain that I also told him that I did not go to college to become a security guard or a police officer, so I was not going to perform a duty that was not in my job description. If it was in my job description, I still was not going to do it. The second major issue I disagreed with was when he instructed me to refer any questions I had to the White managers that were listed. I told him that I did not have any respect for the people he listed and I was not going to do it. I also refused to sign the summary.

Two hours later, the regional manager rescinded the order that I was to assist Loss Prevention Personnel apprehend shoplifters. On my Personal Appraisal, he wrote the following:

"This interview was done to advise Mr. Prophet that his unprofessional behavior will not be tolerated in the future. Mr. Prophet cannot speak to other members of management using profanity or derogatory remarks. Mr. Prophet must understand that he is part of the management team and must function as a cohesive member of that team. Any future actions of an unprofessional nature may result in termination."

Here is the response that I wrote on the Performance Appraisal:

"I feel that Mr. Regional Manager's decision to give me a corrective action interview because of my poor management decision was justifiable. It is unfortunate that my actions were responded to by a transfer. The problem is not with me, but with security and the Kmart management team. There should be more people being transferred. I was not the problem, but the easiest solution. I do not agree with a transfer."

Without question, my behavior on the night in question was unprofessional as a member of the management team. My reaction that night was not as a manager, but as a Black man seeing another Black man being abused by a White lynch mob. As I said before, my allegiance is to my people, and making sure that they are treated fairly. As far as me using profanity and derogatory remarks, I am sure I was provoked. There was never a record of the profanity and derogatory remarks that management said to me and to the other Black employees. It appeared that I was "E.F. Hutton." Every time I spoke, everybody listened, remembered and wrote it down. I never felt that I was a member of a cohesive team. From day one, I did not agree with the way Kmart treated Black employees. I performed the job to the best of my abilities as a team player, but in my mind I was not a part of the team. If I were a true member of the team, it would have meant that I condoned their treatment of Black people. My actions and statements proved that I was not a member of the team. There is no question that my writing letters to the CEO of Kmart accusing them of racism had something to do with my transfer. As far as being terminated, I only wondered when he would finally take me out of my misery. Well, that question would soon be answered.

Livonia, MI

On January 24, 1991, the last stop on my "Introduction To Racism Tour," began. I reported to the last Kmart store I would ever work in. My days were already numbered. There was no question in my mind that it was inevitable that I would be emancipated soon. The Livonia Kmart store did not have any Black management staff and, if I remember correctly, not very many Black employees. Most of the customers were White people. I really felt at home. Yeah, right! I had already came to the store with the reputation of being disobedient, militant, disrespectful and definitely anti-White. I did not hate White people. I hated the way White people treated Black people. It appeared that all the White management staff accepted me amongst their ranks, but that was a lie. Most White people are experts at hiding their true feelings about Black people and work with them like they grew up together. Most Black people have been brainwashed to worship the ground that their White co-workers walk on. It is because some Black people still have a slave mentality. As for me, I could not hide anything! If anyone pissed me off, I had to let him or her know immediately. I did not care if the person was White or Black, my supervisor or a subordinate. One thing I could not be accused of was having double standards I had no respect of person. If anyone upset me, it was on. There were certainly consequences and repercussions for me being candid and outspoken. Everything that is on your mind should not come out of your mouth or be put on paper. That is, if you want to keep your job.

Being an assistant manager at one Kmart store is the same as any other Kmart store. I was responsible for putting out merchandise that we were usually out of because Kmart had one of the most idiotic and obsolete inventory systems of any retail store chain. We would receive cases of the same size clothing. Every time a customer needed a certain size, it was never available. As far as clothing selections, a rock could have made better selections. There were so many markdowns and clearance sales because the fashion buyer made poor merchandise selections or too much of the same items were ordered by coward managers and arrogant executives. This is what I observed at all of the Kmart stores where I grudgingly worked. I explained all of this so I could explain what led to my emancipation and the end of one of the worst employment experiences of my life.

Unlike most Black people, most White people will stick together until the end, regardless if they are right or wrong. It is called a code of ethics. I should have known not to criticize, slander or voice my negative opinion about a White person to another White person. Better yet, you should not voice a negative opinion of any person to any other person. Some Black people have a stronger allegiance to White people than to other Black people. Some of our people have their priorities mixed up. To avoid all of this confusion, do not confide in anyone in the workplace. You go there to earn a paycheck, not to make friends. The most important thing for Black people to do is definitely not to assume that you can trust your co-workers or supervisors, regardless of race. There are exceptions to the rule, but stick with this general rule to be safe and remain employed.

The White apparel manager I worked for at the Livonia store was probably another one of the White men without a college degree who worked his way up from a stock boy. He was assigned the responsibility of gathering evidence against me. This manager and the district manager had worked together for years. They were both a part of the "Good Ole' Boy Network." White men will always stick together to bring down a Black man. Do not ever forget that! Everything I said to the apparel manager or any other employee was immediately written down for the district manager. One of the most irritating problems I had with White employees at all of the stores I worked in was their blatant disrespect and/or disregard for my authority. I would direct a White employee to do something, and he or she would ask another White employees to validate my directive.

In a letter to the district manager, the White apparel manager reported a number of statements:

"Mr. Prophet has stepped beyond his authority by using such phrases to apparel employees as: 'This is your last warning'; 'This is your last strike'; 'If you worked for me in my area, you would be fired.'"

Throughout my three years of employment with Kmart, I cannot recall initiating the firing of one employee. If I did threaten to fire a White employee at the Livonia store, the White manager would have vetoed it. Another statement recorded about me was:

"On 2/16/91, Mr. Prophet was informed of the new programs and possible payroll plans that were discussed at a district meeting on 2/15/91. Upon learning of the changes, Mr. Prophet reacted with a negative attitude, including making the statement, 'We can't do it.' . . . He also stated, 'Slavery is over,' and that he would not work over 48 hours . . ."

I will not lie and say I did not say those things. At that time in my life, it could have been possible. It never crossed my mind that he would write down everything I said, verbatim. As far as the payroll budget, I did think that it was stupid how our store hours were cut drastically. The less hours we had for employees, meant the more physical labor for me. One of the worst things about being a salaried employee without union representation in an "At Will Employment" state is that you can get fired for anything. No matter how impossible or illogical the orders from upper management are, as a salaried employee, you had better make it happen or get ready to find another job. I believe that another person's bad planning should not make for my emergency. In other words, just because someone else messes up, does not mean that I have to make up for his or her mistake. That is why I hate working for incompetent people. Yes, slavery was over and I was not going to work more than 48 hours in one week. Some managers would work up to 60 hours a week and not get any extra compensation. I did not go to college to work for free.

The same White apparel manager was complaining about the same issues that I was complaining about. Since this manager probably worked at Kmart from the age of fifteen, he knew middle-aged White men were "a dime a dozen" and he, therefore, could not work anywhere but at Kmart. This was a lesson to everyone to be careful of what you say to anyone, about anything. I could have only been venting, but he took me seriously. However, I was serious and did not care about my job.

Finally, my prayers were answered. After my three years of servitude, Kmart decided to terminate probably one of the most militant, rebellious and outspoken Black employee who had ever worked on any of the Kmart plantations.

One evening, a Black couple wanted to purchase a crib that was on display, since there were no more cribs in stock. I felt sure that I had authorization to mark down the price of the crib and the accessories inside of the crib, so I did. My rationale for this decision was Kmart's policy of "satisfying the customer." After the markdown, the customers were satisfied. A month later, I was called into the office again to meet with three White men, for the last time. This is an excerpt from my letter to the Michigan Unemployment Agency:

"It took me, and another employee, thirty minutes to remove the crib from the platform. Once we had the crib on the floor, the man asked if additional money would be taken off because it was a display model. He then inquired about the mattress, bumper pad, and the sheet that was with it. After looking at the merchandise, we noticed it was soiled from dust and customers handling it excessively. The crib also had dents and scratches on it. The mattress was an older model, which was supposed to have been marked down several months ago. It was also torn. After going through the department to find identical merchandise and not finding any, I decided to compare everything affiliated with the crib to similar merchandise. Then I calculated on a sheet of paper the price I thought was fair for each item. I came up with a grand total of $100.00. The couple accepted the price."

A few weeks after the sale, the Black male employee who assisted me said that store security questioned him about the transaction. They were insinuating that the couple was friends of mine. I had never seen the people before in my life.

On April 9, 1991, the White apparel manager came and informed me that the White regional manager and White district manager wanted to meet with me in the security office. The regional manager immediately accused me of contributing to the excessive invisible waste problem in the store. He informed me that the merchandise I sold had a retail value of $160.00. Invisible waste was averaged at $745.75 a day. I was charged with $60.00 of invisible waste.

After his accusation, I explained to him how I arrived at the price that I charged the customers. He had already made his decision to terminate me. Then I remembered that, in an indirect way, the regional manager had told me previously that the next time he had to meet with me, I was going to be terminated.

Here is another excerpt from the letter I wrote to the Michigan Unemployment Agency:

"The way I was treated during the interrogation process was unprofessional. I felt that during the entire discussion, I was already guilty and had to prove that I was innocent. The regional manager was not qualified enough to make a decision based on the facts that were available to him. He assumed the positions of jury, prosecuting attorney for Kmart Corporation, and the judge. How could he have had an objective opinion? He stated on one occasion that a question

I had just answered was different from the way I answered it about thirty minutes earlier. I asked him if our discussion was taped. He said no. How is he going to remember word for word what I said during an hour-long discussion? During the entire interrogation process, he continued to look behind me at the district manager to see how he was responding to my answers. The most humiliating part of the day was when I had to continue to ask the manager if I could go to lunch. He said he had to ask the regional manager. That made me feel like a slave, asking the overseer, to ask master if his slave, Conrad, could have some food!! They would not allow me to eat at all. I did not eat until I was terminated at 3:00P.M.

"Throughout the entire interrogation, the regional manager continued to refer back to the written statements that were probably given to him by the infant department employee and the Black employee who assisted me. This employee was with me throughout most of the transaction. On one of the written statements, it was stated that a comforter, a pillow, and a pillowcase were in the display at a certain point in time. It is apparent that they were removed before the transaction took place. I was also informed that I initially stated, I was going to take 25 percent off of everything. I had no recollection of stating that. If I did, it was apparent other circumstances forced me to change my mind. When has it become policy that an assistant manager with almost three years of experience had to justify his or her management decisions to an employee? Every time I make a decision in my mind, I do not tell someone what I am thinking! It was my job to be decisive about my plan of action and implement it. The regional manager took the word of an employee over mine because what the employee stated was what he wanted to hear. The Black male employee has a reputation of telling things incorrectly. His written statement is proof. Recently this Black employee was accused of taking $20.00 from the cash register. If he was accused of embezzlement, how could his statement be considered more valid than mine? The regional manager and those employees had almost a month to prepare their statements. I was given just a minute to reminisce on an incident that I thought was practically standard procedure. If I had been given the opportunity to think about the situation, I could have justified my decision."

The two paragraphs above appear the same as they appeared in the letter I sent to the Michigan Unemployment Agency, except the names are excluded. I noticed numerous grammatical errors that I could have changed, but I did not want to alter the letter to attempt to give the illusion that I was perfect or that I have always had a mastery of the English language. Some areas of my grammar are still weak, even to this day, but I try to improve everyday. One day, I might not need an editor, but until that day, I will never be too ashamed or embarrassed to ask someone for help. The only way to eliminate any weakness is to work on eliminating it; not ignore it or pretend that it does not exist.

Kmart attempted to prevent me from receiving unemployment, but I received it almost immediately. The excellent employees at the Michigan Unemployment Agency in Madison Heights knew I was terminated unfairly. Because of Kmart, I was able to receive $243.00 a week for 26 weeks. I have to thank Kmart for allowing me to have one of the best summer vacations I have ever had.

Advice

What possible advice can I give that has not already been given throughout this chapter? Even in 2003, many things have not changed in corporate America for Black people. I cannot officially state that every corporation is as racist as I alleged that Kmart was. It would be wrong for me to state that the entire Kmart Corporation is racist. From what I read in the newspaper, see on the news, and hear from other Black people, everything that you have just read has happened to thousands of Black people. There is no doubt that most of the problems I experienced were caused by my candidness and desire to make sure that all Black employees were treated fairly and with dignity. My self-defense mechanism was activated because I felt that my pride, dignity, and self-respect were threatened everyday. When I am placed in what I consider to be a hostile environment, I sometimes emulate the tactics of the one who is trying to oppress me. I am always determined to play as good as my competition. I have some regrets about the way I conducted myself at that time in my life. The ill treatment I received from White staff members caused me to view all White people as my enemy.

For those of you who really want to succeed in White corporate America, I suggest that you assimilate as quickly as possible. If you do not know what that means, just refer to the quote from Paul Robeson that I provided earlier in this chapter. Also, look at a number of financially successful Black people in America who have been accepted by the White power structure. If you emulate them, your chances of surviving in White corporate America will be greater.

I have been in the belly of the beast and have read enough books about the experiences of other Blacks to know how to deal with White people. Take my advice and "be like Mike." If any of you young people don't take my advice on how to conduct yourself in White corporate America, 20 years from now, you will be writing a book like this one. I do not have any regrets. I am just glad that I am able to share my experiences with you, so you may possibly avoid some negative experiences and situations. If you do not believe what I wrote, please ask somebody, who has been down the road, I have traveled.

Kmart In 2003

In 2002, Kmart Corporation filed for chapter 11 Bankruptcy. Below are some documented facts and allegations that led to Kmart Corporation filing for bankruptcy:

- Thousands of employees were fired with no severance pay and shareholders lost more than $6.3 billion in equity over two years. Yet Kmart's bankers were paid 40 cents on the dollar, and creditors were given newly issued stock.[3]
- The review, released Friday, gives a detailed outline of how the actions of a few dozen executives resulted in $2.1 billion in losses for Kmart, the shuttering of more than 600 stores and the eventual elimination of 67,000 jobs nationwide.[1]
- Managers never filled out formal applications. No background checks were done and no interviews were conducted, according

to the review. Ultimately, these hires would prove unqualified for their positions and would be terminated.[5]

- Kmart's proposed reorganization plan calls for canceling all the company's outstanding 519 million shares—leaving thousands with worthless pieces of paper.[6]
- One stockholder indicated he bought the stock for about $6 a share and watched it climb to $17 before dropping off to less than 20 cents a share.[7]
- All total, 25 ex-managers were given loans totaling $28.8 million weeks before Kmart filed for bankruptcy in January 2002.[8]

How sad is it that while Black and White Kmart employees were losing their jobs, White male executives were receiving interest-free, million dollar loans. It was the arrogance and ignorance of White men that caused the demise of Kmart. I am happy to state that no Black man or woman had anything to do with the failure of Kmart. All I can do is shake my head in disbelief, because I was terminated for allegedly discounting clearance merchandise for $60.00 below cost.

Experts predict that Kmart Corporation will be out of business within the next ten years. It will be an unfortunate situation for all the remaining Kmart employees, but there are times when, "chickens come home to roost." I am glad that the regional manager freed me before Kmart's downward spiral into the bowels of hell.

This is my last important piece of advice. Starting in 2000, it became more difficult to sue a corporation successfully if you were fired because of your race. Unless it is a blatant act of discrimination, it will be hard to get a lawyer to take your case. The EEOC does not have the personnel to pursue your case in a timely or aggressive manner. In addition, there was a time when the EEOC was headed by Clarence Thomas who is now a Supreme Court Justice; that is a clear indication of how much power the EEOC possesses. Your best bet if you are fired from corporate America is just to "charge it to the game" and move on with your life. The time, effort and money that you use to fight a losing battle in the courts in this country will most likely be in vain. I hope you never have to fight this battle.

Chapter 6

WAYNE COUNTY DEPARTMENT OF PUBLIC SERVICES

"He delivered me from my strong enemy, and from them that
hated me: for they were too strong for me."

—2 Sam 22:18

Introduction

Sometimes only God knows why certain things happen to certain people. In my case, I know why I end up in the places that I do. Attitude! Attitude is everything. After being emancipated from Kmart, I tentatively started pursuing other employment. I was not very eager to return to corporate America after my Kmart experience. When I went on interviews, I let it be known the type of person I was and what drives me. I did not want to give anyone the illusion that I was a person who would tolerate any and everything to obtain a job. That candid and assertive approach did not get me any second interviews.

The Kmart experience had a profound psychological effect on me. The passion to be a manager in corporate America no longer existed. Fighting for respect everyday as a Black man to make an honest living and trying to do my job was more than a notion. I was not ready to deal with that emotional stress just yet. The requirements were too steep for me to cope with so soon after the Kmart experience. One day, I was job hunting and noticed that Wayne County Department of Public Services (WCDPS) was accepting applications for a Typist I position. In junior high and high school, I took typing and became proficient at it. So, naturally I headed for 600 Randolph to apply for the Typist I position. When I took the typing test, I had no problem passing the minimum requirement for this position. There was no concern for securing a job since this was a very large employer and unemployment was low.

Wayne County is the largest county in Michigan, with Detroit as the largest city, in this county and state. The CEO of Wayne County during this time was Mr. Ed McNamara. He was responsible for over 6,000 employees with an annual budget over $10 billion. As I reminisce over my Wayne County experience, you will discover how Mr. McNamara, the CEO of the largest county in Michigan, and an entry level typist had their names mentioned in the same sentence. To clarify the major focus of this chapter allow me say that it is not about Mr. McNamara, for whom I have the utmost respect, nor is it on the blatant racism that was allegedly occurring at Wayne County during my employment. Kmart had taught me all that I needed to know about racism, so the racism I experienced at Wayne County was redundant. Black people will always be subjected to the wrath of racism in the United States. It is a given. The most profound lesson I learned at Wayne County and the focus of this chapter is Black people. There is a phrase that goes, "All my skin folks, aren't my kin folks." This is a phrase you will understand the meaning of by the end of this chapter.

WCDPS—Typist I

On September 20, 1991, I started working at Detroit Metropolitan Airport as a typist for the Director of Airport—Facilities and Planning. Surprisingly, this director was a Black man. Unlike a number of directors and appointees, this Black director had a degree in architecture and was extremely competent and experienced in this field.

Accepting the position of typist resulted in a substantial reduction in pay for me. At the time, I viewed the position as an opportunity. Going from an assistant manager in corporate America to a typist in the government sector, was like going from a Staff Sergeant (E-6) to a Private (E-1) in the Army. If my ego ruled, there would have been no way in the world I would have taken an entry level position as a typist with a Bachelor's Degree in Business Administration. But remember my ego was not my guide and since I never allowed a title, job, or hourly wage to define me, the title of a typist was irrelevant. Initially, some of the other Black employees at the airport thought I was gay because of my position. Certainly this assumption was made based on the relationship between my gender and title. It did not take very long for them to figure out that you cannot judge a person by job description, title, or salary.

Being a typist was a much needed hiatus from management. There was no need for me to lie and embellish on my responsibilities. This job was no different than any other clerical position. I answered the telephone, typed contracts, and performed other minor office administrative tasks. Very simply put, I was a typist. There was no shame in my game. This job provided me with the funds necessary to pay some of my bills and make an honest living. As you go through life you will find that there are times when it becomes necessary to make sacrifices in order to improve.

In comparison to my previous management position, I cherished being a typist for that period in my life. Being in a subordinate position means that you are not responsible for the behavior and productivity of other employees. All I had to do was come to work on time, do as I was told and go home. What my co-workers thought of me was of no concern. The director that I worked for was considered arrogant, aggressive, dominating, and demanding by many. Those were some strong qualities for a Black man to possess and still keep his job. I had a high level of respect for him because he had no respect of person. He treated everyone the same. If you upset him, you would receive his wrath. It did not matter if you were Black, White, male, female, a typist, or another director. We had our heated confrontations regularly. I had to stand my ground and explain to him that between 8:00A.M.

and 5:00P.M., I was a typist and was paid to follow his orders. At 5:01P.M., I was Conrad Prophet and any problems we could not resolve during working hours, we could resolve after working hours when job titles did not mean anything to me. My combative nature would resurface, when provoked.

The rapport I established with co-workers and upper management was harmonious. There was never any animosity between my coworkers and me. I worked on trying to be as non-confrontational as possible. Since I was in a position with little power, most people assumed that my personality matched my title. During that time, I would have considered my disposition to be compliant. What could possibly get a person upset to the point of rebellion in a typist position? Over the years, I have learned to adjust to my environment As the saying goes, "If you don't start none, there won't be none."

Time Analyst

After almost two years in the position as a mild mannered typist, opportunity came knocking once more. I took a test and became a Time Analyst. Initially, the position of a Time Analyst was more challenging. I was responsible for collecting the hours of the employees who worked in various departments and ensuring they were paid correctly. When I joined the department in July 1993, there were twelve Time Analysts. Other than myself, there were only two other men, both were White, and ten women—five Black and five White. Our department manager was a White man and our assistant department manager was a Black woman. At this time in my Wayne County career, race did not play a pertinent role because I was not there long enough to apply for any positions of authority.

One thing I quickly observed when I joined the Time Analyst Department, was that the caliber of White people in positions of authority in Wayne County were considerably inferior to the White people in the same positions in corporate America. Our department manager's personal appearance was totally unprofessional and borderline atrocious. Just like Black people are categorized based on their clothing style, behavior, education, and the neighborhood they live in, White people are categorized the same way. The White department manager who represented us at important meetings was a combination of a "hillbilly" and a resident of a low-class "trailer park." There is no disrespect intended, but his personal appearance gave our department an image of incompetence and a lack of professionalism.

Neudeck Building

My first permanent assignment as a Time Analyst was at the Neudeck Building in downtown Detroit. The people in this building played a significant role in my growth over the next six years. I shared an office with a Black woman, who helped prepare me for the battles that I would soon encounter in the coming years. Her wisdom and knowledge were beyond the capacity of intelligence necessary for the position of a Time Analyst. Periodically, I would ask her why she was still there and did not apply for other positions. As time passed, the answer was revealed.

Daily, we would argue about any and everything. She was very territorial, dominating, and aggressive. Her mastery of the English language and selection of difficult words fascinated me. There were times when she would say a word and I would have to write it down, so I could look up the definition after our discussion. I would ask her why she used a $100.00 word in a $2.00 sentence and she would respond with "because I can." Everyday, I learned something new from her. After four months, the job as a Time Analyst became monotonous for me. It was the mental challenge that I received from a lady, who I now consider a dear friend that allowed me to maintain my sanity.

When we were not philosophizing and discussing issues far more important than our job, we were at each other's throats. On several occasions, either the department manager or assistant manager would have to come down and resolve a dispute. This co-worker and myself had the same problem. We were both stern, stubborn, and had the desire to control our environment. It did not matter to me that she had been with Wayne County for a number of years and had more life experience than me. All that mattered was that she was going to give me respect. Again, like myself, she was from the "show me state" and we had to show each other that we were not easily intimidated. Eventually, we called a nonverbal truce, but in my mind, I was the H.N.I.C. and in her mind she was the H.N.I.C.

My co-worker's demeanor was similar to a girl scout in comparison to the other Black women in the building. Several Black women in the Neudeck Building held upper management positions. Some of them were the most vicious, abusive, vindictive, and power hungry Black women I ever had the misfortune of meeting. Even though the position of Time Analyst did not have much power on paper, we determined when and who received the correct amounts on their checks. At each location, we had our own independence and autonomy. As long as the director's check was correct, everybody else was fair game.

Now, these Black women in power were outrageous. On a regular basis, I would hear about and also see them verbally abusing the Black women who worked for them. I would make a mental note and whenever I received the opportunity to retaliate, I did. It is tragic how petty, jealous, and contrite some women in power can be. If a Black woman in a high position thought a subordinate looked or dressed better than her, all you could do was say a prayer for that unfortunate woman, because she would feel the wrath of her Black manager. There were five specific women at the Neudeck Building whose day I would try to make as miserable as they did for others. In this building, it was every man and woman for themselves. If you could not defend yourself, which most Black women in lower level positions could not, you were at the mercy of the ruthless Black women in power. I am not referring to all Black women, but those who were in the Neudeck Building know who I am referring to.

During one period, I had the opportunity to be the Time Analyst for the Roads Maintenance Yard. This job entailed traveling to various maintenance yards in the Detroit area to check the time cards of the maintenance workers and provide other administrative assistance. The workers in these locations were responsible for the repair of Wayne County roads in the summer and snow removal in the winter. A majority of the workers were Black men from Detroit and other neighboring cities. This was the environment where I felt the most comfortable. I considered myself to be a down-to-earth, hard working, "roughneck" type of brother. When I visited the maintenance yards, these brothers were hardworking and most were not into kissing up to the White man to keep their jobs like other Black men. I had nothing, but respect for these brothers.

On one of my site visits, there must have been an invisible sign on my back that only certain people could read which said, "Try me. I'm easy." I went to one of the maintenance yards one day and an employee was trying to become irate with me over something trivial. I told him, I would take off my tie and whip his behind! Well that was the last time I addressed that issue with anyone. For some reason, people assume that just because a Black man wears a shirt and tie to work, he is less of a man than a Black man who wears work clothes. For those of you who have this opinion, please do not allow the way a Black man dresses to determine what he is capable of doing. Of course, I was not in this position long. There was an opening in another location in Detroit, so I requested and received a transfer. The job of a Time Analyst is important, but once I master a job, I become bored and it is best for me to change my environment to avoid future problems. I firmly believe that an idle mind is the devil's workshop.

WCDPS—640 Temple

Each location in Wayne County possessed its own cultural environment. This attribute was reflected in the mentality of the employees. The employees located at 640 Temple would be no different. As the Time Analyst for the building trades workers, I recorded the hours they worked daily and provided administrative support. The skilled trades workers were assigned to perform work in all of the Wayne County buildings in the Detroit area. The number of skilled trades positions and the number of Black workers that were employed in each trade are listed below:

- 11 Carpenters—0 Black
- 12 Electricians—0 Black
- 5 Iron Workers—0 Black
- 10 Painters—0 Black
- 9 Plumbers—1 Black
- 11 Refrigeration Equipment Mechanics—0 Black
- 2 Sheet Metal Workers—0 Black
- 6 Steamfitters—3 Black

For those of you who are unaware, skilled trades workers are paid extremely well. The question is: Where are the Black skilled trades workers? In Wayne County, the tax dollars pay the salaries of all employees (except Detroit Metro Airport employees). Remember the city of Detroit, the largest city in Michigan, is located in Wayne County, where more than 80 percent of the city's residents are Black. Why weren't Black workers getting a piece of the skilled trades pie?

The director of the skilled trades department was one of the coolest White men I had ever met. He could have kept a white hood in the trunk of his car, but once he sat down at his desk, he treated Black and White workers the same. He did not take anything from anyone. He reminded me of Marlon Brando's character in the "Godfather." This director would walk down to the building trades area and allow them to experience his wrath and return to his office. He determined the mood on the third floor. If a Time Analyst was having trouble with anyone, all we had to do was give him a name and the person was his.

My co-worker at this location was another Black woman, who was nice and on her way to retirement. Her replacement was another Black woman, who I hold in the highest esteem to this day. This Black woman was also nice and sweet, until you crossed her. When she said, "Alright captain," it was a warning that somebody was about to get on her last nerve. After that it was on. I never crossed her and to this day,

I still have no plans of doing so. Working with her was enjoyable because we looked out for each other and there was no territory battle. This work environment for the most part was pleasant. There were times when a White skilled trades worker would come into our office trying to make demands that I found to be hilarious. Some of them thought I was their servant and that my job was to cater to their every need. Once I explained myself in some not so pleasant words, we got a good understanding of each other. Weekly, it seemed like I had to do or say something to get my respect from a White man.

Working at 640 Temple was just a refresher's course on what was in line for me next. From my first day of employment with Wayne County, my goal was to just come to work, perform my job to the best of my ability, and go home. Life was good. Then reality resurfaced. It is just amazing how well White people get along with Black people, as long as we stay in our place, and behave ourselves. Well, naturally every place was my place, so I belonged everywhere. No boundaries and no behavioral guidelines except to "do unto others as others have done unto me." Wayne County had a set of unwritten rules of which I was unaware. Quickly, I learned those rules the hard way.

WCDPS—Department Supervisor IV

In April 1997, I was promoted to the position of Department Supervisor IV at Central Maintenance Yard (CMY) in Romulus, MI. To me this was Hicksville, USA—forgotten by the evolution of progress. I think that some of the Black and White people at this particular location were unaware that slaves were emancipated in 1863. Even before I arrived there, people were placing their bets. Everyone, but me, knew what was awaiting me. CMY in my opinion was the most racist work location in Wayne County. The further you worked from Detroit, the more racist Wayne County work locations became.

I worked with two White managers. One allegedly had prior military experience. "Gomer Pyle" is the character that comes to mind when I think of him. The other was a bonified hillbilly. Wayne County was one of the only places where I knew a White man with an education level that appeared to stop at the sixth grade, could make $50,000.00 or more a year. We had a unique meeting of the minds. My mentality at the time was similar to that of Malcolm X. I worked for two White managers with mentalities almost identical to Strom Thurman, Trent Lott, David Duke, or any other White supremacist who attempted to act out their delusional fantasies in their mind. They seemed to think they were superior to Black people because of their race. They were in for a rude awakening.

Some of the storekeepers under my supervision had taken the same test as I to get the position that I obtained. Two Black female storekeepers had ten years of experience in the stockroom and were qualified to get the position, but because of the sexist beliefs of the two White managers, neither was promoted into the position.

Initially, some of the Black storekeepers resented me for receiving the position. One Black storekeeper referred to me as an "Uncle Tom." Eventually, she would realize that I was no "Uncle Tom." Can a brother elevate to a managerial position without being thought of as a "sell out" to the race? As a supervisor, it was my job to give directives and delegate responsibilities.

My responsibilities as a Department Supervisor IV included supervising the employees of the Central Maintenance Yard Stockroom. This particular stockroom supplied nearly ninety percent of all the supplies needed for most of Wayne County's locations. The stock ranged from office supplies to parts for trucks.

Anytime a Black man or woman who earns a position of authority, fails to follow the unwritten rules of the game, and does not assume an inferior role, they will feel the wrath of the power structure in this country. Being a supervisor at CMY Stockroom did not take years to master. The combination of a Bachelor's Degree in Business Administration and being trained by experienced Black storekeepers, allowed me to acclimate myself to the stockroom system quickly. Thorough tours of the stockroom during my training helped me recognize that some of the methods of warehousing stock were antiquated. After a month, I was ready to implement new ideas that would permit the stockroom to operate more efficiently. All I had to do was treat all storekeepers Black and White with respect and dignity, passing the probationary period would be no problem. The battle lines would be drawn swiftly and with precision. I always told myself that all battles were not meant to be fought. The battleground in Hicksville, USA was different. It was imperative for me to fight all battles. If I did not, it would have only given the managers, who I alleged to be White supremacists, a false sense of security and I never wanted that to happen. The first incident that occurred, which infuriated me, was the inability of the managers to assign me a desk, even though two desks were empty. After three weeks of indecisiveness by management, I assigned myself a desk. When "Gomer Pyle" asked me who assigned me the desk, I told him, "I commandeered it." Commandeer is a military term, meaning something was taken without authority. Immediately, his eyes appeared to cross, his face turned red, and he marched away mumbling to himself. You guessed it. That made my day.

There was a difference like night and day in our management skills. Neither of the White managers appeared to have taken any training courses on how to communicate effectively nor any diversity training on working with people of color and women. It was apparent that just being a White male alone qualified you to become a manager in Wayne County. It also appeared that Black people could not be placed in many positions of authority.

Just like my Kmart days, my decisions were always second-guessed and questioned by the White managers and White employees. It seems that White men have difficulties being told what to do by Black men. I assume some of them still think the rules of slavery are still applicable today. Even though racism continues to impede the progress of Black people, many of us continue to become successful and remain Black. There was an enormous amount of resentment by the White employees in the stockroom because of my work performance. I performed my job effectively and had an excellent rapport with the Black storekeepers. They probably hated the fact that I was not kissing up to them and thanking them for giving me the job. Believe me, when I say it was not because of any generosity of a White person or the influence of a Black person that assisted me in getting the job in the first place. I did not owe any allegiance to anyone. If I owed anyone, it was the qualified Black storekeepers who applied for the job, but did not get it because the White managers refused to see a Black woman in the position of authority in the stockroom.

As I was being trained by the Black storekeepers, I observed how the White managers were showing preferential treatment to the White storekeepers. It was unfortunate that I had to assume the role of a defense lawyer and civil rights activist instead of a supervisor. I always told myself that when I elevated to a position of authority, I would respect and protect the rights of all employees who were assigned to work for me regardless of color. This was a daily battle because these two White managers were determined to make the Black storekeepers lives a living hell. My mindset, from the countless books I have read, life experiences, and conscience would not allow me to stand around and allow injustices to be infringed upon the Black storekeepers.

For almost five months I battled constantly with the two White managers. There is no need to explain in detail the redundant form of harassment and underhanded tactics that were used against me on a daily basis. The reason I am fast-forwarding through what I consider trivial issues is because I had already anticipated that it was going to occur. It was inevitable.

On Friday, September 12, 1997, I was called into the manager's office at 1:30P.M. In attendance were the two White managers, my White union steward, and the White union president. It was almost de ja vu of the Kmart experience six years earlier. This time around I was hoping that the two White managers would be real and bring their white hoods. I truly believed that my union steward and union president were attempting to defend me to the best of their ability. We talked about the allegations against me. For the first time, I saw my probationary period evaluation.

In Part I of the Evaluation Of Performance On Major Duties, the three possible rating categories were: Unsatisfactory, Marginal and Acceptable. I received a rating of "Acceptable" in the all of the four areas: Organizing and planning; Supervising; Training employees; Coordinating with vendors and customers agencies.

In Part II of General Performance Rating, I received a rating of "Acceptable" for the following: Level of Knowledge/Skills/Abilities; Productivity; Attendance; I received a "Marginal" rating in Reliability and an "Unsatisfactory" rating in working with others. My union steward asked me to sign it and I refused. I did not have any problems working with the employees I was supervising. My problems were with the two White managers. Attached to my performance evaluation were 11 pages of statements of "Findings and Determinations." They consisted of statements written by both White managers defending the reason for failing me during the probationary period. Here are comments regarding some of the accusations against me that were made by the two White managers:

"His attitude and demeanor have been unacceptable. He has been antagonistic, contemptuous, condescending, provoking and rebuffing, both towards management and storekeepers, and insensitive to his social surroundings . . . .

Based on incidents during the beginning of his probationary period, I feel there were just causes to have terminated him. However, I was trying to give Mr. Prophet the benefit of the doubt, hoping he would improve. Since he has not, we can not continue to endure having an individual undermine the good will and discipline of the division."

My first response was, "What?" I will refute the following statements individually; "Insensitive to his social surroundings." What were the social surroundings that I was insensitive to? Was he referring to the racist surroundings where Black employees were harassed, belittled, and disrespected daily by White managers while White employees were praised and received preferential treatment? If he was referring to me not allowing Black employees to be treated like second-class citizens, then yes I was guilty.

In regard to the next statement: " . . . undermine the good will and discipline of the division." I never saw any good will. As far as discipline, if that is synonymous with having Black employees working in a hostile work environment where they have no rights, again I was guilty because I never permitted any storekeepers Black or White to be treated unfairly. An employee should be able to come to work daily and work in an environment free of any form of harassment. Again, I am guilty of undermining the illusion of good will at the CMY location. Throughout their "Findings and Determinations" they recorded a variety of relevant and irrelevant statements concerning my alleged behavior. Once they discovered that I was not going to condone and comply with what they were doing, they were determined to have me fail my probation. Here is an example of a planned conspiracy. There were two statements typed on May 21, 1997, but the incidents in question occurred on May 6, 1997 at 3:40P.M. and May 7, 1997. Then there was a memo typed on May 30, 1997 with statements I made on May 15, 22, 23, 29, and 30. I wondered why someone would write down everything that came out of my mouth, unless of course, they had an ulterior motive.

Managers make the decision of who passes or fails his or her probation period. Unfortunately, my fate was in the hands of the two White managers, I considered racist. It would have been different if these two White men had unblemished records and were known to be fair and just people. The two White men did not possess the skills, credentials, professionalism, education, or appearance to be managers anywhere, but in "Hicksville, USA." America's legal system states, that a person is innocent until proven guilty. If you worked for Wayne County and were Black, the opposite held true. Because of the influence of Mr. McNamara, a person would need the legal expertise of Cornelius Pitts, Geoffrey Fieger, Johnnie Cochran, or Willie Gary in order be to proven innocent.

Since I was on a 6-month probationary period, I was not going to relinquish all my rights as a man and assume the role of a Black boy in order to keep my job. I believe that certain qualities are necessary to be a fair and just person: Integrity; Character; Respect; Good morals; Dignity; Pride; Intelligence; Compassion. They were not paying me enough to relinquish the qualities that I am willing to fight for. Some people were for sale and did not stand for anything, but I was not one of them.

Before I was released from the Department Supervisor IV position, a co-worker received a call from a Human Resources Department

Manager, a Black woman. She asked the co-worker the following: "Was Conrad being loud and acting ignorant? Did they have to call the sheriff?" This was only an example of the slave mentality that some of the Black people in alleged positions of authority at Wayne County possessed. This Black woman manager knew the mentality of the White managers, but because she possessed a "House Negro" mentality, she was conditioned to believe everything a White man did and said was right. I talked to the Black assistant director of CMY on the telephone and asked him what was going on. He said, "They do not like to see a Black man, stand up for himself."

A statement made by a Black male employee that infuriated me was that I should have just kept my mouth shut and ignored what was occurring until my 6-month probation was completed. That was the same cowardly mentality that I soon discovered could be applied to a number of Black men who were allegedly in positions of power here at good old Wayne County. There are many façades in the game of politics and the "Good Ole' Boy Network System" has many that are wolves in sheep's clothing. Blacks are still learning that having a prestigious title and a hefty salary does not always equate to power. Power is having the ability to change circumstances and conditions. Either these alleged Black men in power, did not have power or they agreed with the abusive treatment of Black employees.

Now, back to the statement by the Black Wayne County employee. How on earth was I going to turn my head and pretend that all was fine when Black men were treated like boys and Black women were being disrespected. If my mother or sister worked somewhere and their supervisor was a Black man, I would expect that Black man to do everything in his power to ensure my mother or sister could work in a peaceful environment. For all those Black storekeepers who worked at the CMY Stockroom, the Black men in their lives, (whether it was their father, husband, son, or friend) could rest assured that I was going to look out for the Black women they loved. The remark of the Black man was indicative of his gutless, head scratching, tap dancing mentality. He would not have been able to elevate himself without assuming this behavior.

During my remaining hours at the CMY Plantation, I occasionally walked pass the White managers. Something in me wanted to try to tear their heads off with my bare hands, which I was more than capable of doing. Fortunately, my growing faith in God led me to just leave it along. Being demoted was a blessing in disguise. That work environment was so hostile that it was inevitable that something was going to occur. On a number of occasions, I had talked with storekeepers that were actually contemplating doing bodily harm to both of the White managers and the director. I told them to just leave it alone. Throughout those five months, it was difficult to come to work everyday because of the emotional stress. Every Monday, I developed a habit of not coming to work. I could not tolerate five consecutive days of work under those conditions. If you have ever worked in a stressful environment then you know what I am talking about. Being demoted back to the position of Time Analyst was a reduction in pay of approximately $6,000. There is something about peace and tranquility that money cannot buy.

To close out this episode, I will briefly fast forward to a meeting that occurred five months after my departure. The storekeepers had an opportunity to meet with Wayne County's power structure—the Deputy County Executive, Human Resources Director, and Assistant County Executive for Legislative Affairs, concerning allegations of the racism, sexism, and favoritism that were occurring at the CMY Stockroom. Within a year of the meeting one of the White managers was forced to resign. The other White manager had heart surgery. The department head who basically agreed with the management style of the two managers by ignoring all complaints, was killed in a horrendous traffic accident on I-94. One of the Black female storekeepers that worked with me became a supervisor. These changes are evidence that one person can make a difference.

Appeal Process

On Monday, September 17, 1997, I was reassigned back to Time Analyst in the Neudeck Building. The director, a Black woman, just shook her head when I walked into her office. Everyone knew I would be returning. They just did not know when. Being demoted did not phase me. A number of my co-workers understood the circumstances, while others ridiculed me behind my back. What the critics thought about the situation was insignificant. My concern now was with the grievance process.

Here's how the grievance process worked: Depending on the union, the company, and your representative, the grievance procedure can change slightly. In Step #1 of the process, both parties attempt to resolve the grievance immediately. Of course, my situation could not be settled at this step. I requested to have a formal hearing in front of the Labor Relations Board, but that was Step #4. Step #2, was quickly rejected also by me. On Step #3, the Chief Labor Relations Analyst, who was a Black woman, sent a response dated October 6, 1997 to my union president, which was rejected.

Basically, the accusing party lied about when they received my initial grievance and also exaggerated about everything else to justify my probationary period failure. One of the managers stated that I was insubordinate because I called him, "asinine." If I actually referred to them as "asinine," it was only my subjective opinion. When did an opinion become classified as insubordination?

At Step 4, a Settlement Agreement between Wayne County and the Local Union, was presented to me. It read as follows:

In full and complete settlement of the referenced grievances, the parties agree that:

1. Conrad Prophet waives any and all claims related to his employment as a Department IV Storekeeper in the Department of Public Services Division of Inventory and Personal Property Management.
2. Conrad Prophet and the Union will withdraw with prejudice grievance numbers #### & ####.
3. In consideration for items (1) and (2), the County will pay Conrad Prophet, Two Thousand Dollars ($2,000.00).
4. This settlement agreement shall establish no precedent.

When presented with this agreement my response was an emphatic, "NO!" Why should I have to accept a $2,000 settlement when I felt I was unfairly demoted from a position that paid $6,000 more than my current position and would have served as a springboard for higher paying positions in the future? There comes a time in most people's lives when they have to make a choice. They can choose to stand up for their principles and beliefs or sell their souls. This was my time, so I made my choice.

In a letter dated January 9, 1998, the Chief Labor Relations Analyst, which I indicated previously was a Black woman, sent a letter to my union president. She emphatically denied my grievance again. Did she think just because I was on probation that I was supposed to be less of a man during that time period? Was I supposed to stand around and allow White men to impose what I considered to be racist beliefs on me and all of the other Black employees under my supervision just because they were higher than me in the chain of command? That was never going to happen. In her 3-page letter she continued to reference the statements that were made by the White managers. It was apparent that their opinion of me was considered to be gospel. Here are two of the most prevalent statements that permitted her to continue to side with the White managers:

"The Grievant's dealings with Management were less than harmonious. Management uses a number of adjectives to describe the grievant's attitude and demeanor—confrontational, sarcastic, condescending, antagonistic, emotional, easily agitated, and difficult. Management maintains that the Grievant likes to play by his own rules and march to a different drummer."

"It does not appear that the Grievant had any problems performing the technical aspects of his job. However, his interpersonal skills, particularly as applied to his interactions with his supervisors, were such that they were a divisive element in the organization."

Where do some Black people think White supremacists work and live? Let's clear it up. They are not residents of another planet. They live and work in America. And thanks to other White supremacists that elect them to office, they are alive and well right here in Wayne County, Michigan and in every other state in the United States.

It is pathetic that Black people died so we can have the opportunity to vote in America and Black people trivialize the importance of voting. If we continue to neglect our voting rights, we will continue to have White supremacists running this country. When we wake up one day with shackles on our feet, it will be for two reasons: We did not vote and the other reason will be because the Black people we elected to represent us sold us, back into slavery.

In my defense, I alleged that the White managers that I worked for were White supremacist. What White person in a position of authority, would admit that they harbor racist beliefs? That would not be politically correct. With that being the case, why would the Black Chief Labor Relations Analyst expect anything truthful to be submitted by the two White men? Everyone has accessibility to a dictionary and thesaurus so they can use words like confrontational, condescending, antagonistic, and etc., when they are trying to justify their racist mentality.

Mr. Ed McNamara had admitted that there was a pocket (of racism) at Detroit Metropolitan Airport. Does anyone with common sense think that racism was contained at Detroit Metropolitan Airport and not spread to other Wayne County work locations?

When a person's livelihood is in jeopardy, a thorough investigation should be warranted. There were numerous complaints of harassment and discrimination coming from past and present Black CMY employees. I should have been judged by my peers instead of who I alleged to be White supremacists and a Black woman who believed every word written by them.

Here's a hypothetical scenario of what occurred:

> The White slave master of Conrad Prophet would complain to the Black woman Chief Master-Slave Relations Analyst. The slave master would say, "My slave, Conrad is confrontational, sarcastic, difficult, and easily agitated. He

continuously attempts to cause other slaves to rebel and protest being treated like slaves. I find Conrad's attitude to be disruptive to the harmonious working condition that existed on this plantation before he arrived."

In response to the White master's complaint, the Black woman Chief Master-Slave Analyst would say, "Mr. Charlie, you are correct. This slave, Conrad has no reason to complain about picking cotton or complaining about the physical, mental, and verbal abuse that you subject him to. Conrad is an unappreciative slave for being disrespectful to you, Mr. Charlie. Conrad Prophet's complaint has no merit and he will be banished back to the cottons fields, immediately."

Back to the letter of January 9, 1998, where the following statement was written, "Management maintains that the Grievant likes to play by his own rules and march to a different drummer."

Let's dissect that statement. It was not that I wanted to play by my own rules, but rather I did not want to play by theirs. I did not march to a different drummer, my drummer simply played fair, just, free, and equal music. This was something that they obviously failed to recognize. I wanted to play by the same rules that White employees in Wayne County were allowed to play by, but they did not want a Black man to be so privileged. The White managers were upset because I did not play by their rules, which were not necessarily Wayne County's rules. This was their command and they had the freedom to run it as they saw fit. It is just unfortunate that during my time under their command no one else had the insight needed. Black men are not inferior to White men and I refused to lower myself to play that game, even if for only a little while. No, I do not play by the rules of White supremacists. Even if a Black man acquired more education or wealth than a White man throughout his life, the Black man would still be considered inferior.

A week before the arbitration hearing, the White union president recommended that I resign from Wayne County. Could it be that my fate was sealed and he knew the outcome? Does the union work for the employee or the employer? There was an alleged outside mediator who was supposed to be impartial. To make a long story short, I lost the arbitration hearing. The White mediator found no basis to return me to the position of Department Supervisor IV. Actually, I anticipated that verdict anyway. All I wanted was an opportunity to defend myself. The verdict was reached before the hearing ever took place. The hearing was just a formality to make it appear that the scales of justice in Wayne County swung evenly. When the scale of justice swung in Wayne County, it landed on the necks of all the Black employees who were at the bottom of Wayne County's pool of "isms."

Freedom of Speech

Now, I was back in the fields with the other Wayne County slaves. Fortunately, I did not forget where I came from. If I did, I would not have been accepted back with open arms. CMY Plantation taught me a valuable lesson that I should have learned from Kmart. Alone, one Black man cannot fight and defeat racism in America. Racism has been practiced, taught, and mastered in this country since the first African was brought to the shores of this country in 1619. It was ignorant of me to attempt to fight evil with evil. I was fighting against principalities. The battle I was fighting was not mine to fight. The way I was fighting it was wrong to begin with.

As I sat in my office plotting my next plan of attack, Black employees who had also experienced discrimination came to my office or called me. I even had the opportunity to call a truce with the Black women in management with whom I had differences. The vice president of one of the unions, who happened to be a Black man, also contacted me. He knew a Wayne County employee who had connections to *The Michigan Chronicle,* which was a weekly published Black-owned and operated newspaper in Detroit. After a number of meetings with the Publisher and Assistant to the Publisher, I was given the opportunity to submit my first of a series of "Readers Speak" articles. The first article appeared in the February 11-17, 1998 issue of *The Michigan Chronicle:*

Wayne County Is 21st Century Plantation For Black Workers

"Most people consider being an employee of Wayne County government an honor and privilege. For White appointees and management, Wayne County is a prestigious country club. Wayne County, for all but a few chosen Black employees, is a 21st century plantation, which uses the present political structure to demoralize, exploit and discriminate against Blacks. We, the majority of Wayne County employees, are going to tell what taxpayers' hard-earned dollars are paying for.

We have discovered that Wayne County has mastered racism, sexism, cronyism and any other corrupt "ism" that exists in order to oppress Black employees. In Wayne County, we have three distinct categories: The Haves, Have Nots and Blacks Have Less.

The Haves consist of the political appointed cronies. These are mostly White people given authority and salaries that undeniably exceed their education, experience and mental capacity. We can almost guarantee that most of these appointed individuals cannot demand 50 percent of their salaries in the private sector. We also doubt if most of Wayne County taxpayers earn the salaries these appointees are paid. Included in the Haves are White managers, supervisors and other positions of authority that most Blacks are excluded from.

Many of these appointees and managers are incompetent. If you were to look at some of their credentials, there is no way they could justify their salaries. Not only are appointees overpaid, they are given the power to create jobs for family and friends at taxpayers' expense.

There are a few Black employees in the ranks of the Haves. We have to be careful how we define Black. To us, Black is defined as a common struggle we began when our ancestors were first brought to this country. It is a struggle which most of us continue to fight. Even though some of us have fought diligently to rise above the oppression, we continue to fight for the less fortunate, so one day they too can be free from the negative effects of racial discrimination.

The above definition of Black does not refer to Black employees in the Haves category. Once they are appointed, they do not become the pawn of the political game, but the Black square on which the pawn is placed. These Blacks live in fear. They refuse to support or even try to help another Black employee to elevate. They are afraid that if "Master" finds out they are attempting to assist the "Field Negroes," they will be returned to the land of the oppressed. There are also the Blacks in management who are afraid and have forgotten where they came from. We do not dislike, hate or have any animosity for those of our people who assist the oppressor in oppressing us. It is tragic when Black employees receive positions of authority, they lose their First Amendment right, the freedom of speech.

If those of you of the Haves question your Blackness, ask yourself the following questions: What have you done to assist another Black employee to earn a promotion or raise? When a Black employee is being harassed or wrongfully accused by your White superiors, do you come to his or her defense or do you turn away, pretending the situation does not exist? Finally, what have any of you done lately to improve the status of our people?

If you still question your Blackness, take the Blackness test. When you look into the mirror and have difficulties keeping your head up because of humiliation, this means you have sold your soul. With it went your self-worth, dignity and desire to uplift what true Black people call 'our people'.

The Have Nots are the White unionized employees in the struggle for a comfortable standard of living, which the appointees possess, but definitely do not deserve. Like us, their only recourse against unfair labor practices is the union. Time and time again, history has shown the unions are powerless and at the mercy of management when it comes to contract negotiations in Wayne County. While appointees receive substantial raises regularly, union members are forced to practically beg for the meager raises we eventually receive.

For the past two contracts, most locals did not ratify contracts for their members until a year later. Currently, Local 1659 is still without a contract. We empathize with our fellow White union members, who are experiencing similar forms of employment discrimination, but certainly on a smaller scale. One of the advantages White union employees have is that, intentionally or unintentionally, they benefit from the blatant racism which occurs at Wayne County, under the 'Good Ole' Boy Network System'.

The final category, Blacks Have Less, is definitely a disheartening example of what government will be like if we allow the eradication of affirmative action. Never have we experienced and seen the degree of racism which is prevalent within Wayne County. There is a term, glass ceiling, which means there is a boundary where people can see above, but will never reach. In Wayne County, it is the concrete ceiling.

We cannot even see above the boundary line. For the majority of Black employees, the level in which they enter Wayne County is the level they will remain at throughout their career, with minimal advancement, regardless of increased education and experience. There is even an entry-level position called labor trainee. This is the position you start at before you become a laborer. To this day, we wonder if labor trainee is synonymous with slave trainee. You are either a laborer or you are a slave. What differentiates a laborer from a labor trainee? Other than the rate of pay, we do not see any difference. This is just another tactic by management to prevent Black employees from earning decent wages to support their families.

Regardless of Black employees' experience, education or dedication, they usually enter Wayne County at the lowest level and are unable to reach the level of pay and positions of their White counterparts. Black employees are virtually excluded from entry-level positions exceeding $25,000. Another tactic used by management to exclude Black employees from earning more money is by downgrading positions. Whenever a position becomes vacant and a Black employee fills the vacancy, very seldom is the position equivalent to his or her predecessor in wages. Otherwise a majority of the Black employees would not be concentrated at the bottom of Wayne County's jelly bean jar.

We are also subjected to discrimination in promotional examinations and disciplinary action. Whenever a position becomes available, a personnel employee will interview the manager of the particular department to determine the criteria for the position. Usually, the manager has the person he or she wants to promote already selected. The personnel employee will write up the job description so that only this particular person is qualified. Once the job is posted, most employees do not meet the stringent requirements. Most of the questions on the examination are irrelevant to the job and the managers probably do not possess the criteria they set for the employees that apply. If Black employees do qualify, they are eliminated during the oral examination.

In Wayne County there is no due process in disciplinary actions for Black employees. There is severe disparity when it comes to punishment for violations and reporting of incidents. If a Black and White employee commit the same infraction, nine times out of 10, the White employee's offense is ignored. The Black employee is usually punished to the fullest extent. Employees can seek representation from the union, but the reinstatement process is so time consuming that the employees will experience financial hardship before they are vindicated.

The primary reason for the blatant racism in Wayne County is the total disrespect of Blacks by appointees, managers and foremen. No matter where a Black employee works, he or she is going to encounter some form of racial discrimination. The farther away from Detroit a Black employee works, the worse it becomes. It is believed that Detroit Metropolitan Airport is the most racist work location in Wayne County, followed by Central Maintenance Yard. The reason for this is that appointees and others placed into positions of authority who are permitted to practice whatever prejudiced beliefs they possess without fear of prosecution. To be honest, we believe racism is encouraged and rewarded.

It is disheartening that, as we approach a new millennium, a government agency which employs thousands of people, discriminates against Black people. To magnify the problem, Wayne County is close to 50 percent Black and we are allowing this to occur.

We make a plea to all Wayne County employees who have filed a Civil Rights Discrimination Claim, filed a grievance with their union or have experienced any form of discrimination in the past three years to write and explain what occurred. We ask all Wayne County taxpayers to please write and request more information on these allegations of racial discrimination. Unlike Wayne County, we do believe in due process.

If these allegations are proven to be true, it is our duty to exhibit our anger in the coming election. We cannot continue to stand still and allow the efforts and lives of Martin, Medgar, Malcolm and countless others to be in vain. They fought and made sacrifices for our future of those who come after us."

The response to the first article was overwhelming from Wayne County employees, both past and present. During a 2-week period, I received 18 letters. There were even letters from subscribers of *The Michigan Chronicle,* as far away as Jackson, MI. One day, a Black male Wayne County employee that worked in one of the maintenance yards came into my office. He was almost in tears, as he thanked me for what I had done. He was a strong Black man, but he had a family that depended on the fruits of his labor to survive, so he was in no position to become a rebel. I explained to him that being a responsible husband and father was his contribution. The Black family structure needed the father in place for support. There was no question that numerous Black employees were working in fear, desiring to take action, but in no position to do so. I never expected anyone to jeopardize his or her job for a fight that I had selected.

Under normal circumstances an article like mine would have been forgotten the day after it was printed. But these were certainly not normal circumstances. It was an election year for Mr. McNamara. This was not something he could easily ignore, nor was it something others would allow to just pass by. In the March 4-10, 1998 issue of *The Michigan Chronicle,* an article titled, "County exec ready to make change" appeared on the front page. The senior editor asked Mr. McNamara questions about my letter criticizing the county's race relations at Detroit Metropolitan Airport. Here are some excerpts from the interview:

> "'It is a caste system,' McNamara said during the wider-ringing interview at the Michigan Chronicle. The airport has 'created a situation where the guys at the top are all White. We've engaged it and what we found was a pocket (of racism). It feeds on itself.'"

> "Prophet 'made some good points,' McNamara said. 'Now that it has been driven home, we can do something about it.'"[2]

Of course, whether or not Mr. McNamara was sincere about what he said, it was the politically correct statement to make. My question was: If there was a pocket of racism at the airport, why wasn't it acknowledged that there was also a pocket of racism at CMY, which is located less than a mile from the airport?

Immediately after that article, a well known political consultant in Detroit arranged a meeting between the Black vice-president of the union, the Wayne County employee with connections with *The Michigan Chronicle,* Michael Duggan (Deputy Executive Officer), Bernard Kilpatrick (Assistant County Executive for Legislative Affairs), and myself. The meeting was held in the office of Mr. Duggan. In the March 25-31, 1998 issue of *The Michigan Chronicle,* Part II was published:

Wayne County Is 21ˢᵗ Century Plantation For Black Workers

By Conrad Prophet (Second in an occasional series)

"Last month, we had a two-hour meeting with Michael Duggan, deputy county executive and Bernard Kilpatrick, Assistant County Executive, Legislative Affairs. This meeting was arranged by a neutral party outside of Wayne County and was initiated by the county. Throughout the meeting we discussed pertinent issues from the article, "Wayne County is 21ˢᵗ Century plantation for Black workers." (Editor's note: See Michigan Chronicle, Feb. 11-17, 1998.)

One of the first questions asked concerned the tremendous disparity between Black employees in positions of authority in the Maintenance Department and skilled trades at Detroit Metropolitan Airport.

Wayne County has approximately two million residents and 50 percent of them are Black. We stated that Wayne County government was financed primarily by property taxes, federal taxes, state taxes, gas taxes and other taxes.

The question was, "If the Black community contributes equally to the financial base of Wayne County, why isn't money being allocated to the Black community in higher paying jobs?"

Duggan said the top-level positions in Wayne County have a balanced Black employee to White employee ratio.

There is a disparity of wages between the Black employees at the bottom of Wayne County Jelly Bean Jar and the elite appointees at the top of the pyramid. Currently, Black employees entering Wayne County earn less than $7.25 an hour and entering appointees earn more than $20 an hour. Then the gap between Black employees and appointees widens from $7.25 an hour to $50 an hour. There is no justification for this enormous disparity.

Why is entry-level pay so low? Duggan said it was because of the budget. If the budget is important, why are there a number of 1997 Eddie Bauer Expeditions and 50 or more cars assigned to appointed employees at the taxpayer's expense? In addition, Wayne County's top level management receive job perks, such as free parking downtown and gas credit cards. The county should take some of the money at the top and redistribute it to the employees at the bottom. Kilpatrick called us socialists.

But paying employees less than $7.25 an hour has created a Wayne County government class of "working poor." Many people cannot imagine surviving on such meager wages. After employees pay for the necessities of everyday life, there is no money for leisure activities or to pursue higher education. This prevents employees from remaining competitive in the constantly changing work force.

To state that it is advocating socialism/communism is ludicrous. Wayne County is not a private corporation. Wayne County is financed by taxpayers. As taxpayers, citizens and employees can demand parity for the employees who work for the county. Taxpayers are shareholders of Wayne County who demand county employees earn fair wages for a fair day's work.

The majority of the money allocated to salaries should be earned by the employees whose jobs ensure that the citizens' quality of life is maintained and enhanced by the services they provide. The money definitely should not be given to appointees whose only purpose in life is to sponge off taxpayers. Every government agency requires qualified appointees to operate effectively, but the current political regime has lost touch with reality. It is now time for a reality check.

County officials said there were some Black men in prominent positions who African American workers could go to for assistance. The men named were definitely not a part of the solution, but a part of the problem. Wayne County Black men are synonymous with Clarence Thomas and Ward Connerly, the Black conservative in California who led the fight that eradicated affirmative action in California, by having Proposition 209 passed.

As anticipated, the meeting ended with nothing being accomplished. Duggan said he would investigate some of the areas of concern, but many people do not foresee any immediate and sufficient changes occurring. Since employees did not request the meeting, we suspect they wanted an opportunity to size up their opponent. We consider ourselves to be formidable adversaries, but it is apparent the current administration thinks differently.

Since the first letter, other issues of concern surfaced. It appears that the current administration attempts to use privatization to save taxpayers money. If they want to privatize something, Wayne County should privatize the appointed positions at Detroit Metropolitan Airport. Would someone please explain how the appointed management staff earning an average salary of over $80,000 a year, operate the worst airport in the country? Please tell us how.

The current political regime of Wayne County has established a two-class system. The elite upper-class consists of appointees and other employees in authority who elevated themselves to this class in any disgusting way possible. Then there is the lower class which consists of Black slaves and White peasants. What is baffling is why the lower class in Wayne County has tolerated such injustices, discrimination and harassment in hiring, promotions, examinations and disciplinary action for so long without rebelling. Even now, Wayne County's lower-class tolerance still remains too high. This current regime has been pimping the union leaders, employees and the taxpayers of Wayne County for 12 years. Isn't prostitution illegal in Wayne County?

Wayne County does not have a monopoly on racism. What employees experience in Wayne County government is what millions of Black people are experiencing throughout the United States. Not just today but yesterday and tomorrow. Wayne County is the current battleground against racism. Yesterday, it was Detroit Edison. Who knows where the next battle against racism will be fought. Believe it: There will be many more battles.

What is hard to understand is why the Blacks in the position of power continue to sit back and ignore what is happening? Are they oblivious to the fact that the Civil Rights Movement of the 1960's was for equality for all, not just a few? One important fact that they should realize is that they cannot protect their children from the racism and discrimination they escaped by selling their souls.

All concerned Wayne County employees and taxpayers should contact their elected county officials and question them about these allegations.

(Editor's note: County officials confirmed that Wayne County Deputy Executive Michael Duggan did meet with "Conrad" and other members of the Detroit Metropolitan Airport work force, including an American Federation of State, County and Municipal Employees vice president.)[3]

This article also received an enormous amount of attention. Not only were Black employees understanding the purpose of the articles, but White employees were as well. Initially, White employees thought I was against them. To set the record straight, even though I may never win the Nobel Peace Prize, I do not hate or dislike White people.

In Wayne County, both Black and White unionized employees were affected by the cronyism, nepotism and sexism. Black people were affected primarily by racism, which was the major battle I was fighting. Finally, after a month of going back and forth, Wayne County Commissioner George Cushingberry, Chairman of the Committee on Ways and Means, mailed me the Wayne County Summary Sheet (EE0-4) for 1997, Control No. 26200830. This was just what I needed to prove my accusations of the rampant racism in Wayne County. There is pertinent information in the following four tables:

Summary of Wayne County EEO-4 Report
1997 Control No. 26200830

TABLE #1: Salaries	WHITE MALE	BLACK MALE	HISPANIC MALE	ORIENTAL MALE	NATIVE AMERICAN MALE	WHITE FEMALE	BLACK FEMALE	HISPANIC FEMALE	ORIENTAL FEMALE	NATIVE AMERICAN FEMALE
OFFICIAL/ ADMINISTRATION										
$0-15,999										
$16,000-19,999	1	1								
$20,000-24,999										
$25,000-32,999										
$33,000-42,999	4					2				
$43,000-54,999	24	12	1			9	18			
$55,000-69,999	64	19		1		17	13			
(Appointees) $70,000+	110	25		3		52	19	3		

TABLE #2: Salaries	WHITE MALE	BLACK MALE	HISPANIC MALE	ORIENTAL MALE	NATIVE AMERICAN MALE	WHITE FEMALE	BLACK FEMALE	HISPANIC FEMALE	ORIENTAL FEMALE	NATIVE AMERICAN FEMALE
PROFESSIONALS										
$0-15,999										
$16,000-19,999	1	1								
$20,000-24,999	3	4				6	13			1
$25,000-32,999	82	13	3	1	1	71	82	2	3	1
$33,000-42,999	159	52	3	3	1	112	162	1	2	2
$43,000-54,999	169	34	2	1		70	61	1	1	1
$55,000-69,999	74	7	3	1		33	15	3		
(Appointees) $70,000+	18	3	1			16	6		2	

TABLE #3: Salaries	WHITE MALE	BLACK MALE	HISPANIC MALE	ORIENTAL MALE	NATIVE AMERICAN MALE	WHITE FEMALE	BLACK FEMALE	HISPANIC FEMALE	ORIENTAL FEMALE	NATIVE AMERICAN FEMALE
SKILLED CRAFT										
$0-15,999						1				
$16,000-19,999										
$20,000-24,999	61	57	1	1		10	19			
$25,000-32,999	102	31	2			4	4			
$33,000-42,999	51	6								
$43,000-54,999	160	26	3							
$55,000-69,999	5				1					
(Appointees) $70,000+										

TABLE #4: Salaries	WHITE MALE	BLACK MALE	HISPANIC MALE	ORIENTAL MALE	NATIVE AMERICAN MALE	WHITE FEMALE	BLACK FEMALE	HISPANIC FEMALE	ORIENTAL FEMALE	NATIVE AMERICAN FEMALE
SERVICE/MAINTENANCE										
$0-15,999	14	42	1			4	29	2	1	1
$16,000-19,999	18	63				7	27			
$20,000-24,999	89	70	1	1		7	21			1
$25,000-32,999	72	34	3			14	21			
$33,000-42,999	68	17	1			2	2			
$43,000-54,999										
$55,000-69,999										
(Appointees) $70,000+										

My last article with the *Michigan Chronicle* appeared in the April 22-28, 1998 issue titled "What's going on in Wayne County?" In the May 20-26, 1998 issue of *The Michigan Chronicle*, the article "Chronicle endorses McNamara" appeared. Here are the first two paragraphs of the endorsement:

"If anyone can give us one reason why Edward McNamara should not be retained as Wayne County executive, we'd listen to it. We've had our ears to the ground, our fingers on the pulse of the community and don't think anyone has provided a convincing argument for replacing the 12-year veteran at this point.

We think the more than 40 Detroit elected officials who endorsed McNamara's re-election on Friday pretty much have the right idea. We want to add our endorsement to the chorus."[4]

The leader of any company sets the culture of the company. In the case of the *Michigan Chronicle*, the editor-in-chief could endorse whomever he wanted and he chose, Mr. Edward McNamara. I was not upset with the endorsement. All this meant was that I had to find another source to publish my articles. I contacted the *Michigan Citizen* and they allowed me to continue with my crusade for justice. In the June 7-13, 1998 issue, the article, "Wayne hiring shows white preference" (*Michigan Citizen*) stated findings from an investigation which reported figures almost identical to the information that I presented in the Summary of Wayne County EEO-4 Report 1997. Barbara Godre, Director for the Department of Personnel/Human Resources had an article printed—"McNamara lists his African American appointees." The article listed the 94 African Americans that McNamara appointed to his staff. To end this story, Mr. Edward McNamara was re-elected to Wayne County Executive.

I thought the entire process was challenging and educational. It is not often that a person receives the opportunity to challenge the effectiveness of a government CEO who employs over 6,000 people. Throughout it all, there was never any malicious intent on my part nor was there any from Mr. McNamara or his staff. One White male appointee and I had developed a mutual respect for each other over the years. He would always tell me what he felt and I would always inform him of how I felt. During the time I was writing the articles, he would ask me, "Conrad, how is the poison pen coming along?" I would tell him, "It was the pen of justice" and he would burst into laughter.

I am sure for a veteran politician like Mr. McNamara, my articles were no more than a nuisance, at most. If you are going to learn how to do anything, always learn from the best. Mr. McNamara was definitely the best at using all of his skills to get what he wanted. Even if I did not condone what occurred under his administration, respect was still warranted.

Disappointment

I honestly can commend all of the White employees at Wayne County for coming together in solidarity to make sure Black people did not advance. Even though not all White people condoned or actively participated in any form of racism, they automatically benefited from it, just by being White. America's history has taught us what to expect of White people in relation to Black people in this country.

The most shocking realization from this experience, which disappointed me immeasurably, was the lack of support from alleged Black men and women in power. For the first time in life, I discovered that, "All my skin folks, aren't my kin folks." Please remember that although some may consider what you know and who you know as important factors in government and politics, it boils down to who you know that is willing to help you. Not all people who look like you; think like you.

Please do not think that the following statements I make based on my observations pertain to all appointees in Wayne County or any other level of government. It would be unfair for me to categorize an entire classification of people into one group because of the actions of some. I never had the opportunity to interact with every appointee in Wayne County, so I could not accurately assess everyone. There are some Wayne County appointees that have the knowledge, experience, and college degrees that make them qualified for their positions. Then there are the other appointees.

During my CMY Plantation experience, there were a number of Black men and women who were aware of the treatment towards Black employees but just ignored it. The letters that I received from previous and current Wayne County employees, indicated that I was not the only one discriminated against. Where were all the Black people? When they saw me figuratively hanging from a tree, instead of cutting me down, they helped "Mr. Charlie" by kicking the chair out from beneath me. This was our opportunity to stand together and be recognized as a force. It was unfortunate for all Wayne County employees who suffered. No one chose to stand with me publicly.

I can remember when Mike Duggan called out names of African American male appointees who were supposedly there to assist Black employees. He might as well have called out the names of Clarence Thomas, Ward Connerly and any other alleged Black person that has forgotten the sacrifices of our ancestors which helped them get to where they are today. Most young Black people today take the privileges they have for granted. They are not aware of all the Black people who died and made sacrifices for the rights they have today.

Believe me when I say that there were no Black appointees of Mr. McNamara who openly admitted that blatant racism was occurring at Wayne County. Most of the appointees avoided me like I was the Honorable Louis Farrakhan or the reincarnation of Malcolm X.

Here are a couple of examples of how terrified some of the Black appointees were. One Black male appointee passed me in the hallway of the Wayne County Building and secretly shook my hand and congratulated me. Then another Black male appointee expressed his displeasure with what was occurring, but stated that he was powerless to stop it. There was one Black male appointee that was high up on Mr. McNamara's staff that actually hugged me and said he was proud of me. I was shocked and honored that this particular man, placed his pride, title, and ego aside for that one moment to acknowledge that what I did was right.

Most of the Black appointees were out for themselves at Wayne County. The White appointees made sure their assistants and secretaries were taken care of. There were some Black appointees who would not even go that far for those that worked directly for them. Certainly I had nothing coming by way of assistance. It was like they made a contract that stated, "I solemnly swear: Master, if you give me a piece of the multi-billion dollar pie that the taxpayers made for you, no other Black employee will benefit from my fruits. I promise." That is how ridiculous it was.

For the rest of the Black appointees, none of this had an impact on them. It was business as usual. Some resented me but it was not personal. It was like the Black appointees were under a "gag order." Even the Black appointees with whom I thought I had a civil rapport, avoided me. Fighting for your civil rights is sometimes a lonesome battle. I could not waste valuable time worrying about who liked or disliked me. I tried not to burn any bridges. If I did, oh well. Who would want to walk across a shaky bridge anyway?

Some of these appointees both Black and White possessed unwarranted egos and arrogance. A majority of them did not have the experience, knowledge, or college degree to effectively supervise unionized or non-unionized workers who had more years of experience and also had earned their college degree. Several unionized workers earned their college degree in hopes of advancement, but it never came to pass because undeserving appointees received those positions.

I was once offered an opportunity to be appointed to a position. Even though I was qualified, I refused because accepting that position would have meant that I agreed with the mission statement, strategy and goals of the person that appointed me. The only mission statement and goal I have allegiance to is the God that I believe in and people who have the same agenda that I have. If anyone ever appoints me to a position, it will have to be under the high standards that I set for myself. I refuse to lower my morals, abandon my principles, or compromise my beliefs to satisfy man. It is also important that I continue to have my freedom of speech. I must have the ability to say, "yes," when I want to say, "yes" and, "no" when I want to say, "no." I have no problem with agreeing to disagree. I also refused to walk in the shadow of another's man ego. Those are the reasons why I could not become an appointee under the McNamara regime.

The only Black elected politician that publicly or privately came to my assistance was Wayne County Commissioner George Cushingberry. All of the other Black commissioners were aware of the articles and the racial climate in Wayne County, but chose not to comment. Even certain members of Detroit City Council and other Black elected officials in Detroit were aware of my articles. I know for sure they knew because I personally mailed all of them information packages requesting their assistance.

As far as the regular unionized Black employees, I had empathy for them. Like myself, all of them were just the Black squares where black and white pawns temporarily rested, while they continued to advance in the game of life. Even though I was only a black square, I was determined not to allow anyone Black or White to ride me to success. In life, I have learned that people will do whatever you allow them to do.

No More Challenges

After the article writing and Mr. McNamara's re-election, there was really no need to remain at Wayne County. Now I had a reputation and there was no chance anyone was going to hire me into their department because of my article writing. My job as a Time Analyst became monotonous. There was no longer any challenge or motivation for me to remain.

I have always been a person who thrived on obtaining knowledge and making a difference with my life. Wayne County was not going to give me that opportunity, so it was time for me to make my own opportunity. I wanted to be able to reach my maximum potential and I have learned that I am solely responsible for reaching my maximum potential.

One day I was discussing with a co-worker the reasons I was still working for Wayne County. After I weighed the pro's and con's, I did not have a valid reason for staying. The job of a Time Analyst afforded me independence, autonomy, and a peace of mind. Wayne County provided the following; job security, excellent medical and dental insurance, decent salary, paid holidays, generous vacation and sick time, and one of the best pension plans I have ever had. Even though it offered all of that, which most people dream of, it did not offer the one element that I desperately needed: The opportunity to be me.

From all of my work experiences, I have learned that whatever your job title, you are placed in a box by the job description. However, the leaders set invisible parameters within which you are expected to function, without growth or the use of your brain. Regardless of your job function, the salary is set and will not be altered. I have a creative mind and have every intention of using it. I will not dwell happily inside the box or the parameters set by those who attempt to control me.

One of the most important circumstances that permitted me to resign from Wayne County was that I did not have a wife, children, or mortgage. That meant I did not have to stay at a job indefinitely because of family or financial obligations. I am sure there are millions of

Americans, who would resign from a job and go to another one in a heartbeat, if they could. Unfortunately, with life come responsibilities and sacrifices. Leaving a sure thing for a possible was a tremendous chance, but I had to step out on faith, anyway. At Wayne County, I knew what my future would be and it was not going to be a positive one. After I left Wayne County, I was able to control my own destiny. At no time was I threatened or harassed by anyone. I left of my own volition. As with most jobs, you leave behind good friends. Some of the friends and work associates that I made during those years are still in my life today. Most of the time, it is not the job that makes your day brighter, but the people you are blessed to work with and the experiences that you share.

One day, I wondered if my efforts actually made a difference in the lives of my Wayne County co-workers. I heard that the "Labor Trainee" position at Wayne County was eliminated because of the articles. It was also rumored that more Black people were appointed to positions of authority at Detroit Metropolitan Airport. The burning question is: Did any of these Black employees spread their good fortune by reaching out to help others? My goal while at Wayne County was to make it a more balanced work environment for all concerned. Only time will tell if I actually succeeded. If I did not, at least I tried. Like they say, it is better to try and fail, than to fail to try.

Advice For Career In Government

For those of you who aspire to work in government and for some reason are employed there, allow me to share some pertinent knowledge with you. The incidents stated here do not only exist in Wayne County, but government entities all across the United States. It does not matter if you are employed at the city, county, state, or federal level, corruption and all the following "isms" still apply— racism, sexism, cronyism, favoritism, and nepotism. When White people use nepotism, they have the power to bring their relatives in at the top. When Black people use nepotism, they can only bring their relatives in at the bottom. For Black people, if we do not look out for our people, who else will? There are always exceptions to nepotism, but the basic principle applies.

Unfortunately, I have to sadly admit that White people do not have a monopoly on corruption and "isms." The fact is that you will find corruption throughout the game of politics regardless of who is doing the politicking. As with all things in life, good and bad exist. Right and wrong will continue to be measured by personal criteria, and morals and values will always be questioned.

First and foremost, there will always be corruption in government because man is naturally carnal minded. Power, sex, and money are what entice most men and some women into the arena of politics. There are some politicians that truly aspire to serve humanity. Politics is a necessary evil. Without governments, this world would be in worse chaos. Even though it is hard to imagine, it is true. As far back as the Roman and Greek empires and before, there has been corruption. All we can do is hope and pray that we will elect the best candidate. If you do not think there is corruption in government reminisce on the 2000 Presidential election and the state of Florida. I rest my case and I am not even a lawyer.

How does one explain government and politics? It is difficult, but it is simply a game with rules. A game in which we all have a vote that ultimately affects the local laws that govern our day-to-day lives. Let me explain how it impacts the lives of the majority of Black people who will enter the world of government employment at the bottom like I did. I will give it to you straight without any chaser. It may sound depressing, but it is the truth. I dealt with it, so I know you can do the same. At least someone told you what to expect. I had to learn the hard way.

If you are hired in at the entry-level, then the chances of you advancing significantly are slim. Yes, there are exceptions to the rule of course, but the percentage is small. I have seen several employees come in at a particular position and remain there throughout their careers. There are several reasons for this. Some people are satisfied and just want a job that pays enough money to pay the bills and have health benefits. I am not criticizing those people. Some people are happy to have a job that is stress free and they do not want to deal with the stress that comes with managerial or appointed positions. Then you have people that do everything necessary to advance in a government job and the "concrete ceiling" is holding them down. Regardless of the race of the person in power, one or more of these will keep a motivated person at the lowest level-racism, cronyism, nepotism, sexism, or favoritism.

In Wayne County, I witnessed numerous co-workers attending college to earn Bachelor's Degrees in specialized fields of study to advance. Because of all of the "isms" listed above, those positions were not available to most of them. In the Sunday, August 18, 2002 edition of *The Detroit News* and *Free Press*, the following was stated, "As of April 1, 112 of McNamara's 332 appointees had base salaries of $100,000 or more . . ."[5] This is the primary reason why several Black employees that enter at the bottom in Wayne County remain there. Some of the appointees both Black and White moved up through the ranks, but not very many. In comparison to corporate America, only CEOs earned those types of salaries. Those are only the top-end atrocities. Rarely does an appointee earn under $35,000. I witnessed appointees both Black and White that would have difficulties keeping a minimum wage job in corporate America, but were earning $40,000 at Wayne County. In order to operate some level of government, there is a need for skilled, knowledgeable, and experienced appointees with degrees, but a line should be drawn when the money that pays for these astronomical salaries comes from taxpayers who barely make $25,000 a year.

If it was not for blatant racism, cronyism, nepotism or sexism, more than half of appointed positions could be filled by the rank and file of unionized workers who have many years of experience and loyalty. Some unions are at fault for not placing a cap on the number of appointees that an elected official can appoint.

When it comes to unions, I understand the importance of them and their history. Without unions in the United States the poor and working class would be powerless against the rich. In a capitalistic society, it is all about profits. I was not impressed with the union representation at Wayne County. The union stewards appeared to be dedicated, but they did not have the experience or the expertise to represent their members. The elected presidents of some of the unions were pathetic. I do not care what anyone says, behind closed doors, party affiliation is ignored when it comes to a White manager and White union representative when a Black employee is involved. Some of the union members in Wayne County allowed the rank and file to be victimized on a regular basis. If the union was not "in bed" with management, the rank and file would receive better treatment regardless of who was elected. You can ask any Black person who is a member of any union and nine out of ten times, they will tell you something negative.

Even though most unions and the elected officials in some cases are considered ineffective by the rank and file, I feel they are necessary. Without them all blue collar workers like myself would be in trouble. If it were not for union representation, I would never have a job. Unless you do something criminal, the union is usually capable of getting your job back. Sometimes the union is the lesser of two evils, but still necessary. There are still some unions that are racists. If that was not the case, in Wayne County why is there still a great disparity between the numbers for Black and White skilled trades workers. If I am not mistaken, Black tax dollars also pay for the salaries of skilled trades workers. It is only right for minorities to receive more opportunities to work in the skilled trades positions.

Now I will go back to the original point. With most government jobs, if you come in at the bottom, you are likely to remain there regardless of your ambitions. Most people get caught in the complacency trap. They become complacent and the next thing they know, they have been in the government job for five or more years and have not taken a single step toward advancement. The health benefits, paid holidays, and security of a government job are far superior to an entry-level job in corporate America earning the same amount of pay. A government job is just like the military in a way. Once you do eight or more years you might as well stay there because your hourly wages have increased to a level that you probably cannot command in corporate America.

Many entry-level employees are single women with children to take care of. There are also Black and White men who feel fortunate to have a government job to take care of their families. I commend everyone regardless of race for the personal sacrifice of dreams and goals to ensure that their children and people they love have a decent standard of living.

In today's economy, most people are just happy to have a job. If you are still young, single, with no children, I would advise that you do not become too complacent too quickly in any job situation. Make sure the job is something you can be happy with for a number of years before you lease an Escalade or purchase a new home with a monthly mortgage of $1,500. Feel blessed to have your current position, but never lose focus of your dreams. Remember never give up a sure thing for a possible. Always have a back-up plan, because job security no longer exists.

There is no need for me to tell anyone not to confront the power structure of any governmental entity the way I did. Honestly, I do not think there are very many Black men that exist who would do the things I did at Wayne County. It is a difficult road to travel when you are trying to do the right thing. It calls for many sacrifices and the consequences that accompany those decisions. Black people have come a long way since 1619, but we have much further to go and will forever be in battle. It is a lost cause to attempt to fight racism, cronyism, nepotism and sexism from the bottom of any organization. Many of those "isms" that were listed above were actually discreetly written into the Constitution of the United States and they will never change. Some battles will not be won in this country but we must not give up or give in.

If you want a simple life, just go to work, do your eight hours a day and go home. Most people have learned how to do that. Again, I advise young Black people, who are just entering the workforce, not to allow history, knowledge, and injustice to interfere with earning an honest living in this country. Throughout the existence of man, not everyone was chosen to lead. Let me direct you to some leisure reading in the oldest and most popular book: The book of Judges in the Bible will show how the Lord chose certain people to lead the children of Israel. Since 1619, we have had hundreds of Black people to lead us to where we are today. I was never called or chosen to lead. I was just determined to get my respect by any means necessary that was acceptable to the God that I believe in. It was not always in a way that God approved of, but I did make an honest attempt.

For African Americans who are appointed to certain positions in any governmental entity where there is evidence of racism and you ignore it, always remember that the pleasure of sin only lasts for a season. The reason I stated African American instead of Black, is because I think there is a difference between being an African American and Black. Being considered Black to me, means not only sympathizing and empathizing with the struggle of our Black brothers and sisters, but openly admitting that you are concerned about the future of Black people and willing to do whatever is in your power to uplift them. Blackness is a state of mind. I have met White people who are Blacker than some African Americans. Being Black to me is not being afraid or ashamed to mention that you respect, both past and present leaders like Malcolm X, Barbara Jordan, Medgar Evers, Angela Davis, Honorable Louis Farrakhan, Shirley Chisolm, Stokely Carmichael, Sister Soulah, Geronimo Pratt, H. Rap Brown, and many others. Also, Black people are not afraid to acknowledge Dr. Martin Luther King, Jr. in his entirety. I am not talking about the "I Have A Dream Speech," but his other numerous speeches and writings where he opposed the oppression of Black people in this country. We have had some great leaders and they continue to rise. What will be your contribution when your life is done?

If you are an African American who is an appointee of any governmental entity that appears to condone racism and sexism, you are in the position to make a difference, no matter how small. I encourage you to use your power and influence to assist someone who is not as fortunate. I am aware that everyone cannot save the world, but you can make a difference. I applaud those who are already in the trenches of battle, making noise and causing change. To all future African American appointees always remember that you did not get there by yourselves. Whether it is apparent or not, you must accept the fact that someone struggled first to provide you with an opportunity. Be grateful and remember that someone in the future is depending on you. Be aware that while your morals, standards, integrity and dignity are important, you are in a game and it is imperative that you learn the rules before deciding to play. Also, know that in order to change the rules you must first be in the game.

Wayne County 2003

Earlier in this chapter, I listed some important facts in the articles that I had published in *The Michigan Chronicle* and the *Michigan Citizen* in 1998. The same information was confirmed years later in the newspaper articles cited below:

- "McNamara insider to run Metro Airport," By David Josar, *The Detroit News*, Thurs., April 6, 2000.
- "McNamara loyalists mismanage airport—Most appointees lack credentials, experience," By Paul Egan, *The Detroit News*, Monday, December 3, 2001.
- "McNamara aides' pay, perks soar," By Paul Egan, *The Detroit News*, Sunday, August 18, 2002.
- "Taxpayers provide autos," By Paul Egan, *The Detroit News*, Sunday, August 12, 2002.

Once you become familiar with how the media works, you will understand why my information was ignored.

In 2002, the citizens elected, Robert Ficano as new Wayne County Executive. Ficano pledged to restore confidence in government.[6] Only time will tell if his leadership will bring a change. I am curious to know if the 2004 Wayne County EEO-4 Report shows any significant improvements from the 1997 EEO Report. I wish all Wayne County employees past, present and future, the best.

Chapter 7

DETROIT PUBLIC SCHOOLS

"For when for the time you ought to be teachers, ye have need that one teach you again which be the first principles of the oracles of God;"

—*Heb 5:12*

There was no question in my mind of what my next goal in life would be. It was to make a difference. I thought that one of the best ways to make a positive difference would be by becoming a teacher. As I reminisce, I can recall the positive impact that the teachers and principal at Grant Elementary School in Ferndale, MI had on me.

During my elementary school years, I can remember being aggressive. In my words, I was a true "problem child." From kindergarten to the sixth grade, I went to school to fight. If someone asked me about learning, I would have asked: "What is that?" Fortunately, in the 1970's the teachers and the principal utilized corporal punishment. Even though it may have been illegal then, it was still used. At least once a week, I was summoned or dragged to the principal's office for fighting. Once there, I knew what to expect. After I failed to convince the principal that I did not start the fight, he would tell me to touch my toes. He would take his favorite wooden paddle and let it rip into my backside. For those of you who have never been whipped with a wooden paddle, it was not fun. I visited his office so much that I learned to wear two pair of pants or place paper towels in my pants to soften the blow. It did not work. When the principal was not trying to make me become a disciplined student, my fifth grade teacher would try. This teacher would grab me by the back of my pants and tear into my behind in front of the class. He would have me running in the air. My friends and I would get whippings regularly. If I told my mother, she would say something like, "That is what you deserved." If it was not for the principals and teachers throughout my youth, there is no question that I would either be in prison or dead.

Elementary School #1

I had the opportunity to have a positive influence on some young student's lives. Teaching was an opportunity to give back to the Black community. Since I had a Bachelor's Degree and was planning to earn my teaching certificate, I was able to become a substitute teacher in the Detroit Public Schools System. My intentions were to teach history at the high school level. At the time, there was a shortage of elementary school teachers. My first assignment was an elementary school on the eastside of Detroit, in a low-income neighborhood. Since I resigned from Wayne County the first week in June, I had the opportunity to teach the last two weeks of the school year before summer break. I was assigned as a gym instructor. Once the students found out this was my first time teaching, I was at their mercy. For two weeks, some of my students actually made me regret deciding to become a teacher. Everyday in gym class, I had to break up fights. When the students would get suspended, the next day they would ride their bikes back up to the school and continue their aggressive behavior. I would ask myself, "What have I gotten myself into?" Veteran teachers would tell me not to worry because students acted like that because it was the end of the school year and the students were excited about summer vacation. I believed them because I did not know any better.

After a brief summer, I was back at the same school. The only difference was that I was assigned to teach fourth grade math. Even though I was not certified to teach math, I did not find the assignment overwhelming. There was an average of 20 students in my class. As with any class, there were students at various levels of math skills. Some were good at math. Some were a little behind. Some wanted to learn. Some didn't want to learn. Some were like I was in elementary school. They came to school to fight. Guess what? Those were the students in my class. Everyday, the same students were disrupting the class. Teaching was difficult enough for me without the behavioral problems. I would send disruptive students to the principal's office and the next day they would return being more disruptive than before. I would call their parents and the results would be the same. The innocent victims were the majority of the students whose parents sent them to school to learn and respect the teachers. The rest of the class suffered because of the four or five troublemakers.

I would attribute a small percentage of my problem to my lack of experience, but not to a lack of dedication. Everyday, I would tell myself that if I could just have a positive impact on one student, then my day would not be in vain. As I talked to other teachers and observed the students in other classrooms, I discovered that I was not alone in my battle for order. At this particular school, even the veteran teachers with years of experience were having unimaginable difficulties with students.

This pattern of disruptive behavior lasted for the first three weeks of the semester. During my break one day, I went to see the principal, who was a Black man. I gave him the names of the notorious students from my class who exhibited the continual disruptive behavior. Most of these students had a previous problem of disobedience. The principal was already aware of the conduct of these students, but he chose to do nothing about it. After I explained to him what was occurring he stated, "Mr. Prophet, you have to look within yourself and find out what you are doing wrong that is preventing these students from respecting you." His words caused me to have flashbacks to my verbally aggressive behavior in my youth, but I held my peace. I told him that it was not about me, but the students. I asked him how could he accuse me of not being able to control the students' behavior, when half the teachers in the school were experiencing the same problems or even worse. Initially, I was shocked by his response. After I talked to the person who assisted me in obtaining a teaching position there, I was no longer shocked. The next day I informed my union representative of what occurred and she instructed me on how to request a transfer.

Elementary School #2

The shortage of teachers in Detroit was so great at the time that I was reassigned to another school within a week. This school was also on the eastside of Detroit, but it was in a middle-income neighborhood. Later I will discuss the relevance of household income on student performance. This elementary school had twice as many students and teachers. The principal at this school was a Black woman and the assistant principal was a Black man. Both of them were two of the nicest people a teacher could have as supervisors. The entire teaching staff was like a family. To my amazement, there were quite a few White teachers there. At this school, race did not matter. We all were on the same team and had the same goal, to prepare young Black minds for the future.

Health Education

My first assignment was to teach, Health Education. Before the class began, I had the opportunity to receive two weeks of training along with other teachers at an area high school. This time, the class was not the problem, but the location of the class. Since there was a shortage of classrooms, I was responsible for setting up a class on the stage in the auditorium. With the assistance of the head-building attendant, I was able to gather enough usable desks to simulate a classroom. When you are a substitute teacher, you are always assigned the most difficult responsibilities. It seemed like when the students were on the way to my class, they had already made up in their minds to make my day as miserable as possible. They succeeded everyday. As soon as the door opened to the auditorium between 8:20A.M. and 8:25A.M., students would run in. They ran through the seats in the auditorium and jumped on and off the stage. It would take 15 minutes to gain control and finally provide instruction.

I did not blame the students for their behavior. When they saw the auditorium, they saw a place to have fun. Since the class I was attempting to teach was basically an elective, they did not take it seriously. Plus, I was teaching outside of my area of emphasis for my certification in college. The students in my classes were extremely aggressive. A day did not go by that I did not have to break up a fight. At this particular school, even the girls would fight. Never in my wildest nightmare did I imagine that teaching would be this challenging.

What I failed to realize when I decided to pursue teaching was that the students had changed drastically from when I attended elementary school in the 1970's and when I taught in 1999. In the 1970's, I was not exposed to all the negative influences that young minds are exposed to today. With television, videos, video games, music, magazines, and negative environments today, children in elementary school are exposed to sex, violence, drugs, and other forms of negative behavior that are prevalent in society. When I was in elementary school, there were only three stations on the television. All I can remember watching is "Mod Squad," "The Waltons," "Little House On The Praire," "The Rookies," and "Sanford and Son." None of these shows exposed the young mind to drugs, sex, profanity, or glorified violence. As far as music, rap and hip-hop were non-existent. The only video games I can remember were Atari and Intellivision. These were just some of the minor differences.

The most tremendous difference that influenced the behavior of students today and in the 1970's were the parents. In the 1970's, even though some of us were raised in single parent homes, the mothers were older. That meant most children were raised in homes where the mother was more mature and responsible. In 1999, I noticed that children were being raised by mothers who were young. Plus, we have to take into account that a certain percentage of parents of the children who are now in urban school systems were affected by the crack-cocaine epidemic of the 1980's. This and other social ills definitely had an impact on some of the students. I am not stating that a majority of the students were affected by the problems mentioned. If 3 students out of 25 had behavioral problems in a classroom, it caused the entire class to suffer.

Attempting to teach in the auditorium was my worst nightmare. Every night when I came home, I was traumatized. It would take me two hours to recover from the stress of the day. By that time, it was time to get ready for another day. The emotional stress that I experienced from dealing with the students all day was different from any stress that I had ever experienced. When I dealt with racism and betrayal from other Black people in my previous jobs, it was more challenging than stressful because I was dealing with adults. With adults, if I did not get the respect that was supposed to be given to me, I could demand or take it. Throughout my adult life, I was accustomed to interacting with adults. Since I never had any children, I could not relate to the mind of elementary school children.

From the first day, I messed up because I exhibited my caring side. They took this for a weakness and it was over. When children do not respect the teacher, it can be a difficult situation for the teacher. At least, it was for me. The students knew their rights. They knew teachers could not touch them physically or verbally abuse them. Intimidation was out of the question. The only recourse I had was to send them to the principal's office. After a lecture from the principal or assistant principal, the student's behavior would change for two days at the most. Then it was back to pandemonium. To handle the stress from the difficulties we were having with the students, I used to pray with other teachers who were having the same problems. While they prayed for peace, I prayed that I did not lose my mind. I was assigned to the auditorium for approximately four months. Everyday, it took the grace of God to sustain me. I could remember on numerous mornings driving east on I-94 with the sun shining bright in the sky. Once I pulled into the parking lot, even though the sun was shining bright, in my mind it was a dark and gloomy day. One day I asked a veteran teacher, "Could it get any worse?" Many days it just didn't seem like it could.

Team Teaching

Finally, the day came when it was apparent that my prayers were answered. I received an opportunity to team teach a third grade class with one of the best teachers in the Detroit Public Schools System. This Black female teacher had taught for approximately eight years and had recently earned her Master's Degree in Education. She not only had the passion for teaching, but the experience, knowledge, and a maternal connection to the students. If all teachers exhibited her level of dedication or more, we would have a greater number of students excelling in school. The students in our class respected her like she was their mother. All I had to do was basically act as her assistant. I used the opportunity to learn all I could with her as my mentor.

Three weeks before spring break, the administration decided that the students had to be divided between the two teachers in the classroom. Every student in the class was assigned a number. All the even-numbered students were assigned to me and all the odd-numbered students were assigned to the female teacher. When some of the students learned that they were going to be assigned to me, you could see the disappointment in their little faces. The students and I knew that those assigned to me would receive a sub-par education for the remainder of the school year. I did not see how a teacher who had just entered the teaching profession seven months ago could provide the same level of education that a teacher with eight years of experience and a higher degree in the field could. Some of the students assigned to me wanted to be placed with the other teacher. Since I felt their pain, we traded about five students like we were trading players in the NBA. The entire ordeal was unfair to the students that were assigned to me. A week before spring break, I decided to resign so that all the students who were assigned to me could receive the best education possible. It was a financial sacrifice, but giving those students the best opportunity to prepare for the future was more important.

Teachers

In all professions and jobs there will always be people with different work ethics. I said that to say that throughout America we have the same variety of people working in different occupations. Teaching is no different. During my teaching experience at the two elementary schools, I was a part of a team of teachers who had teaching experience ranging from 1 to 25 years. It was apparent that a correlation existed among a teacher's years of experience, their reason for going into education, and their dedication to teaching.

For the most part, the teachers I worked with were dedicated to educating students. Teaching is one of most demanding and satisfying professions a person could commit his or her life to. Regardless of the difficulties these teachers faced, they still came to school daily and gave it their all. There is a saying—"Those that can't do, teach." That is one of the most ridiculous and false statements I have ever heard in relation to teachers. Being a dedicated teacher is not a job or career but a lifestyle. The dedicated teachers I am referring to worked 24/7 to prepare their students for the future. Most people think teaching is one of those 8:00A.M. to 3:00P.M. occupations. That is just half of a dedicated teacher's day. Once the teacher gets home, there are parents to call, papers to grade, and preparation for the next day. There is so much administrative work, i.e parent-teacher conferences, staff meeting, progress reports, preparation of lesson plans, workshops, and other responsibilities that consume a teacher's personal time. For those of you who think teaching is an easy profession and teachers are not doing their best to educate children, please remove those thoughts from your mind Until you have fought on the frontline in any urban public school system across America, please keep your opinions to yourself.

As in most professions, you have some people who are in it just for the money. This was the case for some of the young people who were not certified to teach. When I went into teaching in 1999, there was a shortage of teachers so the requirements to become a substitute teacher were lowered. If you were a person who possessed a Bachelor's Degree in any field, you could teach. In order to be an excellent teacher, it is best that you receive the proper training from an education program in college. Do not get me wrong. There were some excellent teachers that came from other fields and excelled in teaching. I never try to group all teachers into one category. All teachers, just like all people, should be evaluated by their individual character and performance; not in a group. A lot of teachers who did not possess any formal training in teaching were actually like babysitters, myself included. We did not have the four years of learning to effectively deal with all the special needs of young students.

Teaching at the elementary grade levels is more difficult than the high school level. At the high school level, a teacher has to deal with more behavioral problems, but not the problem of developing a young mind to think. If a student was not taught to think during elementary and junior high school, by high school all a teacher can do is pray for that student. Some of these teachers were only there for a paycheck and could have cared less whether or not the students learned. This mentality was reserved only for a couple of teachers. If this was the mentality of two teachers at every school in a system with more than two hundred schools, that equates to roughly four hundred teachers who do not care and thousands of students who are not learning.

Even though there are several different categories of teachers, I will focus attention on this last group. There were a number of teachers who were close to retirement and were just biding their time. When these teachers first started teaching 25 years ago, the students back then were different from the students today. Some of these teachers were so burned out from the daily toll of the mental and emotional drain that they just lost focus of teaching. Since they only had a couple years until they could retire they had no other choice but to persevere.

Students

Regardless of what you hear on the news or anywhere else, more than 75 percent of the students in the public school systems are good students who come to school to learn and are raised in good homes by good parents. It is that smaller percentage who create dilemmas for teachers. The behavior of some of the students was so terrible that the school social worker resigned in the middle of the school year. Everyday, there were fights. Fighting was not the exception but the norm. When it came to the usage of profanity, it was ridiculous. One day, as I was walking towards the bathroom, I heard a student cursing. Too Short, Tupac, Biggie, Snoop Dogg, Eminem, and Fifty Cent were subtle compared to this student. I went in the bathroom and was surprised to discover that the student was in the first grade and barely knew his alphabets, but cursed better than me when I used profanity, "back in the day."

These were the students that the administrators attempted to separate from the good students. I knew this first hand. When I walked down the hall, I would see nice students and wonder why I never saw them in my class. The reason was because the administrators purposely placed all the difficult students in one group and they attended all the same classes together. The inexperienced teachers and the teachers who taught non-essential classes were primarily responsible for these students. That is my belief. If I were an administrator, I probably would have made the same decision. There is no question that the behavior of some students disrupted the learning process of all the other students who came to school to learn. In addition, some of the well-behaved students would learn behaviors that were not a part of their home environment. This would cause parents to come to the school and complain about what their children were learning in school.

I cannot forget about the students that were compulsive liars. Some students would lie on teachers just to get out of trouble with their parents. One student told her mother that I gave her a Coach purse. The parent came up to the school to interrogate me about what her daughter said. After the parent and I talked, it was discovered that the student had taken the purse from another student. There are certainly students that make teaching more difficult than it should be.

The students assisted me in deciding that teaching was not for me at this time in my life. Some of these students brought back the pain of my childhood, since I grew up in a neighborhood with families with low to high income levels. These students came to school malnourished, along with wearing dirty and raggedy clothes. I can remember two students who were sisters and they reminded me of the starving children that I saw on news reports from Ethiopia. Then there were students who came to school without washing up because their house did not have running water or electricity. There were also the students who came to school from homeless shelters or homes for abused women.

Regardless of what previous chapters in this book indicate, I am a compassionate person and these children's pain became my pain. I could empathize with a number of them. Even though it was against school policy, I would give money to students that needed it. If I came to school with fifteen dollars in my wallet, I was broke by the end of the day. It was difficult seeing the pain in these students' eyes everyday and not being able to help every single one of them. Teaching is like being a doctor, police officer, fire fighter, or any other occupation where you have to deal with the suffering of other people. I had to try not to allow the pain and struggles of those students to affect me emotionally. No matter how hard I tried, it was too difficult because of my personal experiences and because I knew the future that was possibly awaiting those students that began life in poverty. Some of those students would go on and have a decent life, but some of them would fall victim to the vicious streets.

Parents

It would be wrong for me to group all parents into one category. There is a correlation between the socio-economic level of the parents and the children's performance in school. Not only were the students facing difficulties due to the low level of income in their household, but many were also a part of a single-parent home or being raised by grandparents. One day I was asking a little girl questions concerning her parents and she told me that she had never seen her father. It is common knowledge that there is a greater hardship for single-parent households. Children may also be psychologically and emotionally affected when they have no contact or relationship with one or both parents. Challenges can arise for the teachers and the students in these instances because the parents' time for being actively involved in the child's education is limited or nonexistent. At times, there may be a difference between a child being raised in a two-parent home instead of a single-parent home. Studies have shown that a child's success may not be better in a two-parent rather than a single-parent home. Student success was and still is influenced more so by their parent's involvement in their education.

At the two schools in which I taught, the behavior of the students and their ability was a reflection of the parents and the teacher. When I was teaching, I noticed that a number of the students came from close to impoverished living conditions. This was apparent from their personal appearance and the appearance of their parents. By talking to the students, you could find out about their individual struggles. I talked to my students to learn more about them and what I needed to do to help them as a teacher. The events and circumstances I heard from the students were true because I saw the homes of some of those students. I would drive up and down some of the streets and see houses that appeared to be abandoned, but children that attended public schools lived in them.

Some of the parents were uneducated and did not know how to properly prepare their children for school. There were students who never did their homework. When I asked why, they would come up with numerous excuses. The most common excuse was that their mother could not help them or they did not want to do it. These were the same students whose parents never came to parent-teacher conferences. Some parents had to work and others just did not care.

On the flip side, were the parents who cared about their children's education and were able to provide a stable home environment. These parents ensured that their children came to school clean, fed, and ready to learn. At the elementary school age, it is the parents who determine how much the child will learn. Parents who care about the education of their children make sure that their children are doing their homework daily. Learning continues at home. When it is time for parent-teacher conference, they will make the necessary sacrifices to ensure that they will be present to discuss their child's academic progress and behavior. It is unfortunate that a child's success or failure in this country is strongly impacted by the status of the parents.

Rationale

The reason I gave a detailed description of teachers, students, and parents is to make an important point. Teachers are hired to teach, not to be parents. It is the parents' responsibility to raise their children in a way that is conducive to learning. Most of the time, the same behavior that students exhibit in the classroom is the same behavior that is allowed at home. Politicians and others attempt to blame the teachers for the sub-standard performance of students, but the first place they should look is in the home. After they look in the home, they should investigate the history of Black people in this country and determine the primary reason for the educational and economic gap that continues to affect Black families.

In 2003, we have a movement in Detroit to open the door for more charter schools in the district. Charter schools will not solve the problems of the public school system. They will only magnify the problem by removing money from an already struggling school system. Only the best of the best students will be permitted to attend these schools. Now in Detroit, there are three high schools that are considered the Big 3, in the Detroit Public Schools System—Cass Technical High School, Renaissance High School and Dr. Martin Luther King Jr., High School. Instead of only three high schools providing a standard of academic excellence, every public high school in Detroit should be providing the same standards. If charter schools are permitted to compete for students with other public high schools, we will have separate and unequal education in Detroit. This will continue to widen the economic gap. This means that all students will not have the same opportunity for a successful future, because the socio-economic status of their household may be a factor as well as the special needs of the student such as counseling or other things. A quality education opens the door to the mind.

Certification

While I was teaching, I was attending Wayne State University to earn my teaching certification. Since my degree was in Business Management, the easiest certification was in History. I had to enroll in four History courses as a prerequisite before I could enroll in certification courses. Attending classes with students straight out of high school, assisted me in determining how much knowledge I had obtained since those days. The History of Europe and the United States were topics I was quite familiar with so I found the courses to be redundant. All the courses did was reinforce the beliefs that I already had. When you attend White colleges and universities you have to learn what they want you to learn. It is up to you to take the initiative and learn the truth and the other side of the story yourself.

The courses that I enrolled in for my teaching certification were informative and challenging. I did not object to most of those courses. The mental challenges were the things I loved most about college. The teaching curriculum at WSU was definitely appropriate for a positive transition into teaching. There was one class that I did not like. The course dealt with the theory of how children learned and behaved at certain ages. These theories were formulated by European professors of the sixteenth and seventeenth centuries. I could not understand why I was forced to learn about something that was irrelevant to solving the problems in the 21st century. None of the professors who created these theories had ever taught in an urban school district in the 21st century. The children these professors were developing theories about did not have the same environmental problems as children in today's urban public schools. Even though I received an "A," the course did not have any relevant value to me. In order to truly understand the challenges of being an educator, hands-on experience is the best teacher.

Advice

Teaching is a career choice that should be made straight out of high school or during college. The reason is that it would be easier to acclimate yourself to the behavior of children and understand them better. Since I was already set in my ways, I could not adjust to the mentality of younger children. If you know it is your goal to teach high school students, try not to be assigned to an elementary school. If possible, do not enter the teaching profession without at least a Bachelor's Degree in Education or your teaching certification. Teachers without the necessary credentials earn less money, receive less benefits, and are still required to deal with the same problems that certified teachers deal with.

Being a teacher is definitely one of the most rewarding careers I can imagine a person having. We need more dedicated teachers to teach our leaders of tomorrow. Without good leaders, Black people in this country will continue to spiral downward to a 21st century form of slavery. Knowledge is the key to success. In order to obtain knowledge, a person must first be taught to read and think. During slavery, Black people were prohibited from reading and writing. The White slave owner knew that once Black people learned how to read and write, we would also begin to think for ourselves. They knew that if they kept our ancestors ignorant, they would not want to escape from the bondage of slavery. Even though we are now physically free, millions of our people are mentally enslaved. That is why we need more teachers and educators to provide knowledge for future generations. However, it begins with asking yourself: "Is this something I would love doing, even if I was not being paid to do it?"

Chapter 8

UNITED PARCEL SERVICE
ROUND 2

". . . Yet is there no end of all his labour . . ."

—Eccl 4:8

I would never have imagined that I would ever work for UPS again. That is why it is best to never, say never. Twelve years later, the reason for my return to UPS was due to a need for medical coverage and not the money. In case you are not aware, the cost of health insurance is astronomical when you do not work for a good company that provides it. During the period of my entrepreneurship, I was responsible for my own health insurance. Prior to working for UPS, my COBRA insurance payments were $311.00 a month. That was placing a financial strain on my already strained budget. I discovered that UPS was hiring at one of its facilities in the Metropolitan Detroit area. UPS still had the best medical and dental coverage for part-time workers. I filled out an application and was given an interview. In a matter of weeks, I was working part-time for one of the Fortune 500 companies, which ranked in the top 50.

Work Environment

Since I had not worked at UPS for over twelve years, I thought I was going to be assigned to the "Blackhole" again. As I mentioned in UPS—Round 1, that was where you unloaded the trailers. At this particular facility, I would not call it the "Blackhole," but the "Underworld" because of the enormous area designated for unloading trailers and the gloominess. It appeared lifeless because of the lack of light. It seemed like the place where hope went and died. The workers that were assigned to the "Underworld," consisted of men from the ages of 18 to 40 and a variety of nationalities. UPS was definitely an equal opportunity employer. If you could sling a box and get to work on time on a regular basis, then you had a job. Nothing changed over the years since I was away. UPS still ran the tightest ship in the shipping business.

The A.M. Shift Facility Manager was aware of my previous UPS experience and assigned me to Line #2 as a preloader. I was responsible for retrieving packages off a slide and loading them into three package delivery trucks. This facility was more modernized than the facility in Saginaw. The packages were still transferred from the unloading area on conveyor belts and then sorted to different preloaders on Line #2. As the packages were sorted, they would be forced down the slide and come to rest at the bottom of the slide, which was three feet from the back of my trucks.

When I started working for UPS in 1985 as a part-time preloader, I made $9.00 an hour. When I resigned in 1988, I was making $10.00 an hour. Twelve years later, preloaders were only starting off at $9.50 an hour. I certainly had a problem with that. Of course, I inquired about why I had to start off at $9.50 an hour even though I had previous experience. The answer I received was not satisfactory. Since I was working there primarily for the health benefits, I did not waste my energy fighting a lost cause. It was amazing that the starting wage for one of the most physically demanding positions at UPS had only increased by fifty cents an hour in twelve years. The hourly wages for preloaders did not increase considerably over the years, but the weight and size of the packages did. In 1988, the maximum weight of a package was about 75 pounds. In 2000, the maximum weight seemed more like 300 pounds if you ask me. UPS would deliver a house if they could make a profit. It did not take long for me to realize what I had returned to.

On Line #2, there were eight preloaders that loaded anywhere from three to four trucks each. I was assigned to the third position on the line. Each of the preloaders on Line #2 had their own agenda and reason for working as a preloader. One young lady was a college student who was just working for the money. About three preloaders were waiting for the opportunity to become full-time drivers. One of the most hilarious preloaders on Line #2 was a guy that reminded me of Joe Pesci from "Lethal Weapon 2." He gave me the nickname, "ABM" (Angry Black Man). Working next to me was this cool Black preloader that came to work nicely dressed everyday. I called him "Preacher Man" and he referred to me as "Black Man." Nothing, that was going on phased him. He just came in, did his job and left.

Our part-time supervisor was a young dedicated White man. We had a mutual understanding—we were fine as long as he did not start trouble with me. Every time something went wrong, his only response was, "Suck it up!" Today, I still hate that phrase. It means that when management makes incorrect decisions, it is the job of the workers to do whatever is necessary to keep the manager from looking bad.

I noticed that one thing which did not change at UPS was the relationship between management and unionized workers. The union situation was still the same. On the national level, the union was extremely successful with getting the full-time drivers everything they wanted at contract time. As usual, the part-time preloaders were on their own. The relationship between managers and the unions at this facility was too harmonious and accommodating. Anytime management and the union are too friendly, that means trouble for the workers.

Drivers

In my opinion, being a UPS driver is one of the most demanding service oriented jobs that I can think of. During one of the Christmas peak seasons, I had the chance to become a driver's assistant. The Black driver I assisted was probably one of the hardest working drivers at this facility. He was all about business. I had never considered becoming a driver. Assisting him just one cold day in December confirmed that I did not want to be a driver. The drivers at UPS were compensated well and they earned every penny. Every time a contract comes up, the union has the opportunity to ensure that the drivers receive raises and other benefits. Sometimes it is at the expense of the part-time workers. One thing about the negotiating tactics of some unions is that they bargain away the benefits of the part-time and future workers to obtain the confidence of the current full-time workers and management. It seemed like the union's philosophy for future workers was: "They cannot miss what they never had."

All three of the drivers I loaded trucks for were totally different. One driver was a White man who always complained. He was never satisfied with the way I loaded his truck. The only thing that would have made him happy would have been for me to deliver the packages for him. Regardless of what job I perform and whether I liked it or not, my integrity will not allow me to give less than ninety percent.

This driver would blame me if he arrived to work and his packages were stacked from the top to the bottom and the front to the back of his truck. Some of his designated stops received multiple packages. On any given day, he could receive fifty boxes the size of a 27" television along with the other 150-200 boxes that I would have loaded in his truck. I would ask the part-time supervisor if he wanted me to load everything and he would instruct me to load every single box. Once I received a direct order, it was out of my control. The driver would come in and see his truck and start whining. I would just laugh at him. This was the same driver that accused me of loading Next Day Air packages in the middle of his load. If he did not deliver a Next Day Air package at a certain time, he would be reprimanded so he conveniently placed blame on me, frequently. Management did not play when it came to having packages delivered at the time a customer requested it. Fortunately, my manager on Line #2 came to our defense and would not believe everything a driver said.

This one Black driver I loaded a truck for was the coolest. On the mornings that he came in early, he would assist me in loading his truck while I explained any adjustments I had to make. He was an excellent driver, but he was not one of those that would bite his tongue if management did or said something that irritated him. When preloaders loaded a truck for a driver that was down to earth and did not think being a UPS driver made him better than them, preloaders would be willing to put forth that extra effort into ensuring the driver had a good day. The preloader controlled a driver's destiny. If a driver upset a preloader, the preloader could just place packages anywhere in the truck and it would still be the driver's responsibility to deliver the packages on time. If not, the driver would receive the wrath of management.

The third driver I loaded a truck for was a Black man that cried all the time. Here he was with a high school diploma, making $60,000.00+ a year. My question was always, "What are you crying about?" Being a driver for UPS affords all drivers, Black, White and Hispanic, the opportunity to provide an excellent standard of living for their family. Plus, if you took advantage of the stock option, you could retire from UPS without a financial worry in the world. Regardless of everything I just said, he would still cry. Some people are blessed and don't even realize it or appreciate their blessing.

Management

The managers at this facility were different from the ones that were at the UPS facility in Saginaw. Most of these full-time managers were in their late 30's or early 40's. The facility manager had a pleasant demeanor and appeared to have a genuine concern for all the preloaders. I never witnessed him using any of the intimidation tactics of verbal abuse or threatening to fire someone, which was a common practice by some. This manager did everything in his power to ensure that preloaders made it to work.

Some of the other full-time managers at this facility had a different approach with the preloaders. One manager would attempt to use reverse psychology by being friendly with you, so when he needed you to do something that went beyond the call of duty, a preloader would most likely comply. When he asked me, I would politely refuse. The demands that management placed on preloaders at times were too strenuous for the amount of money they were paying us. If you exhibited dedication and hard work, management would reward you with another truck. Going beyond the call of duty to impress the managers at UPS was not a goal of mine. The harder and faster you worked, the less money you received but management received more in their bonus checks.

The arrogant way in which some managers exhibited themselves was unbelievable. Some of them actually felt they were better than the preloaders and drivers because of their positions as managers. Some drivers actually thought they were better than preloaders. I have always believed that a person's title or position doesn't make them superior to anyone else.

The management style at UPS was almost identical to the military. All the managers wore suits and the drivers had to wear the brown uniforms. In addition, no manager, part-time supervisor, or driver was permitted to wear a goatee or beard. All of the employees listed above had to keep their hair below a certain length.

Preloaders were similar to privates at grade E-2, while the unloaders would be considered privates, E-1. One major difference between soldiers in the military and drivers at UPS is that the drivers did not carry weapons and after they got off work, they could go home. Other than that, UPS and numerous corporations have organizational structures and styles modeled after the military. Since I was an ex-soldier, I understood the rules of the game.

There is one major factor that management in corporate America, management in government, and officers in the Armed Forces have in common. When they have their management meetings, they are not discussing how to make the workload easier for the rank and file. The usual topics are the following: How can they get higher productivity out of the subordinates and pay them less; How can they motivate the subordinates to work harder to compensate for the ill-advised decision that management made; How can we demand more concessions in reduced pay and benefits, while the pay and benefits for CEO's, stockholders and elected officials continue to increase. Considering what managers have to impose on employees after those meetings, it would be difficult to call yourself a follower of God. The demands that are placed on the rank and file by management are sometimes inhumane. My question has always been, "Why does your bad planning, make for my emergency?" Regardless of where you work, please learn how to "Suck it up" and keep your mouth shut!

Honeymoon Over

It seemed impossible for me to just go to work, do my job, and come home without any drama. From the first day I began working there, I noticed the sorter did not care about the packages that they allowed to come down the slides. On more than one occasion, I requested and then demanded that they do not allow any packages to come down my slide that could possibly cause me bodily harm. My request was totally ignored. This resulted in a serious consequence. After you read the grievance I prepared and delivered below, I will explain the reason why I decided to share this vital information.

GRIEVANCE REPORT

Article of Contract or Rules & Regulations Involved:
Article 18—Safety and Health
Statement of Facts:

On Thursday, April 5, 2001 at approximately 6:10A.M., as I was turning to exit my truck on Line #2, I heard a tremendous crash. Once I exited my truck, I saw a large steel cylinder weighing possibly 25 pounds that had propelled itself off the slide and crashed against the back of my truck. I immediately became irate and proceeded to walk towards the sorter, explaining my displeasure in a loud voice. I asked him why he allowed a package that could cause bodily harm to come down the conveyor belt. I climbed up to the sorter's location and continued to voice my outrage at a re-occurring problem. The part-time supervisor asked me to calm down. I calmed down and explained the situation to him.

I immediately walked off the line and punched out. Then I walked to see my union representative in the unload area. I explained the situation to him and I was informed that there was nothing he could do about the situation. The unload manager, contacted the facility manager and it was arranged for me to meet him in the office.

I will briefly digress and explain what provoked me to react in such a defensive manner. Since I began working on Line #2 on September 29, 2000, I had been experiencing problems with what UPS refers to as "rollers." Rollers are packages that have the capability to roll down the slide. During the week of March 26, 2001, a cylinder approximately 5" in diameter, 18" long and weighing 39 pounds propelled itself off the slide and crashed behind the truck of my coworker. Shortly there after, a cylinder approximately half the length and weight propelled itself off my slide. When the Line #2 Manager came by, I directed his attention to both cylinders and explained to him the possible bodily harm that could result by those types of packages. He proceeded to write something down and that was the last I heard of my complaint.

Back to April 5, 2001. Once the facility manager and I entered the office, he asked me to sit down on two occasions and I refused. I explained to him that I was too emotionally stressed to sit down at the time. He asked me what happened and I explained in great detail the events that led up to the current situation.

I asked him why they allowed such a hazardous work practice to continue. He informed me that the sorters are instructed to yell "roller" every time a cylinder is sorted to an employee's work area. I asked how could a preloader hear anything with the variety of noises that are present at the facility. First, there is the noise of the numerous motors that operate the conveyor belt system. Second, there is the constant noise from preloaders shouting back and forth to each other. Third, on any given day the average preloader is in and out of his/her truck over 400 times a day. I asked what are the odds of the preloader being present at the slide when the sorter yells out "roller." In my case, I did not hear the sorter yell anything.

He informed me that there was nothing they could do to prevent cylinders from being placed on the belt. He said that once they reach the sorters, there is not enough room for them to do anything but send them to the designated employees.

I informed him that we (preloaders) were not getting paid enough to work in an unsafe work environment. I explained that if a cylinder could hit an employee, then there is a potential for serious injury. The impact of a heavy cylinder could easily break a person's arm, leg or cause more devastating injuries.

(Take a moment and think about these worst case scenarios: What if an employee is bending down, looking under his/her belt checking for the addresses of bulk packages and a "roller" propels itself off the slide just as the employee lifts his/her head up? There is a chance that an employee could be hit on the head or in the face by the cylinder. What if an employee is bent over and a cylinder hits the employee on the spine? Can you visualize the incapacitating life altering damage these packages could cause an employee? As a consolation, an employee could sue for millions of dollars in damages; but ask an employee who is quadriplegic or has severe brain damage because he or she was struck in the spine or head what would they rather have: Millions of dollars or the ability to live a normal and productive life?)

I informed the facility manager that just because UPS provides an excellent benefits package, does not mean I want to use it because of a preventable work-related injury. He asked me for suggestions. I am quite sure an employee has brought this hazard to the attention of management previously or at a Safety Committee Meeting. Eventually, he said that the problem would be resolved. Explain to me why a multi-billion dollar, Fortune 500 Company would handle an important issue such as employees' safety by taking a reactionary approach instead of a pro-active and preventative approach. The preloaders at this facility are blessed that no one has been injured with the hundreds of thousands of packages they have loaded over the years. Who wants to be the first worker injured?

After we went back and forth concerning an issue that should not have been an issue, I requested permission to leave for the day, without any negative repercussions. He said that he could not allow me to leave. I explained to him that UPS did not own me and that they only employed my services. He changed his mind and gave me permission to leave and said that in the future he would not allow Conrad Prophet to leave every time he was upset. Then he proceeded to explain to me how he handled his frustrations and suggested that I do likewise. I in turn, explained to him that I did not care how he handled his frustrations and he was not in the position or authority to tell me how to handle my emotions. I also explained that I was quite aware of my limitations and would suffer or benefit from the consequences of my words and actions, accordingly.

Finally, as I was about to leave, I asked for permission to apologize to the sorter for speaking to him in such a loud tone and to explain that it was not personal. He said that the sorter was working and I was not to bother him.

That was the grievance in its entirety. On April 20, 2001, I had a meeting with the district manager for an hour. We discussed the issue that led to my grievance and other issues concerning UPS. The district manager said he would address my concerns.

* * *

Before I continue with my UPS experience, I want to explain why I felt that sharing this incident was important. In certain states, particularly Michigan, there are thousands of people employed in the area of manufacturing or other jobs that can be hazardous. It is important that you obey all safety precautions to prevent injuries. There are state laws and regulations that govern organizational operations concerning employees. OSHA (Occupational Safety and Health Administration) is an agency at the federal level that governs regulations for the safety and well-being of employees within an organization's operations and MIOSHA is the state level agency for the same concerns. From a financial perspective, you do not want to get injured and have to collect worker's compensation. The money you would receive from worker's compensation would be only a portion of your regular pay and it can take weeks to receive your first check.

While you are off on an injury, do not expect to qualify for unemployment benefits, certainly not in Michigan.

One common factor with manufacturing jobs and the job of an unloader/preloader is the repetitive movements that your body performs. After a number of years, that same movement gradually wears on your knees, back, arms, hands and other body parts that are required for your job. This repetitious body movement probably does not affect you now when you are in your 20's and 30's, but if you live to be 60 or 70, it will come back to haunt you.

I recommend that those of you that are working at a job that is physically demanding consider another field of work if possible, unless it is temporary like UPS for a college student. If you are not in this field of work, I would advise you to avoid this type of work. Having a job in which you use your mind more than your body will be best for you in the years to come. Always remember that getting injured can prevent you from working in the future. If you ever see a workplace hazard, please report it immediately to management to prevent you or a co-worker from getting injured. Also document that you did notify someone.

*   *   *

After the facility manager and I had the meeting that was discussed in the grievance above, I did not have anything else to say to him. I considered his treatment of the situation disrespectful. In retaliation, I decided not to speak to him. If it was not a work-related issue, I felt that there was no reason to have general conversation with him. The Line #2 Manager and the district manager felt that it was unprofessional for me not to speak to the facility manager. I explained to both of them that I was paid an hourly wage for working up to the high standards and expectations of UPS management, not if I spoke to management or co-workers. It was my personal right to speak or not to speak and they were not going to coerce me into speaking.

One morning while I was loading one of my trucks, the facility manager continued to attempt to have a conversation with me. I would ignore him as I removed packages off the slide and loaded them into my delivery trucks. On several occasions, I explained to him that if it was not work-related, we did not have anything to say to each other. For some reason, he was determined to make me speak to him. Finally, I could not take his constant interrogation of me. Quickly, I placed the package I had in my hand on the shelf of the truck and charged him. I stopped probably six inches from this face and asked him what he wanted. We stared each other down like Mike Tyson and Evander Holyfield. Physically, he had me by thirty pounds, but I had him in arm's reach. The preloader that worked next to me who I referred to as, "Preacher Man" intervened before it escalated. Neither of us was actually going to initiate anything physical because of the job related repercussions. It was only territorial—"a man thing." I was not going to allow him to disrespect me as a man and he was not going to allow a preloader to disrespect him in his facility. For him to allow me to disrespect him would have only given other preloaders the idea that they could do it also. He could not allow that to occur.

The facility manager was only performing his job and it was not race affiliated. Less than a week later, we both apologized and learned from the experience. From that day on another "roller" never came down my slide again. A month later, the facility manager asked me if I wanted to apply for a part-time supervisor position. Of course, I declined because I thought it was a ploy to remove me from the protection of the union, so they could fire me. To this day, I have the highest degree of respect for this man. I think it is because of managers like him who inspire unloaders and preloaders to continue to be an integral part of UPS.

Overview

There is no question that UPS is one of the best places to work if you are a college student. For a young person, UPS will definitely teach you how to work hard, be responsible, and take orders. UPS is the closest you can come to being in the military, without actually being in the military. For entrepreneurs like myself at the time, it was an opportunity to receive excellent health benefits and still have the rest of the day to myself, because I got off work at UPS no later than 8:00A.M.

I would recommend UPS for anyone who is not afraid of hard work and just looking for something temporary. If you start off as an unloader in the "Underworld," the chances for advancement are not great unless your work ethics exceed those of your co-workers. If you ever receive the opportunity to drive or become a manager, do not hesitate to accept the offer. No matter what corporation you work for, you will have to acclimate yourself to the environment of that corporation. If you are going to work for any corporation in America, you should aim for one of the best and UPS is one of the best in my opinion.

There is no question that I owe the people who made it possible for me to be employed at UPS in 1985 and 2000, a great debt of gratitude for the opportunity. Even though UPS provided me with income and health benefits at two pivotal times in my life, those were not the greatest benefits UPS bestowed on me.

The reason I am extremely appreciative of being employed at UPS is because of the wonderful co-workers who have become lifelong friends from that experience. "Preacher Man" exhibited a different style to me. He had a style of a Black man who was intelligent, respectful and always conducted himself in a manner that made me wonder what gave him the ability to weather the storms that he did. Once I got to know him, all of my wondering ended. It was his beliefs and allegiance to Christ. Today, even though I think he went into full-time management at UPS, I still consider him a vital part in the equation that allowed me to become the person that I am today. Also having the opportunity to meet him caused a series of events to occur that gave me the support, encouragement, knowledge, and determination to write this book. Thank you, UPS and "Preacher Man."

Chapter 9

AUTHOR

"... He did it with all his heart, and prospered."

—*2 Chron 31:21*

For as long as I can remember, I have always loved reading and writing. It didn't matter that I wasn't good at either during my elementary school years. During those years, learning just wasn't important to me. Fighting 24/7 was more enjoyable. My passion for reading and writing developed in high school. Most of my English courses required that I use creativity in my writing. My imagination was always good, so writing an essay or story was always easy. As I stated previously, I started writing letters in college and the Army, which also allowed me to express my thoughts on paper. When you are extremely introverted and not affected by peer pressure, you have more time to focus attention on your true gifts and talents. My years in the Army gave me the opportunity to truly discover myself, without the influence of friends, family, adversaries, and familiar surroundings.

My passion for reading developed in the same way. I remember sneaking and reading some of my brother's Donald Goines' books. Mr. Goines' books always had a gritty, street mentality that took you to the underworld of Detroit. Although his books were allegedly fiction, they told of his lifestyle and revealed many of the realities of life in the inner city. There are some writers who write about events and people that are truly fictional, but Donald Goines' books were too real for him to have not experienced some of the situations he described. Even today, some events that he wrote about are still vivid in my mind. Some people disapprove of the negative events that Donald Goines wrote about, but I have always been able to read or observe something negative and make it positive. It was always a goal of mine to never be like any of the characters in Donald Goines' books, or any of the ruthless characters I saw on the streets. I learned a lot about the hard life on the streets and was determined to rise above it.

After my Donald Goines' phase was over, I began reading Richard Wright, James Baldwin, Alice Walker and Toni Morrison, just to name a few. During the late 1980's, Terry McMillian, Omar Tyree, Walter Mosley and others were not on the scene yet. My first love was for books about Black history that focused attention on our struggles and our victories. If I attempted to list all the Black authors and the books I have read, it would take an entire page. After reading so many books and being fascinated, I decided to embark on the challenge of writing a book myself.

The motivation to write a fiction novel developed through a combination of disappointment, a desire to educate, and a way to maintain my sanity during the turbulent years of my life. I remember reading one of James Baldwin's books and having difficulty identifying with the setting of the south during the 1950's and 1960's. I was able to relate to the racism because, at the time, I was working for one of the most racist corporations in my employment history. I could not identify with the mindset of the Black characters that were depicted in the books I read. I was determined to write a book that would speak to today's generation, as well as future generations.

That was when *Last Year Before Reality (LYBR)* was conceived. The creation of *LYBR* started in 1991 while Kmart employed me. As I thought about what I was going through there, and the plight of Black people in general, I decided to write a book that would educate the Black youths who came after me.

"*LYBR* is a story of African-American youths experiencing life, love and tragedy as they approach adulthood and independence in their last year of high school. The characters are extremely diverse in their personalities, socioeconomic backgrounds, education levels and lifestyles. The chemistry and camaraderie between them is revealed through socializing, holiday gatherings and personal hardships. Pervasive throughout the book are the parents' struggles to prepare their children for the harsh realities of the future that they were unprepared for themselves. The reader is given a ring-side seat as the characters deal with the challenges of life. The development of close friendships and life expectations provide for nonstop action. Hope, despair, dreams and disappointments propel the characters through to the last page of the book. The inevitable result is summarized in the last sentence of the book: For some, it was their last year before reality. For others, it was their last year."

Reminiscing on my high school years, as well as the challenges I have faced as an adult motivated me to assist in preparing young Black men and women for the unfamiliar and unforeseeable situations that most of them will face. I encourage you to read *LYBR*, as it is full of the real-life scenarios that will be helpful in preparing young people for personal, academic, and professional success. I was ignorant to the reality of what America truly had in store for Black people, as they became adults in this country. It was such a devastating shock that it took several years of trial and error to fully process what I was experiencing. My inability to discern the truth earlier was not because of my lack of education or common sense, but it was because I was not informed of the "rules of the game" before I got into the game. While growing up, I was always told that if you received a good education and were a law-abiding citizen, the sky was the limit. No one ever told me that this theory did not apply to all Black people in this country, but only applied to White people and a chosen group of Black people.

I was determined to create a fiction novel that had characters that today's youth could relate to—the book had to be for them and about them. In addition, the relevance of the book had to be timeless, so if young people read *LYBR* in 2011, the themes and lessons would still have some pertinent value. Since most Black people, especially men, do not read, the odds of educating them through literature would be more challenging than I had ever imagined, but I was determined to attempt to effect change "by whatever means necessary."

To my amazement, I was able to create a 594-page novel in my first attempt at writing. Although all of the characters in my book did not glorify God, it was the talents and gifts that God blessed me with that enabled me to accomplish such an achievement. There is no question that the discipline, patience and perseverance that I learned in the Army established the necessary foundation for me to begin and finish a task that, at times, I thought was too difficult to complete. The business management curriculum and instructors at Saginaw Valley State University (SVSU) prepared me for the research and organizational skills necessary for such an endeavor. The most credit has to be given to the English instructors at SVSU, which I mentioned in an earlier chapter. There was one particular instructor who was determined to ensure that I became proficient in English. This instructor provided all of the students with the opportunity to compose papers on a wide selection of topics that were interesting and intellectually challenging. I always selected topics that dealt with societal issues, such as welfare reform, apartheid in South Africa, exploitation of Black athletes, personal life and death experiences, and numerous other thought-provoking issues. It was during this time that my passion for writing and social issues emerged and became relevant to me. There is no question that the instruction that I received at SVSU enabled me to methodically create my first novel.

Believe me, when I say that money was not the motivating factor for writing *LYBR*. I am still operating at a loss from my first novel, and I can honestly say that I gave away close to 20 percent of all the books that I purchased to sell. Writing is a form of art that allows the creator to communicate their view of life to others. As with any other passion, it would be marvelous if I could be compensated for doing what I love to do. Yet, I think it is more fulfilling when you are motivated to do something because you want to make a positive impact on the lives of others. The primary purpose of *LYBR* was to provide Black high school students with a glimpse of reality before they made the transition to adulthood and corporate America. How could money be the motivating factor when my primary concern was to attempt to educate my young brothers and sisters about reality? I wanted to prevent them from living the rest of their lives wishing someone had told them what to expect and helped them to be prepared for the future. For me, money is not the most important thing in the world; knowledge is. With knowledge, wealth is attainable.

During certain low times in my life, *LYBR* was the hope that made tomorrow brighter, even when I did not believe it. I learned that when you have a goal that you are striving for, the trials and tribulations that you face may be insignificant in comparison to your goal. Throughout my ordeals with unemployment, government employment and other jobs that only paid me enough to pay some of my bills, my determination to complete *LYBR* motivated me to persevere. I had one dream, and that was to complete my first novel. It is difficult to determine what will sustain a person until they are able to crawl out of the valleys in his or her life. For some people, it is their children, spouse, family, job, addictions, money or a vast array of things that sustain them until they reach their destination. *Last Year Before Reality* definitely sustained me.

Getting Published

It took a total of ten years to write and finally have *LYBR* published. In comparison to the process of getting it published, writing the novel was the easiest part. When I first started writing it, I never thought it would take ten years. Since I was new at writing and did not know anyone who had successfully completed such a feat, I was unaware of all of the responsibilities of writing a book. I thought I would be able to write a book and publishing companies would be honored to publish it. I thought wrong!

Most, if not all, publishing companies will not accept unsolicited manuscripts. This means that they will not accept a manuscript from anyone except an agent. If you do not have an agent, they will not accept or review your work. Finding an agent to represent you is difficult if you are a first-time author. There are exceptions to this rule, but I was not one of them. At the time, I did not have an editor, so the sample chapters I sent to agents were not of the caliber that would draw the interest of established agents. In addition, *LYBR* was not the type of material that an agent could aggressively market to White publishing companies. Agents are in the business to earn a living, and they usually earn anywhere from 10 to 20 percent of the contract they secure for the author. If you cannot convince them that you have a book worthy of their time and effort, they are not going to sacrifice their time. Just as a sports agent will not represent the twelfth man on a Division II College basketball team, an agent will not represent a new player in the writing game, and that was me. During my quest to find an agent to represent me, I received so many rejection letters that I stopped opening them. I would have someone else read the depressing news. Just like when you are looking for a job. It is not the 99 "No's" that you receive, but the 1 "Yes" that will make the difference.

Since I could not secure an agent, a publishing company was out of the question. White men own most of the well-established publishing companies. As in many other areas of life in the United States, White men are in control. For an agent to successfully market a book to a publishing company, the agent has to convince a White editor, in many cases, that the book will be successful. Unless the book has the potential to be well received and/or profitable, the publishing company is not going to risk the money for marketing, distribution, and other associated costs on an unknown Black author. There are some Black and independent publishing companies available, but without an agent, it is difficult to approach them, also.

The bottom line in the book publishing business, and any other business is profit. If a White publishing company thinks it can make a substantial profit from a book by a Black author, the company will publish it. Today, there are a number of successful Black authors who are published by White publishing companies. I did not write *LYBR* to appeal to White publishing companies. In addition, it is very seldom that first-time writers obtain success with their first book. If I am not mistaken, Walter Mosley's first novel, *Gone Fishin*, was not successful until after his second book, *A Devil In A Blue Dress* became popular. Terry McMillian did not receive acclaim with her first two books. It seems that it was not until *Waiting To Exhale* became successful that she received recognition and established an audience for her previous work.

Finally, the numerous rejections that I received from agents, publishing companies, and Black writing organizations took a toll. For two years, I had *LYBR* stored away, along with my dream of being a published author. Then one day, I allowed two people to read my manuscript and they convinced me to continue to pursue having it published.

Once I sent the completed manuscript to the Library of Congress to have it copyrighted, a number of publishing companies contacted me. One company wanted to charge me $33,575 to have it published. They were going to handle every facet of book publishing, from production to marketing. If I had that type of money sitting around, I would have been doing my writing in the Bahamas or Jamaica, instead of Detroit in the dead of winter.

After comparing self-publishing companies, I decided to go with Xlibris Corporation. The self-publishing deal they offered was unbeatable. The employees on their staff were extremely helpful in assisting me with every facet of having *LYBR* published. The cost was less than $700. Since it was a print-on-demand service, I only had to pay for the books that I ordered. Finally in March 2001, I became a published author. I did not say a wealthy author, but a published author.

Business Perspective

It never crossed my mind when I decided to write a book that I was actually creating a product that I was going to sell to consumers. Therefore, I was now in the book selling business as well, and it was my job to sell my product. This is one of the biggest disadvantages of not having the support of an agent and publishing company. Not only did I have the responsibility of writing the book, I had to perform all of the other important phases of operating a successful business.

If I knew then what I know now, I would have definitely attempted to approach my first book from a different perspective. For people who want to be successful authors, or successfully sell any product, there are some pertinent questions that need to be answered before you begin.

The first question I should have asked myself was, "What is my reason for writing this book?" Most writers do not think about that. I was only concerned with providing a book that was both educational and entertaining. Today, with the high cost of living, not very many authors have the opportunity to write for the sheer pleasure of it, unless they have a full-time job or another significant source of income. Too many hours went into *LYBR* for me to have only considered it to be a hobby. Time is money. I do not have the time to invest in anything that I will not reap from financially or have an opportunity to provide knowledge for others.

I should have determined my market before I started *LYBR*. It is important to know what segment of society would be willing to pay for your book. You have to consider whether or not your book/product has a viable market. Would you get rich selling heaters in hell? I don't think so. When I decided to write *LYBR*, I should have seriously thought about who would actually read it. It is a proven fact that most of the Black people who are avid readers are Black women. The average Black man does not read. In addition, a large number of Black males in high school and college do not read unless it is required reading. Based on statistics, *LYBR* was doomed to fail from its conception because the audience that I was attempting to reach does not exist. Had I thought about it, I probably would have never written *LYBR*.

Another important element to consider is a support staff. When I started *LYBR*, a friend sacrificed countless hours assisting with editing. After a while, it is difficult for someone to invest time in your dream when they are not sure if you will be able to compensate them. Having an editor is definitely important if you have not mastered the mechanics of English and grammar. Today, English grammar is something that I still have not mastered. When I am in a writing/creative zone, I do not have time to think about the correct tense of verbs or the components of a basic, complete sentence. I am concerned with forging ideas and therefore, allow an editor to handle the technical aspects of editing the book.

The last phase of selling a book is getting it to your audience. Without the support of an agent or publishing company, I had to handle distribution and marketing myself. Because of work responsibilities, I was not able to aggressively market it to all of the people and businesses that might have been interested. I had a Website created to advertise *LYBR*, but a large number of Black people do not have access to the Internet, therefore, the number of people I could have reached through that medium was limited. I attempted to advertise through the mail and with fliers, but without a support team and investment capital, it is difficult for first-time authors to get the sales and exposure that is necessary to be successful.

Frustrations

Since the targeted market of *LYBR* was high school students, I sent letters to superintendents of urban schools across the United States, informing them of my book. I never received a response from any of them. On my second attempt, I sent letters to principals of urban high schools throughout Michigan and other states with a majority Black student enrollment. Only two principals requested a book, and I did not receive a response from them after they received the book. Having been educated in the public school system and having taught in it briefly, there is no question that *LYBR* would have been a valuable tool for learning. It is ironic that in Fowlerville, MI, the school board voted to recommend *Whale Talk* by Chris Crutcher into their high school English classes. This book was centered around the same theme as *LYBR*. It dealt with racism and also contained profanity. A student defended the book by stating, "This is the language of our lives. I hear this language day in and day out. Even though it's not appropriate, it's a fact. Most students I talked to can connect with this book."[1] Why is it that a rural school district is open-minded and exercises diversity in their choices of reading materials for their students, and urban school districts are not?

In addition, I sent letters to a number of Historically Black Colleges and Universities (HBCUs), requesting that *LYBR* be considered for African-American Literature courses. I also sent letters to various public and private universities, nationwide. Professor Henry Louis Gates Jr., Chairman of the Department of Afro-American Studies at Harvard University was one of the few professors who exhibited professionalism and courtesy by responding to my inquiry/solicitation. Although it was not the letter that I was hoping for, it was still an honor for a highly respected and distinguished professor to take the time to address my letter. It does not cost anything to show courtesy and professionalism, but it is apparent that everyone does not possess these qualities. Another person who has always exhibited professionalism is Omar Tyree, who is the prominent Black author who wrote *Fly Girl, A Do Right Man* and *The Diary of a Groupee,* along with, several other books. Any time I wrote or called him for advice, he was always available. Even in the storms of frustration, there were people there willing to offer me assistance.

As always, my greatest frustration during my marketing campaign was from my dealings with our people. Black people will spend $150 on a pair of gym shoes for their children and in excess of $200 for electronic game systems, but will not buy them a book that could assist and prepare them for the future. I know several Black parents, personally, who just refused to buy a book for their children. I wish parents would buy books for their children and not allow their children's mind to be influenced by television, movies, video games, and the ills of society. All I can do is shake my head in disbelief as they continue to allow their children to learn about life in inappropriate ways instead of being exposed to life through a book first.

Some parents have actually told me the following, "My son does not like to read." I wanted to ask, "Did you say that your son does not like to breathe?" Children under the age of 18 whose parents are still providing food, clothing, shelter, and the other necessities of life should not be given a choice when it comes to reading. The only choice the child should have is when he or she wants to move out and support himself or herself. When did children obtain the right to tell parents what they are and aren't going to do and still have the ability to sit down or chew their food? Somewhere between 1983 and 2003, some parents have relinquished their rights and responsibilities of being a parent. My conclusion is that either some Black parents do not have a clue about what is awaiting their children or they just don't care.

One parent, a Black man in an allegedly prominent position, purchased a book from me and read it. He said it was good, but it was too coarse for his high school aged son to read. I thought to myself— *What on earth is he talking about?* I had this discussion with him in 2002. The content of *LYBR* is a nursery bedtime story in comparison to what is happening in high schools today. Take a moment to reflect on high school events and tragedies that have occurred in recent years: the Columbine High School massacre; students caught in the act of engaging in sexual activities; students hitting/terrorizing teachers; parents beating up teachers. The list is endless. It was apparent that this particular Black man was oblivious to what has been happening in the real world. As history continues to prove, we are our own worst enemy.

The Next Time

I have learned that it is failure, and not success, that is the best teacher. Every aspect of *LYBR* has taught me, not only how to be a better writer, but a better person as well. By learning from my mistakes, I have finally become a successful writer, and I am able to provide the aspiring first-time writer with some guidance on the do's and don'ts of writing a book. Writing *LYBR* was like a failed first marriage. You learn so much the first time; the chances for success are greater the second time around.

This time around, I knew what to do. My first step was to accurately assess my targeted market. The profanity and length of *LYBR* were immediate turn-offs for the primary market I was trying to reach. The profanity discouraged parents from buying it for their high school children, and the length discouraged anyone, other than avid readers, from reading it. Since I eliminated what I thought were the two major negative deterrents that existed with *LYBR*, I will be able to market this book to any Black organization, school, parent or person who really wants to know "the rules of the game," and not learn the rules through trial and error, like I did.

When it comes to advertising, I am going to use the Internet, radio, television (local/public access, initially), newspapers, magazines, and any other advertising means that I can afford to promote. As for selling, I will emulate the aggressive marketing techniques used by authors and other successful business people. Many other authors sold their books out of the trunks of their cars and went to every hair salon and barbershop that they could. I will have books available at every ethnic festival, convention, expo and any other event that Black people attend. To take it to another level, I will have book sale representatives. If cable companies, religious groups, insurance agents and others can go from door to door, then I can do the same. In America, it is all about a successful marketing campaign and excellent product. I am selling knowledge, and this time, I am going to do it right.

With *LYBR*, I did not approach it with business acumen. This time, I will be selective about when I distribute promotional copies of books. Although nothing is free in America, I wanted to do everything within my power to enlighten others. I did not realize how costly my endeavor could be. Every time I gave a person a book first, I had to almost hunt the person down in order to receive compensation. Most of the time, I just wrote it off as a loss and learned by my mistake.

For those of you who are aspiring to be successful authors, I strongly suggest that you follow, or at least consider, all of the steps that I have defined. Writing a book is primarily about business. Before an agent or publishing company will even consider exhibiting interest in your book, you have to establish your own clientele. If it were easy to become a successful author, everyone would write a book. It is also better not to publicize that you are writing a book. If people know you are writing one, they will continue to inquire about when you are going to finish. It only puts additional pressure on you. Always keep life in perspective when you are writing a book. If you are not getting paid to do it, then do not sacrifice the time you could be sharing with your loved ones in the interest of chasing a dream. It is all right to have goals and dreams, but make sure they are reasonable and attainable and that the sacrifice you make will be worth it in the long run.

Here is more important information that you will thank me for. Always keep pen and paper close to you. I do not care if you are in bed, in the bathroom, driving, walking or anything else, have pen and paper available. Thoughts and ideas will enter and exist your mind and they may never appear again. It is important to write them down immediately. I use 5" X 7" index cards to write down all my thoughts. When cards are not available, I write on anything in my reach, ie. napkins, paper bags, church bulletins, cardboard, etc. Before I start typing on the computer, I categorize the written thoughts in relation to the particular chapter.

Also, always keep a printed copy and three computer disks of all your book material. Whether or not you believe in "Murphy's Law," it does exist. One of the worst things that can happen to a writer is for some terrible reason the chapter he or she just created gets deleted or lost. It is a sick feeling when you know you cannot re-create the original chapter again. If you are on a computer, make sure you save your information periodically to the hard drive and to disks. Each time you save the information to the disk, remove the disk until you are ready to save additional information. The reason I take the disk out is because you never know when your hard drive may crash or require serious maintenance, which could damage the disk. Just in case it does, you still have your information saved on a disk. I also keep disks and hardcopies of chapters in different locations. Fortunately, I have never experienced any of the incidents that I described above, but I still practice the same rituals just in case.

In addition, do not set unrealistic deadlines. If it takes more time than anticipated to prepare the best book possible to a publishing company, it is worth the additional time. Having a book published prematurely will cause an inferior product to be on the market. It will be more expensive to have it revised. Be patient and take your time. Once you allow an inferior book to get on the market, your credibility and the good reputation you are attempting to establish will be in jeopardy.

The most important advice I can give to any aspiring writer is not to expect to receive support from anyone. If you start writing your book with the idea that it is "you against the world," you will not be disappointed. Once you have a completed manuscript, then you will have something to bargain with, and you can begin to seek the aid of an agent or publishing company. The time and effort that you use to solicit an agent could be used to complete your book or to negotiate the best possible deal with a self-publishing company. Make sure you do the research to find out if there is a need or demand for your book. If not, you will be writing a book for your own personal satisfaction. That is not a bad thing, but if you truly want to be a successful writer and get paid, you have to create a book that will be commercially successful and enable you to develop a reputation and establish an audience. Until that happens, do not quit your day job. Starving artists usually starve to death.

Chapter 10

ENTREPRENEURSHIP

*"Though thy beginning was small, yet they latter end should
greatly increase."*

—Job 8:7

The ultimate goal in my life is to operate a successful business.
I am sure this has been the goal of many people and, unfortunately, it
has eluded many. Entrepreneurship is the mobilization of resources
to take advantage of an opportunity to provide customers with new or
improved goods and services.[1] Operating your own business is
extremely risky and challenging, but it is just as rewarding if you are
successful in achieving that dream. There are some questions you
should ask yourself beforehand:

- What do I like to do?
- What am I able to do well?
- Is there a need for the things I like to do and I am able to do well?
- Would people pay me for providing these goods or services?

There were many reasons why I desired to become an entrepreneur.
As you have already learned from this book, my continuous defiance of
authority and low tolerance for most things left me with very few career

choices. Doing anything that could have possibly landed me in the penal system was certainly out of the question. I hope that everyone reading this book will abstain from any illegal activity that would result in incarceration. There are far too many of our brothers and sisters in prison. It should be a "no-brainer"—you must be free to be productive and make a difference or effect positive change for our race.

Independence

At an early age, everyone should be able to determine if they possess the qualities of a leader or a follower. I have always considered myself a leader and independent thinker. Of course, as a child, I had to repress my natural instinct to be an independent thinker and learn how to follow instructions and receive direction. Although I did not follow directions very well, I did work at disciplining myself. Before you can become an effective leader, you have to be a disciplined follower.

In corporate America and government, there are not many opportunities to think independently or have your opinions valued when you are in an entry-level or non-management position. It is difficult to be an independent thinker when you work for someone else. If you question a decision that is made, you will be considered rebellious, disloyal, and not a team player, and find that you have fewer opportunities to speak your mind.

Being an entrepreneur allowed me to be independent and make my own decisions. When you operate your own business, you alone, determine if it will be successful. For me, this meant the end of working for what I considered to be incompetent managers who received their jobs because they were a part of the "Good Ole' Boys Network," and beneficiaries of the "isms": Racism; Cronyism; Sexism; Nepotism; Favoritism. If incompetence were reflected in anyone's work performance in my company, I would be solely accountable. Independence is what most people strive for, but many do not obtain it. You may assume all of the risks as an entrepreneur, but you also reap the benefits associated with successful endeavors.

Maximum Potential

Most likely, if you work for someone else, you will not reach your maximum potential, which means using every gift, talent, or skill to the best of your ability. As I reflect on my work history, I remember working in positions where reaching my maximum potential was definitely not likely to happen. There is no question that I had the ability to perform the jobs of the people who supervised me, but I was not given the opportunity. This may have partially been due to my inability to fully comply with the views of authority figures, and/or my lack of self-discipline concerning my thoughts and views on company operations. But being my own boss allowed me to utilize all my knowledge, skills, and abilities.

Some people will exploit you for their own motives and personal gain. Other people will not allow you to be the best you can be because of their ego, pride, and job security. They would rather pay you a limited, usually unfair salary to come to work, sit idly by, and pass your life away. I have no problem getting up at 4:00 A.M. to work at my own business, but it is difficult to motivate myself to get up that early for someone else's cause. As an entrepreneur, it can be extremely gratifying to know that everything you do is solely because it will benefit you and your customers. To be financially successful, you have to be multi-faceted. If you are complacent and afraid, you will never reach your maximum potential.

Racism and Corruption

One of my greatest motivations for wanting to become an entrepreneur was to escape racism. The truth of the matter is that race still matters, even if you operate your own business. It must be a consideration when it comes to your marketing approach, development of your customer base, business affiliations, and securing financial support.

While companies today may be willing to do business with you if you can convince them of the profitability of your product or service, race still matters. White people generally prefer to do business with other White people, unless the minority business owner is offering a service or product at a price so low that a White business owner cannot possibly compete. As always, there are exceptions to the rule.

"Other cultures are told when they come to America to open a business in the Black community because Blacks do not shop with each other by and large; they would rather shop with anybody else but themselves."[2] Even today, some Black people are conditioned to believe that a White man's ice is colder than a Black man's ice.

A desire to escape corruption is another reason why I left corporate America and government. It is unbelievable what people in power can get away with. Take the White executives at Kmart and Enron for example. The corruption that occurred at both of those corporations caused thousands of people to lose their jobs and life savings. There is no way I want to be a part of events/situations that destroy people's livelihood.

Implement Your Vision

Minority-owned businesses should not remain an underutilized resource in America. "And African Americans are the group most likely to become entrepreneurs. Black men between 25 and 35 with some graduate school work start more businesses than any other group in the country, according to the Kauffman Foundation."[3] Although the greatest revenues are generated by Asian-owned companies, Hispanics operate more of their own businesses than any other minority group. According to the U.S. Small Business Administration, the total number of self-employed African Americans, Hispanics, and Asians is about 2.2 million.[1] Minority groups need to pursue their dreams of being entrepreneurs in order to make money which can generate wealth for their people.

The main reason I wanted to be an entrepreneur was so I could implement my own vision. My vision is to provide a work environment for employees, that is free of the many "isms" that plagued all of the other places in which I have worked. My business would be a place where hard work, teamwork, integrity, equality, commitment, and excellence are not only encouraged but practiced from upper management to entry-level employees, with individuals being awarded on merit. There was a time in America when companies were loyal to their employees and the allegiance was reciprocated by employees. Employees were appreciated, valued, and treated like they were a part of the company. Unfortunately, most of these kinds of companies no longer exist today. The primary goal of corporations is to make a profit for stockholders. A safe work environment, job security for employees and decent wages are things of the past. In my opinion, the present vision of corporate America and government is not beneficial to the working person. Greed is what motivates most businesses in the 21st century. If American businesses could implement slavery again, they would probably do so immediately. However, they have found an alternative, which is to move business operations and jobs to other countries where workers can be paid sub-standard wages. The vision of most American corporations is to continue to make rich people richer and pay the workers as little as possible.

Employment Opportunities

It would truly be a blessing to be able to provide my people employment opportunities. There are too many young Black people who are unemployed because we have not started enough of our own companies to provide jobs and/or career opportunities. Every other race in America provides jobs for their people. We need more successful Black people to step up and make a significant contribution toward the success of our people.

My goal is to meet the challenge of providing jobs for our people. There are countless Black people who have the money, skills, and connections to start a business, but they lack the courage, ambition, determination, and passion to help less fortunate people. If the true leaders, who are blessed with the talents to be entrepreneurs would pursue their true calling, doors of opportunity would open for the people who just want to work. There were several jobs I held and could have kept until it was time to retire. I knew there was more for me elsewhere, so I allowed those jobs to be a blessing to someone else. These positions were simply stepping stones for me to realize my true calling, since I was able to gain knowledge and experience from them. I will be successful, and that will be evidenced by my ability to provide opportunities for others.

Dream Job

Can you imagine having a job that you enjoy and would do, even if you were not getting paid? That is my definition of a "dream job." I think athletes have dream jobs. Some athletes receive millions of dollars a year doing something that they would do for free. My dream job would be to help other people make it in life. I constantly think about developing and implementing plans to benefit others. I hope everyone reading this book will think about what his or her dream job is and implement a strategy to one day bring it to fruition. I remember, on too many occasions, going to work because I had bills to pay. When you have a dream job, you do not even consider it work. Owning my own company or doing what I love to do would be a dream come true.

Being an entrepreneur is not as easy as I may make it sound. If it were, more people would be working for themselves. Most people do not have what it takes, or they are reluctant or afraid to act on their calling. Everybody does not have the desire to own his or her own business. There are many risks, sacrifices, responsibilities, and drawbacks to being an entrepreneur.

Lacking Skills

One of the most essential elements necessary to be a successful entrepreneur is having the necessary skills. If you lack the skills, failure will be eminent. Consider this hypothetical situation. Let's say I want to own a business flying private airplanes. The first problem would be that I do not know anything about airplanes. Secondly, I do not know how to fly one. In order for my business to be successful, I would have to employ pilots and other skilled/qualified individuals to efficiently operate the business. That is why it is imperative that you, or your partner/support person in the endeavor, have the knowledge and skills necessary to operate the business until you establish your customer base and are able to hire the essential people to operate the business efficiently. Entrepreneurs need to be risk takers with healthy self-esteem and a confident attitude to step out into a new venture. They have to believe in themselves and their ability even when others don't. Basic knowledge and an understanding of accounting principles are necessary. Entrepreneurs must be aware of their assets, liabilities, and expenses, as well as the difference between the three. Communication skills are needed to effectively interact with internal and external customers. A basic understanding of supply and demand as it relates to the product or service you provide is invaluable. Research and analysis skills are necessary for making comparisons and studying the market trends for similar products and services which may currently be on the market. The research can also reveal where others succeeded and/or failed in your area of business.

Investment Capital

It takes money to make money. One of the greatest barriers to becoming an entrepreneur is the lack of investment capital. Depending upon the business, the money needed for start-up costs can be as low as $100 or as much as $100,000, if not more. It is important to have excellent credit, should you need to secure a loan to get your business started. Your individual credit rating tends to be viewed as a reflection of your character and integrity. However, excellent credit is still not a guarantee for receiving a loan or capital funding if you are a minority. It is a known fact that minorities encounter greater difficulties in acquiring funding for businesses in comparison to White business owners. "Latino—and Black-owned businesses get rejected for bank loans nearly twice as often as White-owned companies, according to the Federal Reserve."[5] Minorities are also charged higher interest rates in addition to being denied credit more often than White entrepreneurs. Using personal credit cards should be a last resort because it can be costly, although about half of small businesses use credit cards to finance their start-up or expansion. It is important to start saving now if you are seriously thinking about becoming an entrepreneur.

Keep Your Day Job

Before you quit your day job, make sure your business is operating and profitable. Some people have a tendency to step too far out on faith, and fall hard because of the lack of common sense and preparation. If you start a business that will fluctuate due to seasonal peaks, like landscaping or home improvement, steady and full-time employment will guarantee you regular income. Depending on the business you are operating, you may be able to employ people to work for you while you are still working your full-time job. In addition, having a spouse who has a full-time job may keep you from suffering financial hardship during the off-peak season.

Keeping your current job before starting a business is usually a safer move for other reasons also. You have the opportunity to build up a clientele while maintaining a steady income. Health care costs and expenses can be covered by your current job or your spouse's job. In a fluctuating economy, success is not always inevitable, even with the most brilliant ideas. You will still have your current job to fall back on if things don't go well for the business. Sacrificing current full-time employment may be a better choice for some entrepreneurs starting out, but this option should be carefully considered.

Know Your Clientele

In today's economy, people are becoming more conservative with their spending habits. As an entrepreneur, you have to know if your service or product is a necessity or a luxury item for your clientele. Most Black people's spending habits are different from most White people's habits. If your targeted market is Black people, you have to know our spending priorities. It is not wise to develop a product or service before you consider if people will purchase it. You should be asking yourself the reasons that people need your product and service.

You also need to look at the characteristics of those people to see how to market your product/service to stimulate the greatest possible demand. For minorities marketing to others in the same minority group, e.g. women, Black men and/or Black women, etc., there may be an advantage.

Become A Legitimate Business

A number of entrepreneurs start businesses without completing the steps to be recognized as a legitimate, formally established business. The first and most significant step is to file the necessary paperwork to designate the type of business that you are forming, such as: Sole Proprietor; Partnership; Limited Liability Corporation; S-Corporation; Corporation. There are advantages and disadvantages associated with each business classification, and you should investigate each classification to determine which is best suited to your business. One advantage to becoming a licensed business includes the option of being able to separate your personal financial liability from your business liability, which provides personal protection from bankruptcy and lawsuits against your business. Another advantage is that you are able to deduct the operating expenses for your business on your income taxes. There are a number of expenses affiliated with becoming a legally established business, but the costs will be worth it in the long run. For those who desire to start a business that requires a state license, it is to your advantage to obtain those licenses. Individuals, as well as other businesses, are more willing to do business with a legitimate company that is properly licensed and insured.

Business Planning

A clear business plan is the first major task to be completed when starting a business. The initial step, as mentioned previously, is to identify the product/service to be provided and the customers/demand for the business. The next step is the strategic plan, which should consist of a SWOT analysis. The SWOT analysis looks at the feasibility of the business idea by examining the Strengths (S),

Weaknesses (W), Opportunities (O), and Threats (T). If you are not familiar with a SWOT analysis, you should postpone starting your business until you learn more about this valuable assessment tool. After you do a SWOT analysis, you may decide not to become an entrepreneur, to change the service or product that you are planning to provide, or to change your approach to the venture altogether.

When I decided to become an entrepreneur and book writer, I did not complete a SWOT analysis. If I had taken it into consideration, I would not have attempted to be a writer or an entrepreneur with the business I had in mind. To illustrate this analysis, I will quickly perform the SWOT for the idea of a minority operating a "Dollar Store" in the city of Detroit:

Strengths:

1. Market niche—Black owned company in a predominantly Black urban city.
2. Good location—8 Mile and Wyoming; the border of two predominantly Black communities.
3. Retail experience—Know how to control inventory and provide customer service.
4. Good price—All items a dollar. Items affordable in difficult economic times.

Weaknesses:

1. Lack initial investment capital.
2. Competition—dollar store two blocks down the street.
3. Distributors only do business with large franchises.
4. Black people think dollar items offered by White and Chaldean people are better quality.

Opportunities:

1. Start a franchise.
2. Provide employment opportunities.

3. Provide a source to generate wealth in a Black urban community.
4. Give back to the Black community—Set an example for future entrepreneurs.

Threats:

1. Operation expenses (i.e. start up inventory, cost of leasing building, etc.)
2. High business taxes.
3. Lack of patronage.
4. Competition from new dollar stores or other competitors.

Once I complete the above SWOT analysis, I can then determine if a dollar store would be a worthwhile investment. Even if the above information proves to be accurate, I would still need a business plan, which entails a mission statement, vision, short and long-term goals, and the investment capital needed to facilitate the success of my business. Please remember that prior to the implementation of all of the above, you need to exhibit initiative, determination, enthusiasm, diligence, perseverance, and a belief in your dream to facilitate success in your approach. Also remember that these qualities will not automatically materialize just because you decided to become an entrepreneur. I had to develop those qualities before I went into business. Without the right attitude, you will be a hindrance to the success of your own business.

Research

Before you invest time, energy or money into anything, make sure you perform the research that is necessary. In the 21st century research material is easily accessible in a variety of sources. On the Internet, there are several Internet Service Providers (ISPs) that have links to all forms of businesses. There are magazines that cater exclusively to entrepreneurs and people who are interested in starting home businesses. *Fortune Small Business (FSB)* and *Inc.* are two highly reputable magazines. At most large bookstores, there are several books in the business section on how to start your own business. The first investment you make in your business should be for some type of research material.

Mistakes of Others

In life, there is an unwritten rule that you should learn from your mistakes. But a wise person also learns from the mistakes of others. As stated previously, the mission of this book is to provide you with knowledge, which includes specific details of mistakes I have made and lessons I have learned, as a means of helping you to avoid some of the same negative and unnecessary experiences. If you are an honest person with integrity, morals and Christian beliefs, please do not expect all the people you do business with to possess the same qualities. Some people go into business with the intention of trying to exploit you for your goods and services. That is why it is imperative, in some cases, for contracts to be signed or payments made in installments as services and products are provided. A business can actually go bankrupt due to one of their primary clients failing to pay their bills on time.

Also remember that you go into business to make money, not to become a charity. No matter what service or product you are providing, it should not be given away. When it comes to business, it's about dollars and cents, not family and friends. Minorities should not expect handouts or something for free just because the person offering the good or service is in the same minority group. It is all right to barter or sell something at cost, but not for free. If you get into that habit, you will be out of business very soon.

Business Partners

If you do not remember anything else from this chapter, please remember to be extremely selective about who you choose as a business partner. I would not recommend that you go into business with someone with whom you are unequally yoked, meaning a person who does not have goals, habits, desires and thought processes that are similar to yours. It could be a difficult situation if you exhibit integrity and your business partner does not. For example, some people will attempt to make money by any means necessary, which could mean being dishonest or cheating customers by providing inferior products or services. It is inevitable that your different business approaches could lead to conflicts that result in the failure of your business.

When you first start your business, I would advise that you pursue the business alone unless the skills of the partner(s) are required for getting the business off the ground. Once you have established yourself with a steady profit, then you can hire people to assist you. It is almost impossible for other people to be as dedicated as you are to your dreams. While you may be motivated to start your business because of a passion, it may only be about the money with other people. Once there is no more money to be made, those people will be gone.

Lastly, I would like to offer this invaluable piece of advice. Before you go into business with anyone, try to get to know him or her personally. The way they treat their spouse, family, and friends will be the same way they will eventually treat you. If you notice that a person is manipulative, disrespectful or untrustworthy with a spouse, what makes you think they will show more allegiance to you? A snake will not bite you the first ten times you walk past it, but eventually it will bite you. "Once a snake, always a snake." Please be careful. What happens in the business association can have an impact on the relationship you have with the business partners as well. A business failure can easily lead to the end of the friendship, so you should consider that beforehand.

Chapter 11

SHARING KNOWLEDGE

"And they said one to another, We are verily guilty concerning our brother, in that we saw the anguish of his soul, when he besought us, and we would not hear."

—Gen 42:21

The ability to obtain knowledge and use it to your advantage is an art in itself. Knowledge applies to facts or ideas acquired by study, investigation, observation, or experience.[1] Throughout my life, I have had the opportunity to grasp an abundance of knowledge through numerous sources. As far back as I can remember, I have been exposed to a vast array of information, experiences and events which have been both negative and positive. This began my accumulation of knowledge. The primary source was definitely the extensive amount of literature I have read over the years. My family, friends, co-workers, and adversaries have provided knowledge through interaction and my observations of their words and actions. Finally, I have to give credit to the people I have obtained knowledge from who I did not have the opportunity to know up close and personal. To a degree, these individuals influence the way some of us think and act because they are in the spotlight and admired because of their fame. There is no question that people in sports, music, politics, the movie industry, religion, and television (news, sitcoms, etc.) are other sources of knowledge. I am sure that everyone reading this has been exposed to all of the circumstances, people, and experiences that I have listed above. But your analysis may be formatted differently than mine. It is said that, "Wisdom is the application of knowledge." It is also said that wisdom comes from God. Knowledge does allow a person to become wise. The question is what are you wise about? In all honesty, I consider myself to be a "jack of all trades and a master of none." After obtaining a Bachelor's Degree in Business Administration from SVSU and a Master's Degree from the "School Of Hard Knocks," I think I finally have something to share. It is the knowledge from my collection of experiences that I will share to aid others in avoiding some major mistakes. Some will also benefit from the good decisions I have made and use that knowledge to assist them in making a better living with less drama and fewer issues. As always, knowing the rules of the game before the game begins, definitely will give you an advantage in the game of life.

Literature

The most profound book I have ever read was the King James version of the Holy Bible. Even though the Bible has a more sacred meaning in my life than literature, for this illustration I will consider it literature. Bible is commonly referred to as an acronym for "**B**asic **I**nstructions **B**efore **L**eaving **E**arth." There are 66 books in the Bible and all of them provide knowledge about life that will help anyone who wants to lead a more productive and peaceful life. For the atheists and agnostics, the books of Proverbs and Ecclesiastes provide knowledge concerning everyday life. For those who believe that Jesus Christ is our Lord and Savior, the entire Bible provides knowledge on how to live a more spiritual life and how to avoid the tactics of satan. There is no doubt that if I had applied Biblical knowledge to every aspect of my life beginning with the day I graduated from high school, I would not have written this book; or the book would have delivered a different message.

In order to know where you are going, you have to know where you came from. After reading the Bible, I recommend the list of books below. As Frederick Douglas said, "Knowledge is power." The first book I would recommend is *The Destruction of Black Civilization* by Chancellor Williams. In this book, Mr. Williams explains in detail the events, which occurred in Africa that caused Africa to descend from the most powerful continent in the world to what it is today. The next book I recommend is *From Slavery to Freedom: A History of Negro Americans* by John Hope Franklin. This book covers our ancestors in Africa, the slave trade, and the struggles of Black people up to the Black Revolution of the 1960's. To receive a better understanding of America before the coming of the White man, I would recommend *The Last Americans* by William Brandon. This book explains in vivid detail how the land of the United States was taken from the Native Americans and why they are in the predicament they are in at this time in the 21st century. I nearly missed listing *The Mis-Education of the Negro* by Carter G. Woodson. The title speaks for itself. For better insight into financial matters I would strongly recommend *Wealth Management: Merging Faith with Finance* by Ellis N. Liddell.

The most influential book I have read to date would have to be *The Autobiography of Malcolm X*. This book gives the best understanding of what a Black man experiences in his attempt to be a man in this country. Next I would recommend, *Black Labor, White Wealth,* by Claud Anderson, Ed. D. This book explains vividly how White people for centuries have profited from the labor of Black people and are still profiting in the 21st century. *Two Nations: Black and White, Separate, Hostile, Unequal,* by Andrew Hacker, who is a White author, will re-affirm the knowledge that was given in the other books for Black people who do not believe something unless a White man says or writes it. These are just a few of the books I have read over the years.

Each book listed and others provided me with knowledge that reinforced and strengthened the knowledge I had previously. Once you obtain knowledge, it becomes yours. It would be an injustice for me not to attempt to list the other writers who have provided me with knowledge and also inspired me to write. They include Maya Angelou, Alice Walker, Nikki Giovanni, Toni Morrison, Terry McMillian, Sister

Souljah, James Baldwin, Richard Wright, Langston Hughes, Ralph Ellison, Donald Goines, Claude Brown, Walter Mosley, Omar Tyree and countless others.

If it is true that you are what you read, then there is no question that I am a Black man. There are a number of books by White authors that I have read, but Stephen King is my favorite. Everyday, we are bombarded with White people on television, movies, newspapers, and other media outlets. The only escape I have from White people is through Black literature. Reading has become my favorite leisure pastime. After I finish this book, I will take a hiatus from writing and read at least five books before I write again. Not only do I have a desire to acquire knowledge but also to share it.

Magazines

Over the years, magazines have been a significant source of knowledge and research material. It is important to know which magazines provide entertainment and which magazines provide knowledge. One of the best magazines that I have ever subscribed to was *Emerge*. This magazine did not pull any punches when it came to giving its subjective opinion on events that affected Black people. Unfortunately, it was discontinued. If you want to receive similar Black journalism, I would suggest *The Final Call*. Next, I have to say that *Essence, Ebony*, and *Black Enterprise* also provide knowledge that interests me. It is also important to read magazines that White people read as well. *Newsweek, Time, Fortune, Home Business, Money, Bloomberg Markets, Inc.*, and *Entrepreneur* are only a few out of the hundreds of magazines that mainly White people read for knowledge. It is important to be aware of what the competition is reading.

Newspapers

This is where the reader must beware. No matter what newspaper you read, the owner of the newspaper will make sure the writers and editors share their philosophies. Even though newspapers should provide unbiased news, most do not. Newspapers attempt to influence their readers' thinking through persuasive writing. Depending on the circulation of a newspaper, it will attempt to have an impact on all major events that occur in a city. Some newspapers attempt to convince readers to vote for certain candidates in elections. The owners and operators of most large newspapers are rich White men, who attempt to push the Republican agenda. Since Black journalists are few in number, the opinions of Black people are seldom heard. In most major cities there are Black-owned newspapers that employ predominately Black writers, but some of those newspapers cater to specific economic levels or social classes. In Detroit, *The Michigan Chronicle* and the *Michigan Citizen*, are the two most read, Black affiliated newspapers.

The primary motivation of newspaper owners is to make a profit and secondly to provide news and information. Newspaper editors use sensationalism to capture the attention of the average person, in order to persuade the person to buy it. Editors are extremely selective about when and what information will be printed. Some events are not published as soon as they occur. If an important event occurs and it will be detrimental to a powerful person or corporation in a certain city or state, the newspaper will not publish that story until it is given the authority to do so.

A large number of newspapers are unethical and lack integrity. Some will knowingly allow lies to be published in its newspaper, if the price is right. Newspapers are known to give a platform to politicians who blatantly lie about corruption, fraud, personal indiscretions, etc. Some newspapers attempt to vindicate a person, instead of allowing the legal system to do it. Journalist and editors are quite aware that if a lie is printed in a newspaper enough, it becomes the truth to the uninformed reader. A good lie is just as effective as the truth. An excellent example is the invasion of Iraq, which was predicated upon the existence of weapons of mass destruction. Yeah right! Do not believe the freedom of the press hype and also do not believe everything you read until you have researched the information for yourself.

A couple of newspapers in the Metropolitan Detroit area that appear not to have any allegiance to big business or influence from politicians are the *MetroTimes* and *The Spark*. Once a week, both of these newspapers publish whatever is on their writers' minds. They are determined to provide the truth for its readers and are not concerned about what others think.

Even though I placed literature before people as a source of knowledge, this does not mean that literature was my main source of knowledge. I focused attention on literature first in order to move on to more pertinent sources of knowledge.

Family, Friends, and Co-workers

As far back as I can remember—the age of five—I can recall my mental growth process. Since that time, family, friends, and co-workers have been instrumental in my pursuit of knowledge in some way, shape, or form.

While growing up in the 1970's and early 1980's, there was not an abundance of positive role models available for Black youths. Now, in 2004 Black youths can turn on the television, open the newspaper, read a book, or turn to a family member to look for positive inspiration. My motivation for success while I was growing up was to observe the most negative people I was exposed to and make it my lifetime goal to be the opposite of them. By focusing attention on being opposite of the negative influences, it increased the likelihood of me becoming a positive person. Regretfully, those negative role models were not White people. Even before I knew White people existed, it was the negative knowledge that I learned from my own people that began shaping my young mind. That is another story for another day.

Being the youngest of eight siblings and having an extended family of three siblings in Inkster, MI, I acquired knowledge of making an honest living in America from all of them. Their occupations varied from business owners, managers, and public service to many other occupations. My father's side of the family includes doctors, lawyer, judge, and other professions. There is no question that the knowledge was there, but during the important time periods in my life the accessibility was lacking.

Observing how close family members earned a living and what they did with the money they earned was interesting. It all comes down to how you utilize what you earn. Being financially astute is an extremely important factor in one's life. Another important factor is the type of lifestyle you live and your values system. Even today, I am sure some of my family members question the decisions I have made concerning my employment. Just like Black people are not monolithic, siblings are also not monolithic. Because all of us received different influences and knowledge in life, we all perceive life differently. The knowledge I have acquired throughout my life, does not permit me to earn a living the way they do. It is not about one sibling being right and the other sibling being wrong. It is about doing what you have to do, as long as you do not infringe or impose your beliefs, philosophies or ideologies on others. Throughout most of my experiences, which you are now aware, I stood alone. From an early age, I learned that if I was going to make it, it was going to be through my efforts alone. Along the way, I received various forms of assistance from all my siblings.

When it comes to the knowledge I acquired from friends and coworkers, it is endless. While it would be impossible to name all of the friends and co-workers who I have been fortunate and unfortunate to meet, I have learned something from each of them. All of them, friend or foe, young or old, rich or poor, have provided me with a large spectrum of knowledge. Throughout my life, I have traveled many roads with many people. The best thing about meeting a number of people up close and personal is that you can observe their failures and successes and learn from them. I have obtained a tremendous amount of knowledge from the mistakes and poor decisions of others. If I observe or hear about someone making a decision that was detrimental to them mentally, physically, and financially, I would make it a point not to make that same decision, if possible. In life, some people do not learn by the mistakes of others. They would rather learn the hard way. I hope to say that I have finally given up learning the hard way and now learn from other people. That is why I listen more and talk less.

My greatest source of knowledge comes from fellowshipping with my brothers and sisters in Christ. Having the opportunity to listen to others who have been through some of the same trials and tribulations that I have and giving all glory to God is incredible. My favorite days of the week are Wednesdays, Fridays and Sundays. This is when I can just sit back and absorb, as much knowledge as possible and one day be able to share it with others.

I will end this section of the chapter with an anonymous speech that I think sums up everything I have been trying to say:

THE COMPANY YOU KEEP

It Is Better To Be Alone, Than In The Wrong Company

Tell me who your best friends are, and I will tell you who you are. If you run with wolves, you will learn how to howl. But, if you associate with eagles, you will learn how to soar to great heights. "A mirror reflects a man's face, but what he is really like is shown by the kind of friends he chooses." The simple but true fact of life is that you become like those with whom you closely associate—for the good and the bad.

The less you associate with some people, the more your life will improve. Any time you tolerate mediocrity in others, it increases your mediocrity. An important attribute in successful people is their impatience with negative acting people. As you grow, your associates will change. Some of your friends will not want you to go on. They will want you to stay where they are. Friends that don't help you climb will want you to crawl. Your friends will stretch your vision or choke your dream. Those that don't increase you will eventually decrease you. Consider this:

- Never receive counsel from unproductive people.
- Never discuss your problems with someone incapable of contributing to the solution, because those who never succeed themselves are always first to tell you how. Not everyone has a right to speak into your life. You are certain to get the worst of the bargain when you exchange ideas with the wrong person.
- Don't follow anyone who's not going anywhere. With some people you spend an evening: with others you invest it.
- Be careful where you stop to inquire for directions along the road of life.
- Wise is the person who fortifies his life with the right friendships.

Author—Anonymous

Educators

It would be impossible for me to accumulate knowledge without giving credit to the people who have educated me so far through autobiographies, accomplishments, crusades, speeches, and other ways. These sources are too numerous to name everyone. So for all of you that I missed, please forgive me. Here are a few that come to mind:

Nat Turner, Harriet Tubman, Frederick Douglas, Nelson Mandela, Paul Robeson, Malcolm X, Marcus Garvey, M. Joycelyn Edlers, Louis Farrakhan, Herbert Ivory, Dallas A. Walker, Jr., Kenneth Farr, Samuel Davy, Oprah Winfrey, Professor Henry Louis Gates, Jr., Jesse Jackson, Professor Cornel West, George Curry, Tom Joyner, Judge Glenda Hatchett, Al Sharpton, Tavis Smiley, Les Brown, Michael Eric Dyson, Earvin "Magic" Johnson, Dave Bing, and T.D. Jakes.

Sports and Entertainment

How can I mention knowledge without naming some of the Black people from the entertainment world, who have contributed to my obtaining knowledge? Since there have probably been thousands of Black people in sports and entertainment over the years, it will be difficult to narrow down the individuals who have been the most influential in providing me with knowledge. I will attempt to keep it limited to fewer than 40 people:

Muhammad Ali, Jesse Owens, Sidney Poitier, Oprah Winfrey, Tommie Smith, Carlos Jones, Angela Bassett, Arthur Ashe, Althea Gibson, Bill Cosby, Ossie Davis, Dikembe Mutombo, Cheryl Miller, Spike Lee, Danny Glover, John Singleton, Ben Chauvis, Venus and Serena Williams, Denzel Washington, Isaiah Thomas, Anita Baker, Joe Dumars, Stevie Wonder, Tyler Perry, Chris Rock, Sean "P. Diddy" Combs, DMX, Tupac Shakur, Public Enemy, Charles Barkley, KRS-One, Third Eye Open, Jay-Z, Nas, Ice Cube, Queen Latifah, Lauryn Hill, Dave Chappelle, O.J. Simpsons, Michael Jackson, R. Kelly, and Kobe Bryant to name a few.

Politicians and Others

There are many resources for obtaining knowledge. Sometimes these sources are masked because of who they are. We do not recognize the fact that we listen to these people and our thinking and decisions are influenced by what they tell us. By definition, a politician is: one actively engaged in conducting the business of government. 2 a: a person engaged in party politics as a profession. b: a person primarily interested in political office for selfish or other narrow usually short-sighted reasons.[2] When you have the opportunity to relax, think about the politicians that you voted for. I will name some politicians, people affiliated with politicians, and radio personalities who have assisted me in learning more about politics:

Mayor Coleman A. Young, Senator John Conyers, Barbara Jordan, President Bill Clinton, Senator Hillary Clinton, Barack Obama, Ex-Michigan Governor John Engler, Michigan Governor Jennifer Granholm, Ex-Wayne County Executive Ed McNamara, Wayne County Prosecutor Kim Worthy, John Mason, Mildred Gaddis, President Ronald Reagan, President George Bush, Jr., Condoleeza Rice, Alan Keyes, Armstrong Williams, Senator Strom Thurman, Senator Trent Lott, Newt Gingrich, Rush Limbaugh, Clarence Thomas, Ward Connerly, David Duke, and this continues to grow.

*　　*　　*

Consequences and Repercussions

For in much wisdom is much grief:
and he that increaseth knowledge increaseth sorrow.
—Eccl. 1:18

There is no question that if I had not acquired all the knowledge that I have, my life would have taken a different direction. I had the opportunity to be financially successful in a number of the jobs mentioned earlier. If I was docile, complacent or possessed the ability to assimilate, I would have had twenty-one years seniority in the Army, or nineteen years at United Parcel Service, or sixteen years at Kmart, or thirteen years at Wayne County. My knowledge of our people and our struggles in this country prevented me from ignoring the injustices that I witnessed throughout my working career. The consequences and repercussions of being outspoken, defending my rights and the rights of other Black people have been costly. Along with my defiance of the power structure in this country came the sacrifice of financial stability, job security, a comfortable lifestyle, and material possessions. Those are the things in life for which people work and go to college to acquire.

One ironic thing about receiving the opportunity to choose my fate is that thousands of Black people never received the opportunities that I have. Throughout my life I have worked with or seen Black men and women who never raised their voice or a pen to threaten any White person in power in this country and they are still not given the opportunity to succeed. The only common denominator is our color. Regardless of whether you fight against racism or face it laying down, you will still be a victim of racism if you are Black. If I had it to do over, I would choose to fight racism head-on, instead of surrendering without a fight. By not trying to fight for your rights, you are guaranteed to lose.

I would rather suffer the consequences and repercussions of my own words and actions than be quiet and suffer from the words and actions of someone else. That is what happens when our people remain quiet and fail to vote. When you do not vote, you proxy that right to the White supremacists and Republicans in this country. Then you ask: What happened? And you complain about how things are managed or how the laws are affecting you. Well, you need to stand up and be counted. You have no right to complain if you did not vote. Choosing not to vote results in us suffering from the consequences and repercussions of some failing to do what many gave their lives to have the right to do. That causes a domino effect, which will affect future generations of Black people. The bottom line is White racist continue to try to take away the freedoms and rights we now enjoy. That is why voting is a right that all of us must not take for granted.

Failure

To me, failure is just another chance to succeed. There has only been one perfect person who has ever walked the earth. Other than Him, we all have failed at something. If a person says that he or she has never failed, then that person is lying or they have never attempted to achieve anything in life. I have failed at countless things. The most important thing is that I never failed to try. As a word of advice, you should never allow someone else to determine what constitutes success or failure for you. When people do not give a 110 percent effort toward what they are trying to achieve, I believe they are failures.

You would be surprised if you knew how many famous people were fired from a job or cut from a team and later in life went on to become successful. Failure is based on one's perception. Some can view it for what it is: a natural step leading to success because you are learning how to do things better the next time. Others may view a failure as something that ultimately defines you, even if it happens once. If you believe you are a failure then, you are one. I do not consider myself a failure because I learn from my mistakes. As long as God blesses me to see another day, I have another opportunity to succeed. I am not going to stop attempting to be successful at numerous things in life until I take my last breath. When I take what appears to be my last breath, I am going to try to take another one. Never stop trying. When you fail to try, you are guaranteed to fail.

Success

Success is relative to the individual. You are the one who determines if you are successful in life. I think success is achieving your short-term and/or long-term goals in life. I believe that if a person can say that they have contributed to the betterment of mankind, they can truly say that they are definitely successful. What I determine to be success could be considered as a failure in someone else's eyes. My perception is that *Last Year Before Reality* was a success because I achieved the goal that I set out to accomplish.

Everyday in this country small businesses go in and out of business. Even with the deck stacked against us in this country, our people have attempted to be successful. Nat Turner opted for freedom over slavery and rebelled against the institution of one man owning another. To a certain degree, he obtained success because he proved to other slaves that if you are willing to die for what you believe in, others will be encouraged to fight for their freedom. Harriet Tubman was a success because not only did she escape from slavery, but she led others to freedom as well. Mary McLeod Bethune was a pioneer for African-American education. Dr. Martin Luther King, Jr. was successful in his feat of pushing the nonviolent civil rights movement. In more recent times, we have Earvin "Magic" Johnson who is an extremely successful entrepreneur giving back to the Black community. And there are countless others who have gone unnamed here, but are certainly recognized for their efforts and successes. It is not easy being Black in America, with few easy opportunities in existence. However, opportunities can be created.

In order to be successful at any goal you have to be realistic, determined, persistent, and focused. There are always obstacles along the path of success, but that is where the qualities to survive become activated. Sometimes racism is going to be immaterial depending on what you do to become successful. The major obstacle that can prevent you from being successful is you. If you want to be a prosecuting attorney, neuro-surgeon, electrical engineer, or any other occupation that requires intense studying and an abundance of knowledge, it begins with you.

At an early age, parent(s) and guardian(s) should be preparing their children for success. It would be hard for a young person to wait until they are a senior in high school to decide that they want to have a successful medical practice and they have never taken any science courses throughout high school. It is possible, but the likelihood of becoming successful in the area for which you did not properly prepare will be extremely difficult. As early as possible, young people and those of more mature ages should seek exposure to the field of study/work for which they have a natural passion or ability. It takes some people longer than others to realize what is needed for them to achieve their self-actualization. This self-actualization, which is the highest point in Maslow's Hierarchy of Needs, is a point that some people achieve early in life, some people achieve later in life, and some people never achieve. Until you have realized your purpose or calling in life, you may feel like there is still something in the world you are missing, until you reach your destination. For many, the feeling of success continues to elude them until they have reached that point in life.

Challenge

The challenges that I have faced during my life were not as difficult as the challenges that faced our ancestors during slavery. Regardless of what any of us are experiencing during our trials and tribulations, our challenge to be successful in this country cannot compare to slavery. In all honesty, the obstacles that I have faced throughout my life cannot compare to what millions of Black people are facing today. I am truly blessed.

Currently, my greatest challenge is to utilize the gifts, knowledge, and wisdom God has blessed me with to assist others with the challenges that we continue to face as Black people in America. Unfortunately, there are thousands of Black people who think as individuals. They feel that as long as they do not experience racism, who cares about what other Black people are experiencing. Malcolm X said the following:

No matter how much respect, no matter how much recognition, whites show towards Me, as far as I'm concerned, as long as it is not shown to every one of our people in this country, it doesn't exist for me.[3]

All of us face challenges every day of our lives. It is up to each individual to decide how he or she will confront each challenge. Some people ignore them. Some people walk away from them. It does not matter if you ignore them or walk away; they will still be there when you come back the next day. I have determined how I will handle my challenges. One day, you will have to do the same.

Book Cover

I hope that you were able to realize what the cover of this book symbolizes. In Africa, before the coming of the Europeans, our ancestors were powerful African kings and queens. Our ancestors controlled great kingdoms and empires. The destruction of our great civilization in Africa began when, our ancestors were hunted down like animals by our own people and sold to the Europeans into slavery. Since that time Black people have been looked down on by all the other nationalities in the world and classified as inferior.

The object of the game of chess that is displayed on the book cover is to protect your king while trying to place your opponent's king in checkmate. Each player begins the game with the same number of pieces and of course, white goes first. On the book's cover, the black king has to attempt to conquer the white king, but as usual the playing field is not leveled. Assisting the white king is the white queen, the black queen, the white pawn and the black pawn. If you noticed how the pieces are arranged, that is how I perceive America.

Now, I will explain what impact every piece has on the Black man in the 21st century. There is no doubt in my mind that there will always be disharmony between the Black man and White man in the United States. When I state Black man or White man, I am not referring to a particular individual, but a group. Since 1619, the White man has done everything in his power to oppress and exploit the Black man. During slavery it was for our free labor and even today it still applies. Even with Affirmative Action, the playing field is not leveled and it will never be leveled.

The White woman has always been insignificant when it came to the Black man's progress in America. From birth, the White woman was always considered to be sacred and placed on a pedestal. In today's job pecking order, a White man of course would hire a White woman, before a Black woman and definitely before a Black man. Statistics have shown that Affirmative Action helped White women more than it did any other minority group to gain employment. Unbeknownst to some Black women, they are being utilized in an effort to continue to devalue the worth of the Black men in this country. The Black woman, who was once considered a Nubian Queen in Africa, is also used as an agent of the White man. During slavery, Black women began to look down on Black men, because we could not protect them from the violations that the White men committed against them. Now, in the 21st century, some Black women have the same resentment towards Black men. They think that we are less than a man because many of us are stuck in low paying jobs or without a job. But what they fail to realize is that the system in America is not conducive for the advancement of the Black man. The system is designed to keep us down and it is doing an incredible job, with the assistance of other Black people.

In corporate America, nine out of ten White men would rather hire a Black woman than a Black man. In many instances, a White man would not hire a Black man over an equally qualified Black woman unless he was a White male chauvinist. But I am not referring to all White males. Just from casual observation during my lunchtime in downtown Detroit one summer, all I saw were White men in business suits and professional Black women. A Black man in business attire was rare even in a predominately Black city. This is not by chance, but by design. Some Black women willfully assist the White man in keeping the Black man down.

The white pawn represents ignorant White men who are brainwashed into believing they are participating members of the White power structure in America. Since the time that White people arrived in America in the late 1500's, there has been a class system similar to England's during the same time period. A poor White man used to be referred to as a "peasant." In 2004, a poor White person is referred to as a hillbilly or trailer park trash. These poor White men believe the propaganda that the Black men are taking their jobs and by birth they are superior to us. During slavery, there were poor White people and there are millions of poor White people in 2004. For a White man to be poor in America is equivalent and as ridiculous as a fish drowning in water.

These white poor pawns protect the white king because they are ignorant. They have the illusion that because of their color, they are better than the Black man. What they have to realize is that we are all in the same boat together. The only difference is that Black men are at the bottom of the boat on one side and the poor White men are on the bottom on the other side. In every presidential election, the majority of poor White men would rather vote for a Republican candidate that will not do anything for them, than for a Democratic candidate that will at least establish social programs that will assist all poor people regardless of color. That is why the poor white pawn is protecting the rich white king from the black king, because it is misguided.

The black pawn is the most pathetic piece on the board when it decides to protect the white king whose primary objective is to continue to oppress the black pieces. This is an analogy for what is now occurring when Black people choose to forget the plight of our people who have been oppressed throughout history, and they support efforts to continue the oppression. This black pawn is usually referred to as a "Sambo," or a "House Negro." Isn't it enough for the Black man to have to compete on an unleveled playing field against White men without pathetic Black men assisting them? Today, we even have Black men turning on Black men to prove to their masters that even though he is free from bondage, he is still loyal.

I can understand the rationale for White women and poor White men protecting the rich White man, but for Black women and Black men to protect White men in America is an utter disgrace. It is amazing what some Black people will do for money. Throughout my working career, I have witnessed everything that I have described. It is unfortunate but so true. There is more knowledge I can provide on this subject, but it is better for people to see some things for themselves.

Today, in my mind, I consider myself a black king and not a black pawn. As long as I have a queen on my side and know the rules of the game, I can elevate young black pawns to kings. The game is not over yet. In the game of chess, the game is not over until your opponent resigns or you get his king in checkmate. I am not resigning. Even if it was me against the world, I still like my odds because I know the history of our ancestors and have faith in the God that I serve. We need more Black men to stop acting like black pawns and focus attention on advancing our race. You are playing a losing game if you fail to learn the rules. In life unlike chess, no one is forced to lose in order for you to win. Your success in life does not have to come about at someone's expense.

Not By Osmosis

It is safe to assume that everybody I mentioned in this chapter did not obtain the knowledge and abilities that they have to accomplish such extraordinary endeavors by staring at a wall all their lives. If one of them did, I would like the opportunity to meet them.

I will confess that my knowledge came from all the sources and people mentioned above and from the thousands of mistakes that I have made, which I now call experience. If you train your mind to absorb information and develop a way of thinking, your mind will teach itself how to analyze and store anything you give it. What people have to realize is that even with all the advanced computers and technology we have in the 21st century, it was first conceived in the mind of ordinary individuals willing to do extraordinary things. Man created computers; computers did not create man. I said all of that to say that the brain is an incredible organ with magnificent capabilities that I do not have the ability to describe.

Unfortunately, most people at an early age do not allow their brain to grow to its maximum potential. From our birth until our death, the brain absorbs information from the environment that surrounds it. This topic could be a chapter or even another book by itself. I do not have the time to expound on it, but I hope every reader of this book continues with that thought. You are what you see, read, and experience. Too many Black children are exposed to numerous negative influences that mold their minds at an early age. Children should not be exposed to sex, drugs, alcohol, violence, profanity, and other ills of society before the age of 18. There is a correlation between children who are raised in an environment without morals and values and their negative lifestyles as an adult. I cannot tell parents what they should expose their children to, but I just hope that parents are careful of the knowledge that these young minds receive.

A primary example of receiving negative knowledge too soon in one's life is when you have children killing other children without understanding how evil it is. Children's minds today are sculpted in violence from video games, television, the media, and other sources. If a child is shielded from sex, violence, drugs, alcohol, and crime until later in life, by the time they are exposed to it, their mind would automatically inform them that those activities are wrong and they should refrain from doing them. Proverbs 21:6 says *"Train up a child in the way he should go: and when he is old, he will not depart from it."* My understanding of that verse is: If you teach your child right from wrong while her or she is still at home, when your child goes to college, Armed Forces or into the world, they will not be easily influenced by the negative things in this world. That is why positive knowledge is important.

The source of the knowledge is not a factor as critical as having the knowledge, applying it, and sharing it. The knowledge, the source of it and how you apply it can be detrimental to your health, mind, future, and soul. Since I have an abundance of knowledge and know right from wrong, I now know the books to avoid, the places to avoid, and definitely the people to avoid. Since some people are wolves in sheep's clothing, sometimes it may be difficult to evaluate their intentions or ulterior motives. It has been said that you should consider the source. There are young people out there who are experimenting with drugs, alcohol, sex and other things that can cause them more harm than good. If they would learn by the mistakes of others that they see in the media, they would know not to travel down the same road of destruction. But this teaching and training starts at home.

In the news everyday, we are informed of Black people having difficulties with the law. The offenses are numerous. Here are some of the most common crimes or violations that Black people are arrested or suffer public humiliation from: Usage or selling of drugs; Drunk driving; Spouse abuse; Adultery; Child molestation; Crimes committed with guns. The list is almost endless. You would think that a wise person would learn by the misfortunes and mistakes of others. Those of you who are familiar with the Holy Bible are aware of the cause of all of the above situations and problems.

Five years ago, a Black celebrity got in serious trouble with the law because of a White woman. My mind quickly analyzed that information. Now that I am aware of the types of compromising situations that could result from engaging in a relationship with a White woman, I know to leave White women alone, if you are a rich Black man. I agree that love is blind, but America isn't. Many White men cringe every time they see a beautiful White woman with a rich Black man. My question is: If you already know America's history and opinion on interracial relationships and the negative repercussions, why do affluent Black men even enter into those waters? This is just my personal view though I do not oppose interracial relationships.

In 2003, there was another Black celebrity that did not use the knowledge that he was exposed to and today that Black celebrity is suffering because he ignored the knowledge that was available to him and all of us through the media. Why do we fail to take heed to the past experiences of others? Why do some of us have the mindset that "It will never happen to me or I will not be caught?" When the person is caught doing something that God opposes in the Bible, then the person wants to develop a closer relationship with God. If the person were walking with God, instead of with satan, the person would not have been in trouble in the first place. We are all susceptible to the tactics of satan. That is why it is imperative that we stay prayed up and in the Word.

All of us who were blessed with a brain that was not afflicted with a mental condition have the ability to acquire knowledge. In the United States of America knowledge is free to the rich and poor. Public libraries have every book that was ever written on their shelves. Most of the large public libraries even have computers and the Internet. So for any Black person to remain ignorant, it is by choice. Moves have been made to continue to keep the Black race down. If Black people pass on their move or make the wrong move, we will continue to play the game of life like the black pawns working for the opponent. No race of man, in this country or outside of this country, is better than another. The only way for the Black race and other minority groups to move further ahead is through the attainment of knowledge and thereby its application. It's one thing to have it and even share it, but if you fail to use it, you are part of the problem—the continued oppression of your people. I have emphasized what knowledge is and how to obtain it throughout this chapter but it doesn't stop there. Parents should raise their children to be leaders and not followers. For any parent to raise a child and not teach that child how to obtain knowledge so that the child can have a successful life is a travesty!

Controlling Your Own Destiny

It is not my intention for this book to bring me fame and fortune. Its purpose is to provide young people with the knowledge necessary to inspire them to control their own destiny and prepare them today, for the challenges of tomorrow. I pray that this book be the motivating force that ignites a fire in the mind, heart and soul of anyone who possesses the courage to face the challenges of the 21st century with confidence.

Young people the future of the world is in your hands. You will not only determine your own destiny, but the destiny of my generation also. No one can ever determine what anyone will achieve in his or her lifetime. Who would have thought that Dave Chappelle would sign a two-year contract for $50 million to make fun of racism, discrimination, and other dysfunctional problems in America. I wonder did anyone predict that Bill Gates, a college dropout, would one day be a billionaire. Did anyone ever fathom that after twenty-seven years of imprisonment, Nelson Mandela would be elected President of his country—South Africa. Who would have imagined Oprah Winfrey would be as rich and famous as she is today. Finally, who would have thought that an ex-college cheerleader from Yale would one day be *selected* President of the United States. The above examples, merely attests to the fact, that no can control your destiny, but you.

Maturing Process

Throughout life, maturity brings about change. If you live long enough, that natural progression will occur for most of you. There was a time when it appeared that I possessed a great disdain for all

White people. That is not true. However, I do hate the institutional racism that exists in America. I also hate how the White controlled media, racist politicians, and other racists in power continue to use propaganda to keep America divided. The average White person is not racist. They may be prejudice because they are ignorant and believe the lies, but they are not racist. In order to be racist, you must possess the power to control another race of people's destiny. If you look around, most White people cannot control their own destiny.

Throughout my life, there have been numerous White people who provided me with employment opportunities that Black people would not or could not give me. Yes, I did dislike the words and actions of specific White people that I have encountered throughout my life, but believe me when I say that I dislike the words and actions of even more Black people.

So young people please do not allow yourselves to be manipulated by the propaganda of racist in America. Do not be ignorant and hate others just because of the color of their skin. If you do, you could be closing a door of opportunity that you never gave the chance to be opened. Always judge a person by his or her words and actions. If you judge by color, you will be just as ignorant as the racist people who already exist in America.

Some of you may wonder how could a man, filled with so much anger and rage, experience such an extreme change. Here is my reason. After you have climbed the mountain of life for forty years and are finally on your way down the other side of the mountain, you see life differently. Most of the trials and tribulations that I will encounter on this side of the mountain, I have probably experienced already on the way up. If I experience something different, my previous exposures to the situation, knowledge, and wisdom that I have been given by God will see me through. Now that I have matured, I am too wise to allow events that negatively effected me when I was younger, effect me in the same manner, today. I have made a truce with America. I have since learned the rules of the game and now, finally know how to play.

When I suggested that young people of all races not to allow racist to use them in the game of life, that advice was for all of you and not for me. As the saying goes, "Do as I say and not, as I do." I have played the game of life and I am only trying to admonish all of you to play by their rules, until you learn the rules of the game. Oh, if you think I have become soft, docile, passive and have assimilated, you'd better ask somebody!

Chapter 12

YOUR MOVE

*"I have fought a good fight, I have finished my course,
I have kept the faith."*

—2 Tim 4:7

Now that I have made the first move to share knowledge with you, it is now your move. Knowing the rules of the game is only half the battle. Before you make your first move, please think about it carefully. Making the wrong move could place you further behind in the game of life or it could result in it being your last move in life.

There are some moves in life that can make life more difficult. In America, if you are born Black, you already have one strike against you. If you are born Black into a single-parent home and are poor, that is a second strike. In addition, if you are born a Black male, that is already your third strike and you have your first out before you leave the hospital. A great number of Black males should thank God if they are able to reach the age of 18 and graduate from high school. Once you cross the stage and graduate from high school into adulthood, you enter into another game of life where the wrong move can be extremely detrimental to your future goals, dreams, and plans.

One of the most tragic first moves in the game of life is for young Black women to have a baby before they graduate from high school or college without being financially able to support their child. Not only does this put you behind in the game of life, but it will also place your child that much further behind. It is not a death sentence, because there have been countless young women that have raised a child while in high school and eventually became successful. Being Black in America is already challenging enough. So why make life more challenging by having children at such an early age?

For young Black men who were raised by a single mother, it is shocking and disheartening that you would bring a child into this world to live under the same circumstances that you were involuntarily forced to live under. Again, it does not guarantee failure, but it reduces the chances of success for that child.

I applaud all of you who have made it this far in the book. That means you are seeking knowledge. By gaining knowledge, you increase your potential for success. In this country, there was a time in history when it was against the law for our people to be taught to read and write. Unfortunately, today there is a vast number of our people who are functionally illiterate. The White man knew what he was doing when he created that law. He knew that if Black people began to read and obtain knowledge, our eyes would be open and we would see his deception. Once we saw it, we would change the course of our future. The reason the White man did not want us to learn to write was because of all the Black people I mentioned previously. They knew some of us would use our God given talents to educate our people. There is no question, once you are familiar with the tactics of our enemies, you can beat them at their own game. It is tragic that those of us who know how to read refuse to continue to educate ourselves. When you have the ability to read and gain knowledge but choose to remain ignorant, that is by choice.

Now that I have given a general overview, I can be more specific about events and circumstances that effect each group of my primary audience.

High School Students

When I attended high school in the early 1980's, I did not face the challenges that high school students face today in the 21ˢᵗ century. Violence, drugs, and guns were almost nonexistent when I was in high school. We had students who we referred to as "Burnouts" and "Potheads," but nothing serious. A "Burnout" was a student who smoked cigarettes in front of the doors as you attempted to walk into school. A "Pothead" was a student who smoked marijuana. The dropout rate was not high in the 1980's. The rate was 11 percent.[1] When students did drop out of high school, there were jobs available for them or they could join one of the Armed Forces.

As far as entertainment in the early 1980's, the movies on television did not have profanity, sex, senseless killing, and endless commercials. There were only five television stations in the Detroit Metropolitan area at that time. As far as rappers were concerned, all I can remember is the "Sugar Hill Gang." In 1982, the first "Friday the 13th" movie came out. Arcades were just beginning to open in the area. I can remember playing Centipede and Pac-Man. The battle for our minds "back in the day," was nothing in comparison to what today's Black high school students are facing.

In the 21st century, my young Black brothers and sisters are encountering events on a catastrophic level. The violence in high schools today is criminal in many instances. Every year there appears to be shooting with the worst being the Columbine Massacre. Fights occur so regularly in most high schools, that it has become a norm. Teen pregnancy has skyrocketed. Smoking cigarettes and marijuana today is being replaced with crack cocaine and Ecstasy. The dropout rate is unbelievable today. Now, when our Black youths drop out of high school, many turn to selling drugs, joining gangs and living a life of crime. You still need at least a high school diploma or GED in order to join any branch of the Armed Forces.

In 2003, the distractions that are battling for the minds of high school students are endless. Today, there is cable television and DirectTV, which has more than 100 channels. The television movies and programs range from educational to borderline pornographic. The commercials on television today, encourage teenagers to spend money on products that they do not need. Some cable stations show music videos 24/7 and our Black youths are watching them instead of studying. The videotapes and DVD's available today are numerous. Every week a new rapper appears on the scene. The majority of the rappers that teenagers listen to are those who rap about money, sex, violence, misogyny, material possessions, and drugs. The movie selection is countless. Every week movies are released in theatres that promote the same negativity that most music promotes.

The role models and celebrities that these young people are exposed to are a detriment to their minds and future. Young people today are in awe of famous people with material possessions, money, and power. There are two ways to reach this goal. You can either do it legally or illegally. If you want to acquire success legally, that is what this book was created to assist you in doing. If you want to acquire success illegally, I cannot do anything for you.

Once you walk across that stage into reality, you are no longer going to be considered a Black boy or girl. You will be considered White people's, number one enemy. You will encounter experiences that will make what I experienced in life, seem like a luxury cruise. That is why it is imperative that you prepare for the future by learning from my mistakes and take the knowledge I am sharing with you serious! What America has planned for our young Black men and women in 2004 and beyond, is criminal.

Some of you probably think that I am "Old School" and that I don't know what I am talking about. I have been there and done that and that. Many of you already think you know everything and you won't allow anyone to teach you anything. Some of you think your parents do not know what they are talking about. I have weathered my storms and fought my battles. My trials and tribulations have been great, but yours will be greater. It is not time to be scared but to "Man Up!"

In reality some of you are living off the laurels and success of your parent(s). They are the ones that are buying you all the designer clothes, expensive gym shoes, videogames, and the "bling-bling." Technically, all of you are poor because you do not work or earn enough income to take care of yourselves.

Once you graduate from high school and move out on your own and attempt to be an adult, economic responsibilities will knock you into reality. Unfortunately, you have spent your high school years living a fantasy, instead of preparing for a successful transition into adulthood. When will young Black people realize that a $150.00 pair of gym shoes does not make you walk faster than a $50.00 pair of gym shoes. Paying $100.00 or more for a pair of jeans to have someone's name on your butt is outrageous. You can purchase a pair of decent jeans for $30.00-$40.00 and the remainder of the money could be saved for something more important. Answer this question for me. Why do young Black women pay anywhere from $150.00-$300.00 for a designer purse and they do not have fifty cents to put in it?

One day, most of you will reminisce on all the money that was wasted on insignificant material possessions that did nothing to expand your knowledge or assist you to become more competitive in the 21st century. All those expensive clothes and gym shoes did was boost your ego and make you feel like you were, "All that and a bag of chips," or feel like, "Ms. Thing." If it takes clothes to make you feel self-confident, I think you should re-examine yourself. Clothes and jewelry should not define who you are.

All of the hard earned money you convinced your parent(s) to spend or the money you slaved at your minimum wage job during high school was wasted. That money could have been saved for the following: College; Trade school; Car; First home; Starting your own business; Or invested in stocks and bonds, like your White and Asian peers do with their money.

Allow me to tell you a secret. While you are playing Nintendo, Xbox, and Playstation for three to five consecutive hours after school, and from sun up to sun down on Saturdays and Sundays, your White and Asian peers are learning how to create the game cartridges to get your money. All the valuable time that you waste playing those games should be spent preparing for your future, instead of eroding your brain. For instance, you could be studying more, improving your reading, writing, and comprehension skills. This will enable you to pass the newly implemented college essay writing exam which is now necessary to be accepted in most colleges and universities. Countless college freshman have to enroll in remedial college English and math courses because of deficiencies in those subjects. Instead of tuition going towards your core course your freshmen year, hard earned money is applied to remedial courses that you should have learned in high school.

While you are watching music videos and listening to music 24/7, your White, Asian, and Chaldean peers are learning how to start businesses to get your money. While you are talking on cellular phones into the midnight hour, they are asleep dreaming about ways to become rich from the technology for the material possessions Black people strive to have. While you are on the Internet socializing, playing games and listening to music, they are gathering research information on how to become a millionaire by the age of 30. While you hurry to the mall to spend your allowance and hard earned money from your minimum wage job on the latest designer fashions, your White and Asian peers are using their money to buy stock in the companies for the clothes you purchase. While you are spending hours upon hours loitering in the malls because you have nothing to do, your Chaldean and Asian peers are either working at their parent's store or reading a book on how to get more Black dollars from our spending habits. While you are trying to be like Michael Jordan and Mike Vick, your White counter parts are trying to emulate the multi-billionaire Bill Gates and President Bush. While you are trying to look good and learn about sex from the boy or girl next door, your Chaldean and Asian peers are learning how to go straight from high school into their own businesses.

Parents, if you do not monitor your children's education more closely and prepare them for the challenges of the 21st century, your children will be returning home after wasting your money in college. You then will have a second opportunity to raise them again. Just because your child is carrying a 3.8 G.P.A. in high school does not mean he or she is academically prepared for college. At some high schools, teachers just give students good grades and could care less if they earned them. Parents and students, you can either take learning seriously now or suffer the consequences later.

Remember in America, we are no longer only competing with White people for jobs that they received uncontested because of institutionalized racism, Jim Crow Laws, and other forms of discrimination that guaranteed the playing field would never be level for Black people. Our young people are competing against different people from around the world who take education extremely serious and do not have to use racism to secure employment over another race, like White people. These other people, primarily from Asia and India, take education seriously because they are quite aware that in America, if you acquire knowledge and skills, it almost definitely will guarantee success and prosperity.

In Japan and other countries, their students take school so seriously, that they would contemplate suicide, if they are not accepted into the high school or university that they prepared all their lives to attend. Japan and China may manufacturer all the video games that are eroding the minds of our Black children, but they do not permit their children to waste their valuable time playing them.

After reading everything above, do I still have to ask my young brothers and sisters in high school when are you going to finally wake up? If you wait until after you graduate, it is going to be too late. When it is all said and done, and our people are reduced back to slaves, we will only be able to say that we were forewarned. As I stated in the previous chapter, we should all be trying to warn those who are coming after us to learn about our past, so history will not repeat itself.

College Students

It is my hope that the warning I gave to the high school students and the things that they allow to occupy their minds and time are not applicable to you. If these things are applicable to you, you should ask yourself, "Why are you in college." For my educated brothers and sisters, half of this book should have been redundant. It was probably only a refresher course. If it was not, you'd better read it again.

It took me 20 years to acquire the knowledge and experiences that I am sharing in this book. I did not do it intentionally, but like they say: "If life gives you lemons, make lemonade." When I graduated from Saginaw Valley State University, I had unbelievable goals and dreams. Because of the things I described in this book, all of my dreams and goals did not come to fruition. I realized that my will is not always God's will. However, I am striving for my dreams and goals today because I have not stopped living. I have a news flash for college students. In 1988, we did not have all the advanced technology that exists today. When I searched for employment after I graduated, I only had to compete with Theodore and Beth for a job. Now, because of global competition, you have to compete with Theodore, Beth, Adib, Rekha, Ji-Xin, Ho-Phat, Ho-Slim, Majordomo, Ivan, Liliya, Hussan, Sarkis, Makhail, Hector, Rosa and I also forgot, our cousins, Mercedes and Lexus.

Just in case all of you have not taken a course in global economics, the world is now a smaller place. Yes, advanced technology provided more jobs, but it also provided more job seekers. The Japanese, Chinese, Indians and others are now coming to America by the thousands and receiving high paying jobs in all technical areas. Mexicans, Europeans and immigrants from other third-world countries are coming to this country and taking all the low paying and labor-intense jobs.

In addition, American corporations are sending hundreds of thousands of jobs to other countries every year. One of the main reasons that some Black college graduates receive employment's because of Affirmative Action without it, White racist would not hire us even though we possess just as much education and talent as our White peers. For those of you who have been in a daze for the last couple of years, Ward Connerly is attempting to have legislation passed to eradicate Affirmative Action programs. The intended purpose of Affirmative Action was to make up for the discrimination of minorities in the past and increase the opportunities today for them to be employed with various companies and government agencies. Today, the purpose of Affirmative Action has been revised to include various groups of people, i.e. Blacks, White females, physically disabled, low income and other minority groups who are underrepresented in companies and government agencies. That means there will be fewer jobs available for Black college graduates.

Think about this next relevant point. Among the Fortune 500 Companies in the United States, how many do you think are owned or operated by Black people? In 1995, Blacks only held 3.6 percent of the seats on the boards of Fortune 500-level companies.[2] The bottom line is that there are not very many corporations that are going to allow a Black person to receive the position of CEO or president. There were not many on the board then, so how can we influence others without having our representation in these influential positions today? If you are going to college hoping to get the opportunity to run a Fortune 500 Company or any company that is owned by any other race, it is not likely that this is going to happen. If this is your goal and vision, you must start your own company and work to make it rise to the Fortune 500 list.

To sum it up, in order for our people to survive we have to provide jobs for our people. It appears every culture in this country takes care of its own, but us. All we do is take care of other races by giving our money to them. We are a race of consumers and not producers. We allow every other race in this country to exploit and manipulate us for our money and labor. We have to wake up before it is too late because it is the eleventh hour. How many of you college students are waiting until you graduate from college into unemployment until you wake up and take the knowledge that I have shared seriously? If you wait until then to wake up, you will wake up with shackles on your feet.

Young Black Workers

This section is dedicated to my young Black brothers and sisters between the ages of 18 and 30, who are already in the workforce. Now that you have more knowledge to go with the knowledge that you already possess, what are you going to do with it? The odds are great that whatever you are doing for employment today, you will be doing it for the next twenty years, if you have not been terminated from your position.

Black workers do not have any job security anymore. We have more job security in government positions and basically none in corporate America. Nearly all states allow for employers to dismiss an employee for almost any reason, with the exception of a public policy violation, without incurring any legal liability under the basic law of "Employment

At Will." Over the past two years, I have noticed that companies are terminating people for the slightest offense and they attempt to make it appear justified so that the terminated employee will not be eligible for unemployment benefits. Since you were probably getting paid slightly more than minimum wage before you were terminated, you cannot afford a lawyer in order to sue.

I will tell you about the new mentality of corporate America. If they are paying you $40,000 a year, they will terminate you and hire a White high school graduate to do your job for $17,000 a year. By terminating you, the White company president has saved $23,000 and provided a job for someone else, as a favor. Another reason they will terminate you is to hire someone who can be compensated with hourly wages versus a salary or employ the services of a temp agency. Say good-bye, because your job is gone. There is no allegiance in corporate America to anyone today. The three incidents explained above happened to White employees, so you know what would happen to Black employees.

If you are between ages 18 and 30, please be careful of how you spend your money. One day you can have a job and the next day, it could be gone. Do not live above your means and save as much money as you can. After you look around your office or your place of work, you can tell what type of future you will have with that company. If you think there is no room for advancement because of "The Glass Ceiling," then you are wrong. It is a "Concrete Ceiling." I am not trying to depress anyone. I am just trying to be realistic. If you purchased this book, you are getting your money's worth and more.

Millions of our people, including me at different times in my life, are stuck in what we call, "dead-end" jobs. These are the jobs in which your position remains the same from your first to your last day. That is a "dead-end" job if that is how you choose to view it. No matter what your job title is or what you are getting paid, you always have to be determined to give 110 percent and feel blessed to have that job. There are millions of people in the world who would love to have your "dead-end" job instead of no job at all. I am not saying to be happy about your present situation. Be content for a season. A season sometimes lasts three months, one year, or even three years. Regardless of how long the season is, treat that job like you are getting paid ten times your current wages/salary. No matter who you are and regardless of your age, you need to have a vision. Your vision should include what major thing(s) you want to accomplish with your life. Your short-term and long-term goals must work toward your vision. Too many of us are living to help someone else achieve his or her vision because we don't have our own or we are too afraid to strive for it. Depending on the type of job you have, you should think about how far up the career ladder you want to advance and work towards that.

I will use a security guard position for example. If you show initiative, enthusiasm, and a desire to learn, the owner will definitely give you more responsibilities. You can take advantage of those opportunities and obtain as much knowledge as possible. In this scenario, the short-term goal could be to learn the security industry, enroll in classes and request more challenging security assignments. The long-term goal may be to receive licensing necessary for the security industry, collect contacts for possible clientele, and complete research on current security businesses. Your short-term and long-term goals would work toward a vision of operating your own security guard agency. While you are learning the tricks of the trade, do not tell anyone. Remember that everyone is not aiming to open or direct you to the door of opportunity. Just continue to learn. As soon as you realize that America is a capitalist society and it is all about cheap labor and high profits, you will have a better chance of acquiring a better standard of living for you and your family.

In one book, I could not possibly explain everything I know about trying to earn an honest living in America. All I know is if you give up, your life is only going to be about surviving and not living. I have felt your pain and there is no guarantee that I will not feel your pain again. It is the pain of being Black and playing by the rules of a game that is not designed for you to win. One thing I can guarantee is that when I recognize that there is no window of opportunity at a current job and feel the pain from my past, I will be slowly breaking down the wall and creating my own window of opportunity.

Crying, whining, and complaining will not get you anywhere. So you can stop it, if that is what you have been doing. Instead of doing those three, you should be implementing a plan of escape. There is nothing wrong with dreaming as long as you wake up and make that dream a reality. While you are going through trials and tribulations at your place of employment, apathy and complacency will not get you anywhere.

As you can see throughout my life, I have worked at a number of different jobs and as I reminisce, I wonder how I kept going when I wanted to quit. It was only by the grace of God that I was able to persevere. Regardless of how my face and body may appear, my mind and soul have been scarred by the continuous battles I have fought for others and myself. My question to every person who is reading this is: When can all our weary warriors who have fought for our freedom finally rest? When can Rev. Jesse Jackson, Rosa Parks, Nelson Mandela, Maya Angelou, Congressman John Conyers, Randall Robinson, Honorable Louis Farrakhan, Angela Davis and other Black warriors finally rest? Now, they are afraid to close their eyes, because when they open them again, they might be slaves.

Black people in America needs some young leaders and I pray that those of you reading this book will apply for the available positions. Before you are able to lead, you have to know how to follow. In order to be a good and effective leader, you have to possess knowledge and pray for God to give you wisdom. Young people, please allow our seasoned warriors to have an opportunity to see a better America for our people before they depart. Also please prove to the thousands who have died in this country that their lives were not in vain and that the price they paid for our freedom was worth it. It is now your move. You now know the rules of the game. Are you going to use the knowledge that you have received to provide a better life for yourself and our people or are you going to "sell out?"

Young brothers and sisters, I am not suggesting that you do not enjoy life. One day, you have to become mature enough to place things in perspective. Playing video games is probably fun entertainment, but playing four to eight hours continuously is more like an obsession or addiction. If I am not mistaken, there is no job that pays you $25.00 to be a video game player unless it pertains to the manufacturing or marketing of them. I will tell you from experience that life is not all fun and games for Black people in America. Before you start having fun, I suggest that you earn a good education and either seek employment with job security or operate your own business. Once you have established yourself as a responsible adult, then play your video games for eight hours a day; until then, playing video games is a waste of time and money.

To those of you who are a part of the "Hip-Hop Generation" and want to be "shot callers," and everything else they rap about, please be aware that we have enough rappers. Can more of you focus attention on becoming writers, educators, lawyers, doctors, business owners, and other career occupations that will provide role models that our young people so desperately need. There is nothing wrong with rap when it is listened to in moderation. When you are listening to it 24/7 and watching the rap videos, it interferes with your ability to study and learn. Do not think I am anti-rap. During my college years and afterwards, I used to listen to Run-DMC, KRS-One, Cool Mo-Dee, LLCool J, MC Lyte, Salt and Pepper, Ice Cube, Queen Latifah, NWA and Tupac to name a few. Today, the prominent rappers are Jay Z, Mos Def, Kanye West, Ludicrous, Eminem, and 50 Cent. Most of the issues that most rappers are talking about are irrelevant issues to people who are working hard to make an honest living. Rappers are only enticing you give your money to the White business owners who make all of the material possessions that are shown in the videos and mentioned in rap songs.

As far as the lyrics, it is just tragic that young Black people have experiences that are so violent in the United States of America. What went wrong in this rich country that the government will allow any race of people to be subjected to such living conditions? Any time a government has $87 Billion to spend on a war in Iraq, it should have money available to improve the living conditions of young Black people whose ancestors were forced to build this country. It is not my place or responsibility to tell you what to and what not to listen to. Rap is a form of expression just like any other kind of music and I have received an abundance of knowledge from it. All I ask for all of my young brothers and sisters to do is, listen to it in moderation and do not duplicate the negative lyrics and learn from the positive lyrics.

*   *   *

There are numerous Black students who are focused on diligently handling their business when it comes to education despite negativity encountered from the streets, the media, and peer pressure. If you are a young Black person experiencing these things, my message to you is to keep working towards the positive future that you are building the groundwork for with your current mindset. Ignore them when they call you a "Bookworm", "Square", a "Nerd", "Computer geek", or "White acting". These are only names they may use in an effort to discourage you from becoming all you can be. Sometimes it is out of jealousy and envy that they do not have the courage, dedication, or will to be as serious about academics as you. Ten years from now when your hard studying has paid off, they will be envious of your success.

A word of advice on alleged friendship. All of you have to learn when to sever friendships and relationships that can be detrimental to you academically, mentally, physically, financially, or spiritually. It is imperative that you make a conscientious effort not to reap what someone else sows. Meaning, do not place yourself in a situation where you suffer the consequences of someone else's words or actions. Too many times, I have heard where an innocent person was with the wrong person, at the wrong place and at the wrong time. Be extremely careful about who you call your friend and select your friends wisely. You only have one life to live. If you make the wrong decision and are affiliated with the wrong people, your life can be altered so dramatically that it will never be the same. Always think twice before you make a decision that can have irreversible repercussions.

Now that you know some of the rules of the game, only you can decide your next move. Are you just going to be complacent, apathetic, and try to live a quiet life and allow other people to control your destiny? Or are you going to be dedicated to acquiring knowledge so you can become successful and make a positive difference in other young Black people's lives?

In the 1970's and 1980's almost any Black person could easily get a job at Ford, GM, or Chrysler. The plants are what attracted Black people from the south to Michigan and other industrial states. Working 30 years at a company no longer exists in the 21st century. Job loyalty and job security are things of the past. In America it has never been easy for a majority of Black people to find decent employment. That is why the unemployment rate for Black people has always been double that of White people.

Please do not be misled by all the success and prosperity of Black people you see on television and those in the suburbs of America. According to the Bureau of Justice Statistics, there were approximately 872,000 Black males and females in the nation's prisons and jails in 2001.[3] If we continue at this rate, our people will serve in three capacities; Entertainers in sports and comedy; incarcerated; and menial labor jobs of servitude. If any of you will closely observe futuristic movies, then you will notice that there are only one or two Black people. This shows that many White people do not want or expect us to be around in the years to come.

We are not going anywhere. Our ancestors contributed more to this country than any of the other races combined. If White people are willing to take credit and have pride in their forefathers who brutally enslaved our people for capital gain, then that only confirms what most Black people believe of the evilness of racist White people.

This is my last plea to my young Black brothers and sisters. Please wake up and carry on in the footsteps of Dr. Martin Luther King Jr., Mary Church-Terrell, Malcolm X, Mary McLeod Bethune, Honorable Louis Farrakhan, House of Representative Barbara Jordan, Medgar Evers, Congresswoman Shirley Chisholm, Dr. Ben Carson, Professor Henry Louis Gates, Jr., Ida B. Wells, Muhammad Ali, Rosa Parks, Dick Gregory, Mayor Coleman Young, Oprah Winfrey, Bill Cosby, Professor Cornel West, Randall Robinson, Spike Lee, Earvin "Magic" Johnson, Gordon Parks, Dave Bing, John Singleton, Tyler Perry, Tavis Smiley, Judge Hatchett, George Curry, Ice Cube, Queen Latifah, and countless other Black people who have and are contributing to make America a better place for us to live.

Young people, we are all in this together. Yes, there are some Black people who think they have left the race, but we just have to ignore them. You are our future. I have made my best attempt to assist you in learning some of the rules of the game. The rules will continue to change to the detriment of Black people, but the game will continue to be the same. The game in the United States of America is to make a conscientious, methodical and planned attempt to keep Black people down. In order for us to prevent this, we have to prepare leaders of tomorrow, today. There is no question that our people desperately need future leaders. Please gain as much knowledge as possible, so not just one of you, but all of you can apply for the job!

If our current generation does not prepare for the responsibility of leadership, the following will be asked:

> *"What became of the Black People of Sumer?" the traveler asked the old man, "for ancient records show that the people of Sumer were Black. What happened to them?" "Ah," the old man sighed. "They lost their history, so they died . . . ."*[1]
>
> —*A Sumer Legend*

Epilogue

What do you say when you don't want to say good-bye? Do you say, "It was fun, but I have to run?" It is unfortunate that I had to devote the contents of this book to the trials and tribulations of trying to earn an honest living in the United States of America. I wish I could have presented a less serious side of myself—like my sense of humor, multi-faceted personality, and compassion for all people, and animals. My life has not only been filled with anger, frustration, disappointment, tears, and battles. I think I recall seeing the sunshine a couple of times, and I did stop to smell the roses once. That was fun. Now back to reality, because that is what America has branded into my mind!

Throughout my life, a few major factors significantly contributed to the way I have dealt with every challenge that I have encountered. Those factors include the mentality I inherited from my father's side of the family, the environment I grew up in, and allowing sin to be my best friend for most of my life. There is no way in the world that I will give any person—man or woman, Black or White—enough power to control my destiny.

I could have easily used being Black in America as an excuse for my numerous trials and tribulations. But what do I need an excuse for? God has blessed me with talents and gifts that have enabled me to endure the storms of my life. Yes, racism is prevalent in America, but I am too wise and experienced to allow it to deter me from reaching my goals in life. If you want to use it as a crutch, that is certainly your choice, and your cross to bear.

As Black people, we cannot allow racism and the actions of White people or others to consume our thoughts. The average White person is not worrying about Black people. In 2004, White people are worrying about the same things that Black people are. For instance, they are concerned with their own job security, so they can support their family. They are also worried about whether or not President Bush is going to continue to allow Black and White soldiers from the low and middle class America to die in the war in Iraq that was motivated by power and greed. The White power structure in America uses propaganda and lies to keep the Black and White people divided.

The average White male does not know who his true enemy is, and this plagues America. In many instances in the history of America, a White man's loss of employment was attributed to a Black person or some other minority. In 2004, White people have to start looking at the president they selected to run this country in 2000. Since 2000, approximately two million Americans have lost their jobs. Majority of them were White people; because millions of Black people were already unemployed due to racism, inferior education, insufficient preparation for career success, and a multitude of other circumstances and barriers, some of which were self-inflicted.

When will the poor and middle class White men finally realize that being a Republican is synonymous with corporate America and being rich? The Republican Party uses the "Reverse Robin Hood Concept." They tax the poor to give to the rich. If I were a rich, greedy, atheist, Republican who worshipped money, I would probably agree with a policy that taxes low and middle class White people in order to make rich people, richer. Since I am none of the above, I vehemently oppose that concept because I am in the same boat as the middle class White people.

Adding to the aforementioned problem, every week, we hear about corporations closing plants in America and moving operations to Mexico or some other country. The reason for this is to increase profits by decreasing labor costs, thereby, generating higher dividends for stockholders. Do you think that one corporate CEO genuinely cares about the blue collar, White male worker who has a family to support? I don't think so. Because of the new global economy, corporations and places of higher learning are hiring computer programmers, engineers, scientists, professors, and doctors from other countries to perform the jobs that were dominated exclusively by White men. Are the rich Republican corporate presidents saying that other workers educated in other countries are mentally superior to the average White man, and that the advances of technology have surpassed the thinking capacity of every White man, other than Bill Gates?

"Almost 500,000 white-collar American jobs have already found their way offshore, to the Philippines, Malaysia and China . . . American computer programmers earn about $60,000, while their Indian counterparts only make $6,000."[1] So for all of the White computer programmers that have lost their high paying jobs, please do not blame Black or Hispanic Americans, or even people from India. The majority of the presidents of American corporations that are sending jobs overseas or are hiring foreign workers are White Republicans. They are the ones to blame for the loss of those white-collar jobs. "IBM has expanded offices in Bangalore, India, to handle engineering work, and is reportedly considering a big offshore push. Hewlett-Packard has 5,000 employees in India, doing research, developing software and staffing call centers. The companies say they've had Indian workers for years."[2] In addition other high paying, highly sought-after jobs often require advanced degrees and years of study to attain. But instead of paying 6-figure salaries to trained workers in America, more companies are shelling out $10,000-$20,000 to get cheaper employees an ocean away. Other jobs that were previously held by White people that are now going overseas are financial analysts, architectural drafters, telemarketers, accountants, claims adjusters, and home loan processors just to name a few.[3] White people are finally experiencing first-hand what it is like being Black and trying to earn an honest living in America.

In Greenville, Michigan Electrolux AB announced that it will close its Greenville factory next year and move most of the work to a new $150-million plant in Mexico. The result will be 2,700 people losing their jobs. The company estimates wages in Mexico are 10 times less expensive than the $13 to $15 an hour plus benefits it pays its Greenville workers.[1]

Before every average White man votes in November 2004, they should ask themselves if the candidate they are voting for is concerned about the best interest of big corporations or the average blue collar worker. It is impossible for the President of the United States to support "big business" and the "little man," simultaneously.

The first assault on the American worker was in the high salary technician jobs and the blue collar manufacturing jobs. Now, the current president is attempting to assist small companies by introducing a new immigration policy that will have an adverse effect on both Black and White American citizens. The ulterior motive of this new policy is to increase the support of Hispanic voters in November 2004. This new "temporary worker program" would allow either one of the estimated 8 million illegal immigrants that are already in the United States or people from abroad to apply for the right to work legally in this country for a 3-year term that could be renewed . . . The employer must show that no Americans wanted the job.[5]

In essence, this new immigrant policy, if passed, will take thousands of additional jobs away from American citizens. Companies will generate greater profits because they will be able to pay a "guest-worker" minimum wage instead of the higher hourly rate that a skilled unionized or educated American citizen would require.

The stipulation for an employer to show that no Americans wanted the job is ridiculous. In America, people attend school or pursue other development opportunities to increase their career options. For most Americans, a menial labor job is not a dream occupation, but a job that will pay the bills until they can obtain a better job. For "guestworkers" from another country, the jobs that will be offered will be a "dream job" compared to the career choices that are available in their country. While Americans will suffer because of the availability of this new cheap labor force, owners of companies and corporations will benefit enormously.

Again, America is not about Black and White, but rich and poor. Rich White men in corporate America and government create the laws and make the decisions that control the destiny of all poor people—Black, White, and other. They cannot empathize with us, so how can they serve our best interest? The government of the United

States and corporate America is conveniently legalizing a form of indentured servitude that places millions of Americans, regardless of color in the working class, poor. Until low and middle-class White men accept this fact and stop allowing the rich White men to manipulate their minds, America will continue to spiral downward. While America continues to focus its attention on perfecting racism and sexism, India, Japan and China are perfecting excellence and taking millions of jobs from American citizens.

I thought that it was necessary to take a moment to discuss what is truly ailing America in the 21ˢᵗ century. Now back to my passion, Black people!

*   *   *

As Black people, we have to learn how to "agree to disagree." Now is not the time for us to continue to be divided. Regardless of political affiliation, level of education, sexual preference, annual salary, portfolio, religious beliefs, lack of beliefs, or anything else that separates us, we have to place those differences on the "back burner." When you are attempting to catch a taxicab in New York in the middle of the night, the driver does not stop to pick you up because of any of the aforementioned reasons. He does not pick you up because you are Black. "'You cannot run or move away from being Black; you cannot graduate from being Black; and you cannot gain enough wealth to remove your Blackness.' Unfortunately, some of us think we can, and we are sadly disappointed when we find our efforts are futile."[6]

In 2004, policies and practices that will ultimately hurt minority groups have been enacted in White America under the leadership of the exclusively White Republican Party. They are attempting to eradicate Affirmative Action with the assistance of the alleged Black leader, Ward Connerly. For those of you who may not be familiar with Affirmative Action, I will provide a brief history. In essence, Affirmative Action is based on programs designed to enhance opportunities for groups that have suffered discrimination in the past.[7]

In 1961, John F. Kennedy was the first president to use the phrase "Affirmative Action" when he issued Executive Order 10952, creating the Equal Employment Opportunity Commission (EEOC), and directing federal contractors to take Affirmative Action to ensure that applicants and employees were treated fairly and without regard to race, creed, color, or national origin.[8]

Now, back to 2004. Ward Connerly, who leads the initiative to have Proposition 209 passed in California, is attempting to do the same in the state of Michigan, with his referendum. There is no question that if the citizens of the state of Michigan vote to have Affirmative Action dismantled, it will cause a domino effect. It will accelerate America's inevitable transition to a system of apartheid. The consequences of it would be catastrophic. Black people, women, and other minorities are already victims of the institutionalized racism and sexism that exists in America. Elimination of Affirmative Action will result in a totalitarian government, where White men will rule exclusively. They already possess that power with institutionalized racism and sexism.

The war against racism in America will never be eradicated because we cannot control how other people perceive us. We have to focus attention on a war that we can win. This war has to be fought on three different fronts—education, employment, and politics.

From its conception, the educational system in America was never designed to provide Black people with the necessary skills and education to compete in higher education and the job market with White people. I will not even elaborate on the struggles our people have battled since slavery, to receive an education. There is definitely a correlation between the lack of adequate education and the high incarceration rate of Black people.

The next front we have to fight is employment. "We must unite around economics if we are to realize the benefits: $800 billion could create 400 Fortune 500 type companies that are making $100 million or more."[9] Black people have to come to the realization that no other race in America is going to place our financial well-being over their own. Until we are able to provide millions of jobs for our people, many of our unprepared people will continue to struggle to make a living, or engage in criminal activities that will eventually lead to incarceration.

The last issue that I want to address is politics. We have to stop trivializing how important voting is in this country. Our ancestors and also dedicated White people died in this country, so that we could have the right to vote. Now that we have the right to vote, too many of us fail to take advantage of it. That is the reason why President Bush was selected, not elected, in 2000. Had more Black people voted, it would not have mattered that those "wanna be" Republicans in Florida could not count and threw away thousands of Black voters' ballots.

Also in the political arena, Black people have to scrutinize the Black candidates that run for various political offices. We cannot continue to allow television, newspapers, advertisement, and speeches from excellent orators to determine who receives our votes. Many of these politicians are wolves in sheep's clothing. They may look good, dress nice, and speak well, but their ulterior motive is to gain accessibility to power and money that is affiliated with the office they are seeking.

* * *

It is time for each and every one of us to take personal responsibility for our lives. Since no man has a heaven or hell to place you in, please do not allow anyone to judge you or determine your destination. You, alone, will either benefit or suffer from the consequences of your words or actions. Individually, all of us must decide what our purpose in life is, and stand behind any beliefs that we may have. From Revelations 3:15-16: "*I know thy works, that thou art neither cold nor hot: I would thou were cold or hot. So then because thou art lukewarm, and neither cold nor hot, I will spew thee out of my mouth.*" We cannot vacillate on the important issues that define us. You cannot be a Democrat in public, and a Republican in the closet. You cannot be Black around your Black friends, and a "sellout" with your White co-workers. You cannot be a sinner at the club on Saturday night, and a Christian at church on Sunday morning. Be true to the game, 24 hours a day, 7 days a week.

Although you already know, before I was a college graduate, assistant manager, author, Christian, or anything else, first and foremost, I was and will continue to be Black—inside and out. If you are ashamed of how you were created, all a person can do is pray for you. Every nationality I know of is proud of the history of their race. I think the historical achievements and perseverance of Black people are equivalent to, or surpass, every other race on the planet. When people consider the Black race, they only want to examine our history from 1619 up to 2004. If anyone would take the time to search legitimate history books and not "his story" books, they would discover that Black people in America are descendants of a great and strong African race.

Tragically, although we were emancipated from physical bondage in 1863, millions remain mentally enslaved, and continue to rely on the White man for guidance. In 2004, we still have some Black people who think like the Hebrews in Numbers 14:4—"*And they said one to another, Let us make a captain and let us return to Egypt.*" They chose to select someone to lead them back into bondage and we have Blacks who are following suit. For those of you who are knowledgeable about Black History and current events, you may be familiar with alleged Black leaders, educators, and people in power who think that it is more advantageous for us to return to serving the White man, instead of becoming independent and self-sufficient.

As a people, we have to learn how to say "No" to the dollar when other races in this country attempt to pay you to humiliate yourself, your family, and our race. When other nationalities in America, and around the world see and listen to us on the news, in movies, through music, and other forms of media, we are unofficial ambassadors for all Black people in America. Every time a Black celebrity is recorded conducting himself or herself in a negative and irresponsible manner, it reflects on each of us, regardless of the fact that a majority of Black people conduct themselves in a mature and professional manner.

All of us should have a purpose in life other than just to exist and pay bills. After it is all said and done, what will be your legacy? Each of us cannot be in one of the occupations where people receive fame, fortune, and accolades, but we can make a positive contribution to the human race.

It is my purpose and mission in life to continue to educate our people, especially young people, through literature. My plan is to continue to proceed in this area, if it is God's will. I have such a passion for reading that I have set up reading initiatives for select junior high and high school students. The primary purpose of my first novel, *Last Year Before Reality*, was for high school students to read about how the characters in my book deal with real life situations, to better prepare them to deal with similar situations in their lives. Only time will tell if a number of students have benefited from the knowledge they gained as a result of reading *Last Year* Before *Reality*.

Some people have a mission in life to acquire fame and fortune, but mine is to create and successfully operate a religious-based, non-profit organization. The primary purpose is to offer young people a caring and learning alternative to the negative influences that they encounter on the street.

In closing, I can guarantee that I will be a lifetime servant of God and a member of the Black race. It is my hope that all of you who have read this book, from beginning to end, have seen my transition and know what influenced such a miraculous change in me. I do not and have never advocated any hate or violence towards any man or woman, of any race, and it is my hope that all readers of this book share the same feeling. No, please do not think that the "Angry Black Man" that you met at the beginning of this book changed to a "House Negro" or someone who would tap dance for "Mr. Charlie" for a dollar like thousands of other Black people have done in America. I have never rolled that way and have no intentions of rolling that way. I want for us as Black people to start loving and respecting ourselves. If we do not love and take care of ourselves, history has proven time and time again, that no one else will.

Until the next time, and I do pray that there is a next time, I pray that there was some knowledge in this book that possibly inspired someone to make a positive change in his or her life. Knowing the rules of the game is half the battle. If you know and are obedient to the will of God, your battle is already won!

Acknowledgments

First and foremost, I would like to give all glory, honor and praise to my Lord and Savior Jesus Christ for blessing me to be born into a strong and persevering race. I would also like to thank my Brothers and Sisters in Christ for their prayers and words of encouragement. To my Brothers and Sisters in the Struggle: We must continue to fight the good fight, regardless of the odds against us, or those who turn against us. To John Brown and the thousands of other White people who have fought valiantly to bring equality and justice to every citizen of the United States, regardless of color: Thanks to all of you.

The greatest love goes out to Vanilla Prophet and Lillie R. Williams whose combined love and effort set the foundation for making me the man that I am today. To my sister, Regina Lewis who has been my best friend, confidante and personal advisor, since we were children— Thank you for being there all my life.

A special thanks goes out to the following individuals for their support, encouragement and assistance on this project and through the years: Advisor: Kenneth L. Farr; Calvin Prophet; Valerie Pilot; Marvin Mayberry; Esther L. Jackson; Gerald Prophet; Roderick Drane; Petrena Boone; Dr. George Gibson; Pamela McColla; Dallas Walker, Jr.; Donna Squalls; Keith Willams; Francis Cureton; Derrick Williams; Michael Henderson; Ortheia Ward; Samuel L. Davy; Phillip Gibbons; Annie Pullins; Curtis Perry; Charlie "Chuck" Thornton, Jr.; Adolf Mungo; George Cushingberry; "Bonnie and Clyde".

Herbert Ivory, Principal of Ferndale High School; Staff of Xlibris Corporation; Detroit Public Library; Charles H. Wright Museum of African American History.

Brother in Christ, Will McCants of Conglomerati Ink, for designing the Book cover and website.

Sister in Christ and soon to be best selling author, Lisa Drane, *The McGallister Fiction Series—Book One: Only A Man*: I wish you the best and I know that God is with you;

Zakiya Greene—Shrine of the Black Madonna; Members of the Akwaaba Center; Aziz Adisa Masai, M.Ed.

The entire 1225 Corp Support Battalion—Priscilla A. Swan, Ricci Moore, Christa Moore, Lydell Tinnon and Phillip Sangster.

Now a moment of silence, while I give respect to the following people whose names I did not know, but I still feel their misery and pain. To all my African Ancestors who died during the voyage from our Motherland Africa to what some call America, the land of the free: This was our Holocaust. To all my ancestors who were forced to labor for free to make the United States of America the powerful country it once was, my heart goes out to you. To all my innocent brothers, sisters, mothers, fathers, daughters, sons and relatives who were raped, whipped, beaten, lynched and murdered for the last 385 years: I say a prayer for you. Even though none of you were recognized by name, your spirits dwell in those of us who continue to make sure your death was not in vain. I will never forget the sacrifices that you have made for our people.

To all my co-workers at the State of Michigan Unemployment Agency—Branch Office #3, Detroit RIC, Cadillac Place—Thank you for supporting, *Last Year Before Reality*. Thank you for all of the love, family atmosphere, encouragement, and motivation to write this book. Thank you goes out to "Tina, from Ike."

Thank you to all of my teachers, instructors, professors, fellow students, co-workers, friends, and adversaries at all the places discussed in this book and etc. I thank all of you for providing me with the knowledge, experiences, trials, tribulations, and challenges that made this book possible.

The list of family of friends that I have and made over the years is almost endless. If I missed anyone, please charge it to my mind and not my heart.

Here are the families:

Anderson; Anfield; Archer; Atkins; Banks; Bishop; Bonner; Boone; Brown; Burden; Cain; Calhoun; Carter; Clay; Clemons; Coleman; Cunningham; Daniels; Davis; Davy; Denson; Dockery; Duncan; Evans; Farr; Flowers; Ford; Fox; Gibbons; Gibson; Hall; Hamilton; Hampton; Harris; Hawkins; Henderson; Hewitt; Hickman; Hollie; Hughes; Hurst; Ivory; Jackson; Jeter; Johnson; Jones; Kennedy; Kirby; Lee; Lester; Lewis; Littlejohn; Lloyd; Longmire, Love; Mayberry; McChristian; McColla; McGrady; McNair; Morgan; Murphy; Nelson; Ogburn; Oldham; Parham; Patterson; Phillips; Pilot; Powell; Price; Reid; Ross; Simmons; Simpkins; Snow; Snowden; Tate; Thomas; Thornton; Walker; Waters; Wells; White; Williams.

Thank you to all my friends and family in Royal Oak Township, Inkster, Detroit, Saginaw, and St. Paul, Minnesota.

Now for a time of forgiveness to our ancestors in Africa who sold our people to the Europeans to be used as slaves. Forgiveness goes to our ancestors during slavery who assisted the slave owners to oppress us, instead of fighting with us. Forgiveness goes out to the Black brothers and sisters today in the 21st century, who continue to assist the White men in America to oppress us and gradually turn back the hands of times to 1862 and before. All I ask is when will you finally wake up? Forgiveness also goes out to all my Black brothers and sisters who continue to engage in Black-on-Black hate. Can we please stop the violence?

To those of you, whose ancestors enslaved, beat, raped, lynched and oppressed us, can you now in the 21st century, call it a truce? There are some of us who are patient enough to wait for Judgment Day, for peace and justice. Then there are other Black people who will not wait until tomorrow for what we should have had yesterday. Our fight for justice in America will never end, because some of us will never quit until we receive it!

Until the next time, peace, to all.

Conrad Prophet

*　　*　　*

To contact the author or for more information on book orders, book signings, seminars, workshops, speaking engagements, and large group sales please write:

Conrad Prophet
"The Prophet Group"
P.O. Box 02442
Detroit, MI 48202

E-mail at: *conradprophet@msn.com*
Visit the website: www.conradprophet.com

Notes and Sources

Scripture quotations taken from King James Version of the Bible

Chapter 1: Northwood University

1. *1980 Census of Population: Characteristics of the Population— Michigan.* D.C.: U.S. Government Printing Office, 1983.
2. Toppo, Greg. "Low-income College Students Are Increasingly Left Behind." *USA Today,* January 14, 2004.
3. "Ibid."
4. Manhattan Institute for Policy Research. "Grade Inflation Cheats Students As Employers Get Wise to Scam." *The Detroit News,* November 12, 2003.
5. http://www.alligator.org/edit/issues/96-sumr/960718/b07dropo.htm (12/31/03)
6. *http://www.univsource.com/mi.htm* (9/3/03)

Chapter 2: United States Army

1. *Manual for Courts-Martial.* United States. 1995 ed.
2. *www.dfas.mil/money/milpay/pay/2004paytable.pdf* (1/30/04)

Chapter 5: Kmart Apparel Corporation

1. Robeson, Paul. *Here I Stand.* Boston: Beacon Press, 1958.
2. *1990 Census of Population: General Population Characteristics— Michigan.* D.C.: U.S. Government Printing Office, 1992.

3. Guest, Greta. "Kmart advisers bill $138 million." *The Detroit Free Press*, October 3, 2003.
4. Dybis, Karen. "How 'Frat Boys' drove Kmart to ruin." *The Detroit News*, January 26, 2003.
5. "Ibid."
6. Smith, Joel J. & Karen Dybis. "Kmart plan guts investors." *The Detroit News*, January 19, 2003.
7. "Ibid."
8. Guest, Greta. "Suit seeks millions from ex-Kmart execs." *The Detroit Free Press*, October 24, 2003.

Chapter 6: Wayne County Department of Public Services

1. Prophet, Conrad. "Wayne County is 21st Century plantation for Black workers." *The Michigan Chronicle*, February 11-17, 1998.
2. Goodin, Michael. "County exec ready to make change." *The Michigan Chronicle*, March 4-10, 1998.
3. Prophet, Conrad. "Wayne County is 21st Century plantation for Black workers, (Second in an occasional series)." *The Michigan Chronicle*, March 25-31, 1998.
4. "Chronicle endorses McNamara." *The Michigan Chronicle*, May 20-26, 1998.
5. Egan, Paul. "McNamara aides' pay, perks soar." *The Detroit News and Free Press*, August 18, 2002.
6. Moore, Natalie. "Transition snags Ficano." *The Detroit News*, January 25, 2004.

Chapter 9: Author

1. Pardo, Steve. "Banned Book Awaits Vote." *The Detroit News*, October 3, 2003.

Chapter 10: Entrepreneurship

1. Jones, Gareth R. and Jennifer M. George. *Contemporary Management* 3rd ed. New York: McGraw-Hill, 2003.

2. Willard, W.L. "Can Black Americans Pull Together Economically?" *The Final Call*, December 29, 2003.
3. Daniels, Cora. "Minority Rule." *Fortune Small Business*, December 2003/January 2004, 65-66.
4. http://www.usatoday.com/money/smallbusiness/news/2001-03-06-minority.htm (1/2/04)
5. Daniels, Cora. "Minority Rule." *Fortune Small Business*, December 2003/January 2004, 65-66.

Chapter 11: Sharing Knowledge

1. *Merriam Webster's Collegiate Dictionary*. 10th ed. Springfield: Merriam-Webster, Inc., 1993.
2. "Ibid."
3. West, Cornel. *Race Matters*. New York: Vintage Books, 2001, p. 53.

Chapter 12: Your Move

1. http://www.ed.gov/pubs/OR/ConsumerGuides/dropout.html 1/2/04
2. Reed, William. "Should we boycott firms who oust Blacks from major corporate boards?" *The Final Call*, December 29, 2003.
3. Dowdy, Zachary R. "Crime & Punishment." *The Crisis*, July/August 2002, pp. 33-37.
4. Williams, Chancellor. *The Destruction of Black Civilization*. Chicago: Third World Press, 1987.

Epilogue

1. http://abcnews.go.com/sections/wnt/Business/jobless030729_offshoring.html 2/2/04
2. Armour, Stephanie and Michelle Kessler. "USA's new money-saving export: White-collar jobs." *USA Today*, August 5, 2003.
3. "Ibid."
4. Bennett, Jeff and Jamie Gumbrecht. "Mexico wins factory state fought to keep." *The Detroit Free Press*, January 17, 2004.

5. Frandson, Jon. "House opposition likely will block plan this year." *The Detroit News*, January 8, 2004.

6. Clingman, James. "Being Black When No One Is Looking." *The Final Call*, June 17, 2002.

7. Morris, P. Fiorim & Paul E. Petrson. *The New Democracy.* Maryland: Allyn and Bacon, Heedham Heights, 1998, pp. 563.

8. Cooper, Desiree. "How We Got To This Point." *Metro Times*, June 17-23, 1998, pp. 14-15.

9. Lillard, W.L. "Can Black Americans Pull Together Economically?" *The Final Call*, March 25, 2002.